Italian
Folktales
in America

Wayne State University Folklore Archive Study Series

Janet Langlois, General Editor

This volume inaugurates the Wayne State University Folklore Archive Study Series, first conceptualized by folklorists Michael Bell, John Gutowski, and Robert Teske in the mid-1970s. The series is envisioned as a way to make the rich urban folklore materials housed in the archive more accessible to the reading public than they might otherwise be. Two titles previously published by Wayne State University Press, Susie Hoogasian Villa's *100 Armenian Tales* and Harriet M. Pawlowska's *Merrily We Sing: 105 Polish Folksongs,* point to the success of translating archival resources into book form.

The critical introductions to the volumes planned for the series situate the folkloristic data within a sociocultural and historic framework. They also ground the data in appropriate theoretical models. Here authors Mathias and Raspa use the model of social change to structure the shifts in Clementina Todesco's storytelling style as she moves from the Old World peasant stables of the Veneto to the New World urban experience in New York, Detroit, and Phoenix.

Italian Folktales in America

The Verbal Art of an Immigrant Woman

ELIZABETH MATHIAS

AND RICHARD RASPA

FOREWORD BY ROGER D. ABRAHAMS

WAYNE STATE UNIVERSITY PRESS
DETROIT

01 00 99 98 97 96   7 6 5 4 3 2

Library of Congress Cataloging-in-Publication Data

Mathias, Elizabeth.
    Italian folktales in America : the verbal art of an immigrant
woman / Elizabeth Mathias and Richard Raspa : foreword by Roger D.
Abrahams.
        p.   cm.—(Wayne State University Folklore Archive study
series)
    Includes 22 tales as told by Clementina Todesco.
    Bibliography: p.
    Includes indexes.
    ISBN 0–8143–2122–4 (pbk.)
    1. Todesco, Clementina. 2. Italian Americans—Folklore.
3. Tales—United States. 4. Tales—Italy. 5. Storytellers—United
States. 6. Storytellers—Italy. 7. Italian American women—
Folklore. I. Raspa, Richard, 1940–   . II. Todesco, Clementina.
III. Title. IV. Series.
[GR111.I73M37 1988]
398.2′08951073—dc19   88-6598
                                                              CIP

To Bruna Todesco Baroni
WHO COLLECTED THESE TALES
WITH AFFECTION AND DILIGENCE
AND IS THE SOURCE OF THIS BOOK

Contents

Foreword

Italian Folktales in America: a modest title for a truly unusual work. The reader will not find here just another collection of European-style wonder tales which happened to be collected in the United States. Rather, this is a record of the repertoire of a remarkably animated and artful storyteller, Clementina Todesco, as recorded by her daughter, Bruna, on the encouragement of her folklore teacher, Emelyn Gardner, and put in an archive some forty-four years ago. Once it was rediscovered, two resourceful folklorist-ethnographers, Elizabeth Mathias and Richard Raspa, were able not only to find the original storyteller and re-interview her but to return to the community in which this gifted tale-teller grew up, and to cobble together an extraordinarily full and interesting set of memories (as well as additional stories) by old-timers there, about the setting and occasions on which these stories were told. Though we must give appropriate credit to Emelyn Gardner for having recognized the quality of the stories brought to her, and the industry and exhaustiveness with which Bruna Todesco carried out her recordings by hand, this work as we presently have it is guided by the vision of Mathias and Raspa, for it is they who gathered all the materials and put them into place.

From an ethnographic and folkloristic perspective this is a textbook on how to carry out memory-culture collecting: how to gather lore from those who no longer perform and use such fabrications by having the informants discuss the world that lay behind the lore and to gloss the stories themselves, to talk about the meaning of specific characters and incidents, and to recall what point was being made in telling these tales at this time and in this specific setting. The collector-editors are able not only to reconstruct how life was lived in a specific peasant village at a specific time and place but also to explain how the lore of that village might be used as the baseline for an understanding of culture changes as they impact on the lives of specific villagers. And most remarkable, for the reader, the work of the memory is rendered in such a human fashion that both the tales of wonder and the reminiscences of hardships and horrible experiences reinforce each other, making up a mood document that will surprise greatly those who come to this work expecting simply to encounter examples of the northern Italian folktale repertoire.

Not just made up of the recorded texts, the book is also built on the reminiscences of that storyteller and of some of her old neighbors in her birthplace, and is a record by two resourceful fieldworkers of what it takes to study memory culture. The result is a work that greatly enriches our understanding of who told (and tells) märchen to whom, why and how they are told, and, perhaps most important, under what conditions.

It would be neither fitting nor useful for me to go on at any great length about the implications of this material for the future study of folktales. The texts and the enveloping materials are voiced eloquently by the informants and artfully focused and arranged by the editors. But one dimension of the information and its analysis, where the editors fill us in on the life conditions and, specifically, the village economy in which these stories lived, seems so rich in implications and so suggestive for future study of märchen that I cannot resist making a few remarks adumbrating theirs. I mean ''economy'' in the larger sense of the process of household management, for this book enables us to see so clearly that tales, in conjunction with other value-laden symbolic activities, may be usefully regarded as part of the expressive budgeting that goes on within traditional scarce-resource communities. That is, they enter both directly and indirectly into the way in which work and responsibilities are assigned and land, labor, and other resources are allocated.

The activity of storytelling itself is carried on in the stable, seemingly a mean place, one which hardly seems an appropriate setting for these wonder tales. But in Faller, the town in which these stories were told, the stable was in fact the center of social activity: as the editors put it, "the stable was like a comfortable family room . . . a free zone [which] functioned to mediate the intimate gestures of home life with the formal rituals of public interaction." The warmest place of domesticity, it was also the area most readily accessible to both family and people from outside the household as well, and was the place where most of the important community exchanges took place, including the telling of old stories: "In the stable women sat on tiny seats in a circle around an oil lamp. They brought chests filled with material and would sew, knit, and teach the girls how to embroider linens for their trousseaux. The central activity of the stable was the *filo*, the spinning of hemp on a spindle or spinning wheel."

Not coincidentally, all of the activities in the stable were called *filo* as well, the sewing and weaving standing for the whole of the social occasion, the "time" set aside by the villagers for interacting with one another easily but significantly. And it was in the stable, at the *filo*, that the cloth, woven at the local weaver's, was embroidered in red thread that announced that the object had now been made into a property of the household. And it was here, too, that stories were spun and woven: the trope is not a conceit, for it is the traditional way in which storytelling is described in most of the world in which weaving is done. This working of the fibers in Faller, as elsewhere, is a central act transforming the natural and unformed into the crafted and stylized object that says clearly, "Human beings made this!"

In the stable actions occur and ideas are put forth which are to be judged in terms not only of whether they are right or wrong, but also of whether they are well-done or sloppy, beautiful or ugly. For here not only is work going on but the range of expressive acts and events most significant to the community is carried out: from gossiping and other kinds of bringing in the news to singing songs and telling the old stories. Here a young bride would come "carried like a bundle of logs" into her husband's household and be shown how to work in the right manner, how people ate in that household, and eventually, how they cooked in it. Moreover, the *filo* was a more directly message-laden event, in these cases, for then "the young bride listened to the conversation of her in-laws and discovered what she did wrong, how she did not work properly, and how she was to operate differently."

And at the stable, these stories were told in fairy-tale terms, but they alluded to real problems of daily life: the conflicts that often arise between motives of individual initiative and family responsibility; the strong impediments to marriage that occur within this social system because of the threat of the growing scarcity of basic resources; and the imaginative ways that young men and women invent that address the social binds attending such conditions of scarce resources, ways by which they are able to detach themselves from their families sufficiently that they may move, start their own households, and (at least as far as the conventions of this narrative form would have it) "live happily ever after."

Thus, in the stable, not only are some of the most significant everyday activities carried out but inherited stories are recounted which comment directly and indirectly on the life problems of individuals living in communities with limited economic resources. Here the cultural and social dimensions of the local economy are put into action, where words become counters in an active exchange system that operates by family values and sets of expectations, a system in which the most important rule of thumb is that the young must invest time and energy now to expect a payoff in the distant future. This is not an economy marked, then, by the need to bargain or even to contend. But it is a scarce-resource economy in which everyone is expected to do his own task in good spirit. It is a world in which one parent or another is often taken away, by death or the need to go elsewhere to war or to work. Never have I understood as immediately or as power-fully what "stepmother" connotes in these stories, for stepmoth-ers took an important place in the Faller household economy, in which so many mothers were lost in childbirth and it became necessary so often to merge families. In such cases, attention and affection become as rare a commodity as other dimensions of the household economy, for children now find themselves in competi-tion with stepbrothers and sisters newly arrived and with the offspring of new marriage. The descriptions of Faller life also dramatize in a poignant manner the situation of a family left without a father, making those stories which begin, as does "The Devil Gets Tricked," with a simple description of a mother living alone with her children in poverty and powerlessness come alive with the urgency of living in such a borderline economy. Indeed, virtually every story here not only begins with a reference to a family's poverty but also relates it to the loss of one or the other parent of the protagonists.

There are a great many details of homely life which seep into these tales, the minutiae of household life which undergirds an attitude toward relationships and individual achievement that must be understood as a reflection of poverty, and a response to its accompanying sense of powerlessness to affect one's own life. Moreover, these problems are most fully encountered by the youngest and therefore the most powerless members of the family, the ones who will wait the longest to gain rights and responsibilities even under the best of conditions. Indeed, the problem of poverty is, as it commonly turns out, most fully faced by the youngest ones of the family, and it is they who must exhibit the greatest degree of wiliness in order to transform their situation.

And that is what these stories are about, aren't they, the transformation of life situations for the poorest and most powerless members of the family and community? As they pit the powerless and childlike against the ones with greater resources and control, they have been siezed upon by both Marxists and Freudians as projections of a power imbalance and of traditional ways developed by the weakest members of social units in a scarce-resource situation to fight back through the use of their wits. But, as the editors point out so well, these stories are concerned not just with the *furberia* of the young peasants, their wiliness, adaptability, capacity to take risks, and to find help when it is needed; their wiliness is tempered by *osservanza*, a willingness to live within the traditional code of family and community obligations. The usual problem for them is to find the wherewithal to make an advantageous marriage while being able to do something about the poverty of their families.

If the protagonists in these stories display wiliness, the *furberia* is not carried out in the style of the rampant individualist going it on his own; rather, acts indicating initiative are accompanied by those in which a kindness is offered to an older and more powerful (if scary) figure. Such kind acts exhibit motives of both *furberia* and *osservanza* leading (usually indirectly, for Signora Todesco is a master storyteller who knows the best, most dramatic

forestalling tricks) to a marriage higher up on the social scale for
the protagonist. If these stories are models for any kind of basic
life activity, then, it is not so much that they show how to grow
up by establishing individual autonomy on the psychological
level; nor is it learning some kind of trick by which the apparently
powerless peasant overcomes the hegemony of the ruling class.
Rather, they show how initiative, wiliness, and willingness to
accept and capitalize on help will enable young men and young
women to get together to start their own families and to have a
life of their own. If there is a social and historical lesson here, it
seems to me that it is a model for people living within scarce-
resource economies to accommodate themselves to the added
goods and resources brought into the system through the incur-
sions of the extra-regional marketplace.

It has long seemed to me that one of the major problems of
folklore study has been that we have regarded texts as being capable of speaking for themselves, as if they are works of art which
can be understood regardless of their economic, social, or cultural
underpinnings. They are the artistic products of individuals living simpler lives than our own, and we have allowed ourselves
the ethnocentric luxury of assuming that we, as ideal informed
readers, will instinctively understand and factor into our encounter with these texts, the details of this more circumscribed community and economy. We are attracted to these confabulations
precisely because of their directness and simplicity of means, and
it has seemed most important to us to address ourselves to questions of the retention and transmission of these expressive objects.
This attitude was encouraged strongly by our essentially nostalgic
ideology, which saw such evidences of tradition as examples of
the world we lost in becoming modern. This book strongly
opposes such a perspective, allowing us to recapture the life of
some wonderful tales as they operated actively in a peasant environment not so very long ago.

There is no doubt in my mind that folktales do indeed reflect
human concerns and problems, and if calling them "anxieties"
allows us to connect the stories to other artifacts and processes of
culture, that is all to the good. My problem with both the Marxist
and psycho-analytic perspectives is that they depict folktales as
dreamwork-like projections of inner conflicts (within the self or

society). Both ideologies thereby encourage us to overlook the ways in which these tales operate in a more immediate and instrumental fashion within the cultures that maintain them as part of their expressive economy, as items of performance to be played with and enjoyed by the entire community, not just be children. Moreover, to think of the stories, the tellers, the audience, as childlike is to denigrate them and to make no effort to understand the dynamic by which the stories are generated and regenerated, learned and maintained in the memory.

To me, then, these stories are just what the editors show them to be: expressions of a people going through the horrible and sometimes exciting transition between the traditional world in which one specific place, the stable, provided a center for necessary work activities as well as those in which important social and aesthetic information was exchanged and the cosmopolitan world in which one has to search for a kitchen in which to tell these stories, but in which other kinds of fictions come to take their place. Certainly, in the social transformation, something has been lost. One of the unique features of this unusual book is that we are not asked to weep over this change but to see it for what it is: a pilgrimage away from a system of scarce resources and limitations on personal advancement, though it always offered a nurturing sense of community, to a more fractionalized, less family-oriented world, yet one in which a greater number of real-life choices have become available.

Roger D. Abrahams
Scripps College
Claremont, California

Preface

In 1941, while studying folklore at Wayne University with Professor Emelyn Gardner, Bruna Todesco collected from her mother, Clementina, the twenty-two märchen and legends presented in this book. Bruna, her mother, and her father, John, immigrated to America in 1930 from their native village of Faller in the Veneto region of northern Italy. Bruna remembered her mother's tales well and had always wished to have them published. When she died so young, in 1961 at the age of thirty-nine, the project deposited in the university's Folklore Archive was forgotten.[1]

In 1974 John Gutowski, then director of the archive, discovered Bruna's collection of tales and immediately realized their importance. Here was the first ethnographic study of a northern Italian storyteller. The only other English-language study of the performance of Italian folktales north of Rome is Alessandro Falassi's work on the Tuscan *veglia* (story occasion) in an area about two hundred miles southwest of Faller. Falassi's *Folklore by the Fireside: Text and Context of the Tuscan Veglia,* published in 1980, contributes to our understanding of the performance dynamics of the narrative within the family context.

We were invited to work on the collection because of our long association with Italian culture and ethnography. We were both Fulbright scholars in Italy, did extensive field work in both northern and southern Italy, taught for periods at Italian universities, and have lived in the Dolomite region, where Clementina Todesco was born. We have continued our field research in Italian-American communities in Illinois, Michigan, Minnesota,

New York, Pennsylvania, and Utah. A quarter century after Bruna Todesco Baroni's death, we are privileged to have this opportunity to present the tales Bruna recorded and to evoke the life of our storyteller, Clementina Todesco, and her odyssey from a rural Italian village to the great cities of the New World.

Acknowledgments

Our greatest debt is, of course, to Clementina Todesco, our storyteller, who with grace and patience allowed herself to be interviewed for this book. John Todesco, her husband, was supportive and encouraging. Ben Todesco provided the photographs of Bruna, Clementina, and John. The people of Faller provided valuable information about the history of this North Italian village. We are especially grateful to the ten present-day storytellers in the village who continue to tell stories and who recounted their tales with great charm during our interviews: Brigida DalZot, Cicilia DalZot, Flora Moretto, Filomena Slongo, Florentina Slongo, Stella Slongo, Carolina and Piero Todesco, Ruffina Todesco, and Maria Trento. Mariotti Pedrazzoli of Val di Sole, Mezzana, made a superb translation of the tales and information collected in the Faller dialect into standard Italian.

Dott. Mara Bini Babi and Dott. Bruno Valente of the Discoteca di Stato kindly allowed us to use the folklore archive in Rome, and Cipriana Scelba, director of the Fulbright Commission in Rome, provided a summer stipend to complete the research. Professor Leonard Moss's incisive perspective on folk beliefs and Italian ethnography was most appreciated. We thank John Gutowski, former director of the Wayne State University Folklore Archive, who secured permission from John and Clementina Todesco to have this material published, and Janet Langlois, the current director, for their support.

Scholars and friends who broadened our understanding of ethnography and folklife include Roger Abrahams, Jan Brunvand, Linda Dégh, Kenneth Goldstein, Michael Owen Jones, Joseph

Lopreato, Rudolph Vecoli, and Eric Wolf. Rose Ann Maly made elegant suggestions and encouraged us while typing the original manuscript, and Alberta Asmar and Frances Small typed the final version. We acknowledge Doreen Broder for her fine editing of the manuscript.

In addition we thank the many people who were helpful here and abroad, who will recognize their part in the making of this book: Elizabeth Abell; Richard Arndt; Luigi Arru; Lee and Danny Aubuchon; Paula Baffigo; Nancy, Mary, Laura, Ann, James, and Thomas Todesco Baroni; John Baroni; Joe Beatty; Carla Bianco; Judy Bockenstette; Jack Boland; Meg Brady; Estelle and Eli Brown; LynnKay Brown; Rae and Don Buck; J. M. Cameron; Maria Teresa Catte; Anton Hermann Chroust; Giovanni Cicala; Lori Clarke; Joseph Comprone; Lynn and Lou Cristaldi; Arline Cullen; Frank D'Angelo; Tommy and Johnny Davis; Walter Davis; Tammaso and Maria-Celeste Delogu; Mario and Ann DiFiori; Aleks, Nico, Rudolub, Wilma, Lilijana, and Givan Dimitrijevic; Frank, Margaret, Helen, Henry, Nick, Ruth, David, Nicolo, and Rachele DiOrio; Vic and Isabel Dirita; Silvana Donaera; Gerald Doss; John Dunne; Sue English; Werner Erhard; Maria Ferraroni; Connie Gefvert; Debbie George; Alma Giannini; Joseph Goodstein; Betty Green; Olga Guarnieri; Don and Lois Haynes; Bob and Dixie Huefner; Pat Mathews Jamieson; Tom and Deanne Kemp; Ken and Lucy Khoury; Mary Jane Kirschner; Leon and Ginny Kortenkamp; David Kranes; Dave, Lisa, Susie, and Kate Kranz; Leroy and Barbara Kuehl; Joseph Labriola; Archie Loss; Thomas Loughery; John and Tina MacDonald; Lou, Joanne, and Ian MacKenzie; Alistair MacLeod; Joe and Marilyn Mammola; Mario and Nicolette Manca; William Mulder; Rachel, Bernie, Steve, Cathy, and Stephanie Muratore; Ed and Linda Neenan; John Nelson; Philip and Maria Notarianni; Rae and Walter Orzek; Nick and Helen Papanikolas; Morisse Partee; Cornelia and Giovanni Pedrazolli; Marilyn Phillips; Shirley, Jimmy, and Johnny Qualls; Katherine and Harry Raspa; Catherine and Vittorio Re; Jerry and Ceil Rescigno; Amy and Phil Richards; Rose Ann and Evan Roarty-Collins; Jim Robinson; Mary Rondello; Lee and Max Seltzer; Hezzi Shoshani; Dave Stanley; Laszlo and Lucy Steiner; Wayne and Betty Strong; John

Tallmadge; Terry and Elizabeth Thompson; Zak Thundy; Dave, Enea, David, Debbie, Elizabeth, and John Tierno; Edi and Gerry Tikoff; Joe Trimmer; Ed Vasta; Angela Vistarchi; Marilyn Williamson; Alice Wilson; Bob Winans; Mike and Joan Yetman; and all our students at the University of Sassari, University of Bologna at Urbino, St. John's University, University of Notre Dame, University of Utah, and Wayne State University.

We thank Joseph Lay, Elizabeth's father, for having graciously delayed his string bean harvest in deference to work on the book. Olga Raspa, Richard's wife, took the photographs of the Alps and the people of Faller which appear in the book, dazzled us with her culinary artistry, and inspired the completion of the work. And Nicki Raspa, Richard's daughter, sparkled and reminded us, when we forgot, that the moment is the only thing that counts.

Part I
Background

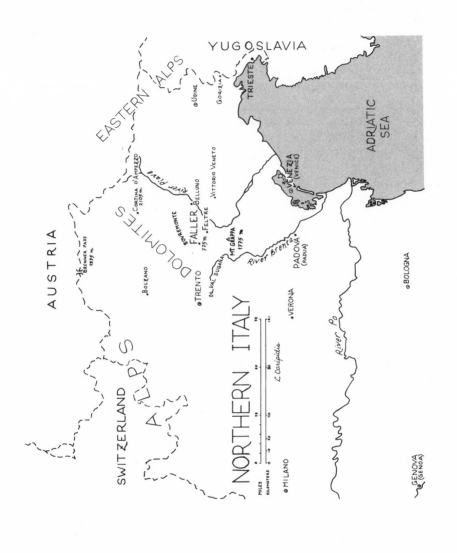

YUGOSLAVIA

EASTERN ALPS

AUSTRIA

SWITZERLAND

ALPS

•UDINE

GORIZIA •

TRIESTE •

ADRIATIC
SEA

River Piave

•CORTINA D'AMPEZZO
2105 m.

River Piave

BELLUNO
•FELTRE

•VITTORIO VENETO

SOVRAMONTE

FALLER
775 m.

MT. GRAPPA
1775 m.

VENEZIA
(VENICE)

BRENNER PASS
1375 m.

DOLOMITES

•BOLZANO

©TRENTO

DI VAL SUGANA

River Brenta

PADOVA
(PADUA)

©BOLOGNA

•VERONA

River Po

L. Garipidis

NORTHERN ITALY

MILES

KILOMETERS

©MILANO

©GENOVA
(GENOA)

Introduction

Alpine winters were long and cold, and night came early to the mountains. The upper pastures had long since filled with snow, and the cattle came down to the village stables. As night fell, women prepared dinner in the kitchens and carried the food to the stables. There the family ate together in the warmth furnished by the animals and in the light provided by the oil lamp. After dinner, others arrived from neighboring homes to join the family. Most were from the village, but a few journeyed through the starlit night from nearby towns to join the family for an evening of activities which might include games, singing, dancing, certainly conversation, and perhaps, storytelling.

At the same time people were free and close during the winter season. In Faller, an Italian Alpine hamlet, the agricultural year set the time and designated the space for social events. The round of seasons and of crops provided the rhythm for heavy outdoor labor in the summer and light indoor tasks in the winter. Evening winter gatherings in the stable were organized around work. For people to play and express themselves artistically, work furnished the occasion, the time, and the space. Villagers even referred to the gathering in the stables as the *filo,* from *filare* (to spin wool or hemp). "Are you going to the *filo* tonight?" men called to each other as they passed on their way home for supper, and teenagers eagerly queried their friends, seeking to know if a special friend would be present at the *filo* that evening.

In the stables, women spun and embroidered, and men repaired rakes and other tools. Folk narratives developed in just such an atmosphere of communal work. Groups of people doing tasks in the same time and place furnished and structured the occasion for the production of the material goods needed for family use—thread, rakes, *zoccoli* (wooden boots). They also provided the framework for artistic expression—märchen (magic tales), legends, and personal experience stories. Village morality and world view, embedded in these narrative genres, were re-created as stories and were told again and again.

Sometimes an especially good tale-teller would come to the stable to entertain all with his performance. The raconteur would speak on, spinning his story, building the suspense, elaborating further at points in the story when he noticed increased audience interest, or shortening the tale a bit with a decline in attention. He elaborated his narratives out of the dreams of never-never land mingled with the materials of everyday life in the village, transforming the exotic into everyday life and the every day into the exotic. This Alpine village is the setting of our study of an Italian folk artist, Clementina Todesco, and her stories.[1]

In interviews in Italian and English Clementina recalled her village traditions as well as the transmission of the tales in Italy and America. She recounted her childhood experiences in Italy, her immigration, and her early American experiences. The Todesco family moved in 1930 to New York City, where they lived in apartments at several locations. Then in 1938 the family moved to Detroit and until 1944 lived in a multiethnic neighborhood known as Delray, which was peopled primarily by Hungarian-, Polish-, and Armenian-Americans. It was here in a small, white frame house on Rademacher Street in 1941 that Bruna began to collect her mother's folktales.

When she returned in the evening from classes at Wayne University, she sat by Clementina in the kitchen as she prepared dinner or washed dishes and wrote down word for word what Clementina recounted to her in the native dialect of Faller. Then Bruna would translate the tales into English, frequently checking with her mother for accuracy. In the final stage of her project, Bruna refined the oral transcriptions, making stylistic changes and additions which transformed the natural cadences and tones of the folk artist into something more closely resembling a literary text (in the familiar fashion of the Brothers Grimm). Naturally, since she was not using a tape recorder, performance variables such as pauses and verbal intensifiers were not noted. The content of the tales, however, was scrupulously maintained. In our approach we are presenting the Todesco material intact, exactly as it was deposited in the Wayne archive by Bruna.

Since the tales were still immersed in the family atmosphere at that time, neither woman realized the value of the stories. Clementina had to be persuaded to tell the tales, and Bruna had to be urged by her Wayne professor, Emelyn Gardner, to collect them. And Clementina did not recognize the brilliance of her own storytelling and performance style. She still regarded tale-telling as it had been seen in Italy—an integral part of kin and community life, a private talent to be exercised and appreciated within the intimate circle of the family. Storytelling to Clementina was really no different from cooking traditional Venetian foods, such as sausage and polenta (corn meal mush). She enjoyed both tales and food preparation as things to be done and as a part of her role in creating family joy. It was Professor Gardner who convinced Bruna and Clementina that what they casually dismissed as unimportant was actually an extraordinary treasure to be shared with the world.

This book is the product of an interdisciplinary collaboration. We proceeded along the lines of Fernand Braudel's recommendation that the many paths of the social sciences must converge.[2] Thus we drew upon literary, anthropological, and folkloric theory to understand the boundaries of the narrative traditions of Faller and to analyze the repertoire of stories of the artist Clementina Todesco who created within those boundaries. The focus of our study is the individual artist and the development of her creativity in the various physical and social environments in which she lived. To supplement Bruna Todesco's texts of the tales, information was gathered over a ten-year period from the residents of Faller, from collections of tale variants in Italy, from analogues in published and archival sources in Detroit and Rome, and from interviews with Clementina Todesco herself.

In addition to the märchen and legends which Bruna collected, we have included in the last section of the book a group of Clementina's personal experience narratives told in Phoenix, Arizona. They help characterize Clementina as a folk artist, her personal, social, and cultural experience, her audience, the structure of her tales and the view of humankind and the world contained in them, and the range of narrative genres in which she performed. In this way the tales could be presented in the context of their environment—the work and leisure life of Faller—and could reveal how Clementina learned the stories at the side of local narrative artists and transmitted them, the tale-telling setting of the stable, and the place of the tales in the life of the community. Her tales were partly drawn from the locality and partly from a composite of peasant and industrial societies. Her personal experience stories illuminate critical aspects of the emigration experience and the corresponding process of social and artistic change as she moved from a rural farming community in Europe to an urban industrial setting in the United States, from an oral-aural culture to one in which writing and mass media are the major means of communication. Rooting artistic communication in its cultural matrix allows us to approach the problem of style and selection without, as Eric Wolf puts it, "falling into the error of letting style refer mainly to the parts of culture that have an aesthetic or intellectual content and of ignoring the economic, political, moral, religious, and familial content."[3]

Our intention in writing this book is to contribute to the growing body of literature on the history and ethnography of work and its relationship to play and other artistic forms. While we recognize the value of semiotic, structural, and other current approaches to human behavior, our discussion does not formally incorporate the methods or the issues raised by these theories. We have chosen to focus on one tale-teller and the transformation of her art over time. Our approach is based upon Braudel's notion of history in the "long term," which, for our subject, means beginning with the economic history of Faller and with the artist as an individual who occupies a place in the rural work of the community, a relationship which produces both material goods and symbolic forms.[4]

Fallerese perception of their own oral narrative tradition is historical. They say the stories have been passed down from generation to generation for hundreds of years, *da tempi antichi* (from olden times). Oral narratives are a record of a people without a history, that is, a history not formally written and only to be found in what is left to us in their folklore.[5] The tradition issues from a reservoir of wisdom of the people and is generated from them.

When one surveys the themes and the world view represented in the narratives, it becomes obvious that they evolved in earlier epochs within different types of economic organizations. Antonio Gramsci, the twentieth-century Sardinian sociologist, understood this distinction and drew much of his information directly from the life of the people. He was concerned with what themes the local *poeti* (shepherd-poets who improvised) were using in their performances each year. Since they were selected by Sardinian villagers, these themes revealed the immediate concerns of the peasants and, thus, the present state of the folk culture.[6]

In the oral narrative-history relationship, Giuseppe Cocchiara notes in his commentary on the work of Vladimir Propp that the unity of composition of the fairy tale may be found in its historical reality: its motifs must be viewed not as immobile, fixed facts but as ever-changing processes like history. Propp analyzed fairy tales for insights about their development through time and not for their origins. This is an important point, for he has been misread as one looking for "relics" from past cultures. In Cocchiara's view, Propp's contribution to folklore scholarship is that he saw the problem of studying the märchen in "concrete material terms," seeing them as documents containing information regarding social stratification and change. Propp recommended that folklorists study not actual historical happenings through folklore but, instead, explore the conditions in the past which produced and nourished folklore. Propp's distinction between conditions, a long-term state of being, and happenings, a single occurrence in time, approximates that made later by Braudel between the long term and the event. The fundamental point upon which Propp's theory of folklore was based is the reciprocal interconnection of all phenomena in the world:

> tales may be understood only with the analysis of social life, entering into social life not only as constituent parts, but in the eyes of the tribe, as one of the conditions of life equal to their tools and to the amulets they conserve and guard like the most sacred things.

> Not by the theory of diffusion, not by that of the unity of the human psyche proposed by the anthropological school can this

problem be resolved. It is solved with historical research on
folklore in its connection with the economy of material life.[7]

Folklore needs to be examined in connection with material life if
there is to be an understanding of the märchen and of the human
beings who created narrative forms. Propp's thesis is that only a
historical approach that focuses upon the interrelationships and
parallel transformation of life's material and symbolic dimensions
will give a true picture of the human condition, past, present, and
future.

Following Propp and others, then, we have explored the net-
work of material and symbolic connections in the context of the
community of Faller in northeastern Italy. Historically, we established the relationship between the manner in which the villagers
organized themselves to produce the materials needed for the
continuation of life and the way in which they produced artistic
forms. We then followed the tale-teller to the United States and
concentrated again upon the connection between symbolic and
material expression. Once severed from the community where
the tales were nurtured in a social matrix of shared work and play
which had a focal time, evening, and place for human gathering,
the stable, the old tale-telling tradition did not survive. In the
United States Clementina Todesco shifted her focus to immigration epics and autobiographical stories. This genre of the personal experience narrative emerged in Faller as young men
emigrated to northern Europe or crossed the Atlantic and
returned periodically to the village, bringing back reminiscences
to share with the townspeople. The transformation of the oral
narrative begins in the village at the time the industrial world
begins to affect the rural economy. Whereas in the Italian hamlet
the tales were part of the agricultural daily round of work and
life, in the American urban environment, work and tale-telling
were no longer complementary. Clementina continued to perform the märchen and legends central to the oral tradition of Faller as long as she had an audience. Eventually, however, as
occasions declined, so did the tale-telling. The narratives were
called forth and set down in writing only years later, when her
daughter, Bruna, began to collect them.

In any community the traditions people share are given form

by tradition bearers.[8] There will always be certain members of the community who possess particular talents of memory, verbal skill, and power to evoke the traditions of the group. These individuals are marked as exceptional people. While they work within the community's aesthetic boundaries, they stand out as artists. As Ruth Finnegan points out:

> the poet's language, style, mode of composition, local poetic theory, role, type of training and mode of reception are surely socially and not individually generated. They are moulded and developed (sometimes changed) by individual poets, without whom the conventions would not persist. But no poet creates in a vacuum, looking only to himself and never to the social and economic world within which he must practice, the audience to which he must direct himself or the acceptable artistic conventions on which he can draw.
>
> The position of poets in society is incorporated into the wider social, political, and economic institutions in which they practice.[9]

In Faller the storytellers Zio Patrizio and Zio Bepi were born into the unique oral traditions of the community and excelled in giving expression to its narratives. Our subject, Clementina Todesco, distinguished herself as an extraordinarily talented folk artist by her ability to learn from these two traditional storytellers, to conform to the aesthetic limits established by the village, and to articulate the rich narrative traditions of the people.

Several important questions stand out for our analysis. In what specific ways do Clementina's narratives relate to real life? What are the points of connection between village life and her tales? In what way have the narrative forms incorporated details of the culture of the societies where they have flourished and been nurtured?

Three forms of the narrative verbal art of Faller are represented in Clementina's repertoire: the märchen, the legend, and the personal experience story. Dynamic structures, narratives have absorbed details of the local environment and attitudes as they were told and changed along with the society. In the nineteenth and twentieth centuries, storytelling was primarily an activity for the very poor. Linda Dégh notes that storytelling was class linked. Enjoyed by the socially underprivileged, it was shunned by those economically better off.

This is to be seen in the content of tales—in their social tendencies, in the message they express, and in the fact that the work occasions of the poor generally furnished the storyteller with the framework of his tales which appeals to the imagination of the storytelling community. The well-to-do peasants in the village have little respect for the folktale. They will tell anecdotes during their get-togethers but only laugh at the long magical tale. The respectable peasant wants to hear something "true," a historical event; he reads newspapers and no longer listens to "lies." His way of thinking is rational. He has access to modern mass media, education, and a comfortable standard of living, and as a result he is able to seek more than oral entertainment. . . . The working conditions of the peasant who possessed land never provided the same conditions for storytelling as occurred with the agricultural workers and other day laborers. Under these circumstances, we should not say that the folktale is alive mainly among European peasants, but rather that it lives among the lowest social ranks of the people.[10]

As Joseph Lopreato discovered in the oral narratives, sayings, and proverbs of his native Calabria, the märchen and legends of Faller reflect the attitudes and world view of the landless peasantry.[11] Roger Abrahams says that "in oral cultures, storytelling is a fundamental way of codifying hard-won truths and dramatizing the rationale behind traditions. Thus, the tales will often end with a 'message' or a point, a truth, to remember as one confronts life's problems."[12] They embody local beliefs, village morality, and survival strategies. The village where the tale is told, Dégh explains, becomes the village of the tale, and the characters are very much like the local inhabitants; "motifs from real life serve to connect phantasy with reality and to bring the anachronistic world of the tales up-to-date."[13] Ethnographic facts and village mores from past and present times are thus documented in the narratives.

The social and political history of this part of northern Italy, combined with a relentless agricultural cycle and geographical isolation, produced an extremely conservative religious system and peasant morality. Märchen and legends developed in a social and political atmosphere historically characterized by devout belief in the supernatural, polemic distinctions between good and evil, and belief in supernatural intervention in human affairs.

People believed that divinity would assert itself, either in punishment for wrongdoing or in assistance to holy people in the presence of evil. This world view furnishes the basis for the plots of the legends, permeates the märchen, and finds its way into the personal experience stories. Clementina's true experience narratives in particular reveal both communal religiosity and personal ethos, as seen in these excerpts from her autobiographical stories:

> I grew up dominated and subjected to obedience, but all the same I could not agree with some of the old people because they were too religious—fanatical. They spoke of God day and night and prayed all the time. Most of them are too religious, I mean holy. Pray, pray all the time. I said, "Sure I pray" when they asked me. But when you're young, you don't think you have to do it to stay out of hell.

And speaking of the devil:

> The devil has his own reign and his own power and that is why I think God put us here in this world. People have different ways of thinking. I think life is like purgatory because we have to put up with each other. . . . If you are good and love the people who are around you and treat people well, you'll be happy. It's necessary to create your own happiness. True love, the love of God, is the summit. Perfect love brings perfect joy in every way.[14]

Central to these beliefs about God and the devil is the matter of power, both temporal and cosmic. The peasants of Faller were poor. For centuries they had been dominated by the nobility, by marauding armies, and even by their own conviction of the inevitability of human subjugation.

In the legends and the märchen, power differences give form to the plots and recommend to the powerless the wisdom of obedience. Power relations are presented in the stratified relations that occur between people and the supernatural. The tales of magic express the traditional dominance of the nobility over ordinary peasants. In the legends each member of the community is accountable to other community members and God. Bad actions, such as refusing to say the rosary, were thought not only to displease God but also attract the attention of the devil, who then enters the community to capture the sinner. Violating moral imperatives is likely to threaten the health of community members, since it was believed individual illnesses or epidemics were a symbol and a consequence of divine retribution. Unfaltering devotion to God and the liturgical calendar was the only path to safety in the secular world and to salvation after death. The daily saying of the rosary was not so much a customary act of devotion as it was a local law.

Although the magic tales and legends stress obedience, there are differences in orientation. While the legends tend to emphasize conformity to established patterns of village behavior and vividly describe punishments for transgressions, in the märchen a balance is struck between obedience and ingenuity, and ultimately both qualities are rewarded. The disobedient character is often later revealed to be clever and resourceful, and he or she is then praised for the accomplishment, though the praise is indirect and paradoxical. In such stories success achieved by any means other than self-discipline is tolerated but ignored. The linkage so often made in the märchen between *osservanza* (obedience) and *furberia* (wiliness) is found throughout Italian peasant society. This joining of personal traits appears time and time again in Italian folktales and other verbal genres such as proverbs, sayings, and songs, showing that intelligence and quick wit, when not obviously displayed, are highly valued. Legends and märchen, then, reveal details about the physical and social environment of the village and represent the reservoir of knowledge of the group. Roger Abrahams says of narratives in other societies:

> and just as each person knows everybody else's "business"—that is, their personal stories—so everyone is presumed to know all the tales of their group's traditional repertoire. The storyteller also will assume such knowledge on the part of the audience except when it is composed exclusively of children, knowing that because the stories are all familiar, listeners will be constantly judging his or her ability to tell the tale. In short, there is continual monitoring of the telling of stories—whether of a tale or just of gossip—in manner similar to that in which actual behavior is judged all of the time. This is the way of the small community worldwide, for the well-being of the group resides in the sharing of this kind of knowledge, through which family and friendship networks are woven into the web of community.[15]

12

Clementina's legends are also folk religious narratives. In Faller they personalize the abstractions of Catholic dogma, instructing children and reminding adults of appropriate communal behavior. Originally performed from on high in the medieval pulpits, the narratives are now brought down to earth and performed on the stable floor. Framed in the natural environment of the village with its surrounding fields, paths, and outbuildings, the action of the legend dramatizes human encounters with supernatural beings who are always present and nearby.

In Clementina's legends, priests and monks, highly respected in northern Italy, are depicted as good, pure, modest, generous, and self-denying. God may give an exceptionally good priest the power to perform miracles. He can control material objects, influence nature, ward off hail or frost to save the crops, as in "The Good Priest and the Rich Stranger," and even raise the dead, as in "The Monk and His Cloak." Daily battle is waged with the devil, as in "The Old Man and the Rosary" and "The Old Man Who Couldn't Die." Legends that focus on irreverent acts and on devilish punishments in Clementina's corpus are "The Story of the Black Sheep," "The Old Man Who Couldn't Die," "The Old Man and the Rosary," and "The Dark Men." Those that describe miraculous power and the extraordinary behavior of village priests and monks include "The Good Priest and the Rich Stranger," "The Monk and His Cloak" (in which priestly modesty is described), "The Monk and the Mason" (unusual because of its urban setting), and "Saint Peter Gets His Way."

The legend from Clementina's repertoire that most fully reveals the religious ethos of the Fallerese is "The Monk and the Mason," which shows profound belief in the power of goodness. A local hierarchy of the priesthood is the subject chosen to demonstrate how goodness and miracles are linked, how goodness is recognized and rewarded by God, and how goodness and the ecclesiastical hierarchy are connected. In this story a poor but good monk sees a mason slip and fall from his scaffold and halts his fall. But the cleric cannot bring the man safely to the ground until he receives permission to do so from the brother superior. The people watching now run to the monastery to ask for this permission, while the mason, through the monk's power, remains arrested in midfall. The villagers' view of the power of goodness is incorporated here. While human beings must respect earthly hierarchies, God need not, and may even specify that one of lower estate be able to exercise more power than those higher up. That the monk, unlike his superior, had the ability to perform miracles was a sign of divine destiny.

Rebelliousness, as seen in "The Devil Gets Tricked," is an invitation to the devil. It gives him permission to entrap the rebel. If the devil comes after someone, he or she is personally responsible for the pursuit, as Satan is drawn to the person by a weakness revealed and is repelled by piety displayed. We learn more about village notions of the devil in "The Good Priest and the Rich Stranger." Here the good country priest and Satan struggle violently over the crops. The priest is victorious by a sheer act of will but is so weakened by the struggle that he sickens and dies. At the end of the legend he is taken into heaven in spirit and in body as well, manifesting the vividness of the peasants' belief in the resurrection.

Generally, the legends honor modesty, practicality, piety, faith, kindness, humility, generosity, honesty, deference to superiors, obedience to God's will, or acceptance of things as they are—all traditional Roman Catholic virtues dating from the Middle Ages. The motif of submission to God's will is connected to the idea of perfection in "Saint Peter Gets His Way," and in the "Bloodred Evil Elf" the theme of obedience is extended to the mother.

Many details of daily life are woven through the legends. Men emigrating to find work and women staying behind to manage households in the village are historical facts which appear as motifs in the "Bloodred Evil Elf." In "The Story of the Black Sheep," the stable is described as a meeting place for work, play, and verbal art. In this legend visitors come from a nearby town, and the recitation of the rosary ends the evening. Stable visitations and the rules of personal comportment are also explored in "The Old Man Who Couldn't Die." Of all the legends, "The Old Man and the Rosary" is the richest in ethnographic detail. Here transhumance (the seasonal movement of herds to higher pastures in the summer and lower pastures in the winter) is explained and the communal life and work of the male herding crew, which stays together in a *capanna* (hut) in the higher mountain pastures, is described. This legend speaks of male work organization and the cycle and timing of duties and also reveals the remarkable religiosity of the males in this part of Italy. After their long work day, the five shepherds gather together to pray and say the rosary.

The märchen, like the legend, is set in or near a village and absorbs the features of the peasantry there. Rules that govern everyday occurrences in the country also guide the aesthetic movement in the märchen. People listening in the stable may see a parallel morality in these stories, which ultimately serve to reinforce communal ethos. This cyclic relationship between the real community and the content of the narrative ties the stories closer and closer to the life of the village.

The märchen is a historical document. Its content probably reflects the life of rural people more fully than the legend. While the legend began its life in written form and then passed into oral tradition, the märchen was born in speech and remained free from the interference of scribes for hundreds of years. Dégh notes that "the mores of the magic tale recall the dominance of the medieval church. Pious, God-fearing heroes personify Christian virtues: innocence, constancy, righteousness, fidelity."[16] In addition, the chivalric code of honor applies specifically to the nobles in the stories, who must keep their promises regardless of the circumstances. This insistence on the code of honor for royalty appears in "Margherita" and in "The Ducks That Talked."

The märchen gives us vivid pictures of the medieval practice of punishment and retribution. "The Ducks That Talked," "Margherita," "The Cats under the Sea," "The Cherry Tree and the Pumpkin Vine," "The Gourd of Blood," and "The Dark Men" all reveal a code of proportional morality which demands an eye for an eye. In the märchen the expansiveness of a magical world in which anything is possible contrasts with the real world of the village, where the limitations on supplies of food, periods of rest, and clothing were hard and clear, as seen in "The Forty-One Robbers." Ethnographic details regarding emigration and absent fathers appear in "The Story of Little Peter," "The Devil Gets Tricked," "Margherita," and "The Cherry Tree and the Pumpkin Vine."

The primogeniture model of inheritance, in which the firstborn son receives the father's property, is a factor in "The Gourd of Blood." In this tale an older brother has inherited the father's property and is greedily hoarding most of it after giving the poorest part to his younger brother. After the older brother takes his own life, the younger brother inherits all of his property and marries the most beautiful girl in the next town, who, as the tale tells us, finds him quite a bit more attractive now that he is rich.

Attitudes toward property and honesty merge in tales such as "The Story of Little Peter." After the witches have burned to death, Peter may keep their gold in good faith because "they have no relatives to leave it to." What the gold made possible was decent clothing and freedom from hunger. In "The Twelve Doves on the Mountain of the Sun," the poor boy hesitates before gathering up the jewels because he has been brought up "religiously and with strict ideas about obeying the law." The boy's good fortune is magically provided, but he secures the goods through his own ingenuity. Treasure may be kept by the finder as long as it is known that the treasure was stolen originally.

Village organization of production is described in a number of the märchen. "The Three Brothers and the Fig Tree" speaks about the developmental cycle of the fig crop, for example. In this tale Clementina's touch shows up in the use of several unusual features. There is a tiger in the tale, and a king is seen reading. The tale ends with the princess marrying the peasant boy and going off to live with him in his house—a reversal of the common prince-marries-peasant-girl pattern. This last characteristic may reflect the patrilocal residence pattern of Faller families. (As noted in "The Storyteller in Italy," when John Todesco emigrates, leaving Clementina in Faller, she goes to live at her father-in-law's house.) The king who reads in this tale is unique in Clementina's repertoire, and the tiger may have been added to the tale in Faller by Zio Patrizio, who read a lot, or by an emigrant returned, like Zio Bepi, or perhaps put in by Clementina herself in order to please her children.

In "The Stone of Gold," "Barbarina," and "The Cats under the Sea," we see girls at work. In the first the young girl helps her father do the plowing, and in the second the main character, Barbarina, and her four sisters assist their father in the grazing pastures and are responsible for milking the cows and getting them into the stable at night. Picking vegetables and cooking them are also tasks for young girls. That the father is rearing his five daughters alone is a switch from the more common theme of a mother alone with her children. "Barbarina" calls to mind Clementina's description of her own duties as a peasant girl in Faller, but the tasks in the tale seem light in comparison with the work described by Clementina in her personal experience narratives. In "The Cats under the Sea," the young stepdaughter goes to the river to do the family's laundry, a hard task because it is autumn and the river is icy. The description is similar to that given by Clementina in interviews, where she recalled how there were times when she went to the village fountain to do the laundry and had to break through the ice before she could begin. In "The Ducks That Talked," one of the heroine's jobs is to go into the woods to gather firewood to last her family for one week.

Wood gathering also appears in "The Old Magician Sabino." Here we see an echo of the feudal commons, or perhaps even the actual government forestlands, where people could gather wood, stones, and edible herbs. Cenco, the main character in the tale, goes to a nearby forest to gather wood. In "The Forty-One Robbers," a poor landless man, a miller's helper, gathers wood and pine needles to sell in order to have money to buy corn meal to prepare mush to feed his twelve children. He works for farmers of the district and is paid for his labor with food. Thus, he barters his energy for his family and to replenish himself for yet another day's grueling labor.

In this tale we also see the combination of the barter and monetary system characteristic of peasant economy in Italy before World War II. Before the period of industrial expansion, many villages, especially in southern Italy, did not use money or used it infrequently. The husband and wife in "The Forty-One Robbers" do not count money because they don't know how to perform the computation; they are forced to borrow a peck measure for the job. The treasure that the miller's helper finds is in gold coins and in paper bills, a mixing of two levels of exchange.

Other ethnographic facts touched upon in Clementina's märchen are hunting and the use of horses and carriages for noblemen in "The Ducks That Talked," "The Cats under the Sea." and "The Twelve Doves on the Mountain of the Sun." Burial practices are mentioned in "The Forty-One Robbers." Elements of modern culture appear in several tales, such as the one about the tiger and the king who reads. There are references to policemen in "The Gourd of Blood" and "The Forty-One Robbers." A surgeon is mentioned in "The Three Brothers and the Fig Tree," and cities appear in "The Cherry Tree and the Pumpkin Vine" and in "The Cats under the Sea."

While legends and märchen uphold the peasant social and political order and its accompanying ideology, personal experience stories are generally a response to conditions and events outside the village and tend to undermine village boundaries and beliefs. Responses to the society and economy of urban centers, when they are articulated in narratives by skilled raconteurs, bring new ideas into the community. Personal experience stories instruct village youth: these oral histories are linked with the cycle of leaving and returning, and since travel in search of work and return has been for centuries a dynamic of the Faller male community and to a certain extent of the female community as well, personal experience narratives have, no doubt, been told for many years. In this genre the tale-teller becomes the hero or heroine. The stories are no longer physically located in the village and socially woven into the life of the peasants. No longer primarily concerned with supernatural beings and magical solutions, the characters are human, and the solutions are human.

In the stables of Faller, the autobiographical epics entertained all ages and informed potential travelers about what they could expect to find outside of the confines of the community. Whether a man went to work as close by as a factory in a neighboring town and returned home every evening to work in the fields before supper or journeyed as far away as Argentina or the United States, the move was much more than just physical. It was to a new society and life style. The stories of returned emigrants were usually humorous and positive, and as such they encouraged others to experiment with the idea of emigration. They not only had pragmatic value in explaining where work could be found but also symbolic appeal in reflecting success in the New World. The teller returned to tell his tale and to display his cleverness to family and friends. Like Odysseus, who traveled for over twenty years, experienced many rich and strange cultures, and returned home to recount his adventures, Fallerese males have emigrated and returned home to tell their epic tales.

Speaking of the personal experience story or "true story," Linda Dégh points out that new forms of tales are emerging in the modern industrial world economy and that new approaches are being developed in the study of folk narrative. She observes that

> we are no longer so concerned with functional changes produced by traditional folk communities or with ethnic changes due to the diffusion of narratives—it is rather with the degenerative and regenerative process that occurs as genres lose their old meaning and are reformulated to fit new social settings. In the industrial community many of the traditional forms have survived because they are given a new meaning. . . . folklorists today seek the personal experience stories of raconteurs whose lives have changed from a rural to an urban style, as they move from traditional isolation into a pluralistic environment.[17]

Clementina's journey did not involve a return to Faller, but she found audiences in New York, Detroit, and finally, in Phoenix to whom she could tell the stories about her life. In the personal experience story the action takes place in the present. The storyteller is both narrator and the central figure in the story. In telling about events in Clementina's life, which fall outside of the beliefs that she learned to hold as a child in her mountain village, her reminiscences logically fall into two parts: Old World stories and New World stories. In her tales she becomes a folk hero, repeatedly confronting adversity and triumphing over hardships. For her there is no final resolution of life's dilemma. To be human means to be willing to confront the totality of human experience. Clementina was a woman who was deeply situated in her mountain traditions, and her childhood and adolescence of rugged adversity prepared her to confront the immensity of life with resilience, compassion, and endless creative energy.

Context and History

The Village Faller and the Alps

Clementina Todesco was born in 1903 in Faller, then a village of some six hundred inhabitants in the province of Belluno, which is part of the Veneto region in northern Italy. One hundred miles northeast of Venice in the Dolomite mountain range, the town is one of five villages snuggled along the slope of a mountain called Sovramonte (higher mountain). At an elevation of 2,225 feet, Faller is surpassed in altitude only by the village of Aune at 2,585 feet. The other three villages—Servo, Zerzoi, and Sorriva—are all at lower elevations.

The Dolomites have a special character which distinguishes them from other Alpine glacial and rock forms, such as Mont Blanc or the Matterhorn.[1] Deep green conifers cover the hillside, and pastures slope upwards; then suddenly the timber line halts, and sheer walls of dolomitic pinnacles stand like megalithic bows arching the valleys and lowlands. Stretching from the Veneto in the east to Lombardy in the west, the Dolomites' unusual configurations and colors are due to their composition of calcium magnesium carbonate. Similar to limestone but heavier and often crystalline, the Dolomites are actually transmuted coral reefs which plate tectonic forces pressed out of the sea and into their unique folds during the Miocene epoch.[2] On a typical day as the mists evaporate and the rays of the sun touch the mountain and flood the dark valleys with light, the bare porphyritic rock displays hour by hour the changing colors of the spectrum, from white and gray to blue, pink, gold, lime, and purple.

Faller is situated in the Belluno basin, sometimes referred to by geographers as the pre-Alps.[3] Eighty-five miles to the north of Faller by mountain road is the center of the Dolomite region, Cortina D'Ampezzo. Cortina may be reached by traveling through Val di Fiemme and Val di Fassa, where Ladin rather than Italian is the native language. The Austrian border is twenty-five miles to the east of Cortina. From Faller going west, the main highway leads to Trento through the Val Sugana and enters the dolomitic group of Brenta. To the east is Vittorio Veneto, where the decisive battle of World War I was fought, and further east is Udine, the capital of Friuli. One hundred and twenty miles east of Faller on the Yugoslavian border are the city of Gorizia and the Julian Alps. One hundred miles south of Faller is the city of Venice.

Faller may be reached by taking Highway 50 from either Feltre or Trento and then following the provincial road for seven miles through Fonzazo to a fork in the road. Here a winding dirt road ascends to Faller. The distance that would require a half hour on foot takes no more than five minutes by automobile. According to the Fallerese, this dirt road was built in 1884, and modifications were made in 1909 to widen it. At irregular intervals along the stone embankments of the incline are cannon posts dating from World War I. From the lookout post about half way, the Venoi, a stream where excellent trout, pike, and perch may be fished, is a channel of blue meandering through the valley and bending at the Pointe di Serra Hotel, glistening white by the river's edge. Young women of Faller have long furnished a domestic labor force for this hotel, working as chambermaids, laundresses, and cook's assistants. Further up the Sovramonte, the panorama of Faller opens to the eye as a flock of white and red houses against a carpet of green meadows and trees. Apple, pear, and peach trees cluster in the fields just below the village, and ribbons of pine trees fan up the sides of the mountains. A folk belief claims that the first families came to Faller, or Fallero as it was called until the sixteenth century, to produce charcoal from the abundant treasure of evergreens.[4] Golden haystacks, squared and piled into tiny shelters, dot the countryside like windowless straw houses. These small mounds are constructed by farmers with only four poles stabilized by four-foot-square miniature gable roofs. The woods, thick with the fragrance of pine, lean densely against the mountainside, breaking high near the top to reveal crags and bare white walls of sparkling dolomite like enormous Roman ruins.

There is a legend in the town that the *sanguenell* (bloodred elf) took bad boys and girls up to these peaks and abandoned them. At the top of Monte Velazza (6,300 feet) to the north is a lake, the source of the brook which murmurs through the center of the town, past the old church in the piazza with its eighteenth-century bell tower. Village houses used to be built mainly of stone and wood. Today they are constructed for the most part out of cement blocks, given a white or pink stucco treatment, and appointed with pine balconies. Like many mountain homes, the balconies are lined with terra-cotta pots of red geraniums and loaded with pyramids of logs. On a bright day the village and the vast expanse of the valley are a delicate sheath of rainbows.

Historically and politically Faller has been tied to the fortunes of the largest city of the province, Feltre, some ten miles to the east and the administrative capital of the area.[5] Because of this political connection between the larger town and Faller, the historical circumstances of Feltre are essentially the same as Faller. There is no specific history of Faller; therefore, we are relying upon the data from the larger town to locate the village in a historical context.

Feltre is strategically situated along the main Roman road from Oderzo to Trento where the Brenta mountain range and the Piave River are at their closest point. For hundreds of years this city was the object of barbarian attacks by Vandals, Lombards, Ostrogoths, Visigoths, Franks, and Huns. Feltre was plundered by Alaric, king of the Visigoths, in 409, and by Attila the Hun in 451. It was occupied by Alaric, the first barbarian ruler of Italy, in 475, by the Franks in the sixth and eighth centuries, and by the Hungarians in the tenth century. In the Middle Ages, the city was governed by bishop princes. Like many other northern Italian cities, it was the theater for the struggle between the Guelphs, who formed the church party and supported the papacy, and the Ghibellines, who supported the German emperors. In the fourteenth century, the city surrendered to the duchy of Austria. The Venetians seized Feltre in the fifteenth century and held control until the eighteenth century. It was occupied by Napoleon from 1797 until 1814, when it fell back into the hands of Austria. In August 1866 the Italian troops entered Feltre and united the city and the whole region of the Veneto with the newly created Italian nation. This political unity was not supported by the Vatican and therefore was not supported by the people of this zone, who were fiercely loyal to the pope.[6]

In the twentieth century Faller figures prominently in the two world wars. People from the village recalled that from 1915 to 1917 Italians fought along the entire mountainous front.[7] In October 1917 the Austrians invaded Italy and pressed through the Italian defense at Caporetto, now a city in Yugoslavia called Kobarid. Faller was not far from the line of resistance, drawn back to the Piave River, with the center at Monte Grappa, about eighteen miles south of Faller. Faller became an important recuperation center for the Austrians in June 1918. After intense fighting on Monte Grappa, the Austrians would return to Faller and send out fresh reinforcements. In October 1917 the final victory was secured at the battle of Vittorio Veneto, fought about fifty miles southeast of Faller, which signaled the end of the war.[8]

During the Austrian retreat in 1918, women exchanged jewelry, embroidery, handkerchiefs, stones, earrings, and scarves with the enemy for food. People remembered that food was in very short supply and that the Fallerese were desperate, eating whatever was available, even potato peels and leaves. Children would beg Austrian soldiers, *"Pise Prot,"* which is the Italianized version of *bitte Brot* (some bread, please). Clementina gives further details of this period in the town's history in her personal experience stories.

Faller and the whole province of Belluno was important in World War II. Partisan resistance was extremely strong in this region. One woman recalled that when the Germans suspected someone of harboring a partisan, they would burn the house and execute the suspects.[9] In a village near Faller, a partisan had killed a Nazi trooper, and in retaliation ten men were hanged. At Quero, a village near Treviso, a day's journey from Faller, another woman recounted that, as she was pushing a cart of apples which she intended to exchange for polenta, she saw along the road the hanged bodies of partisans.[10] The Fallerese aided the partisans at great risk to their lives.

It is interesting to note that an agreement in 1939 between Hitler and Mussolini permitted the German population of Belluno, Trento, Bolzano, and Udine to choose German citizenship and emigrate to the Reich or to stay in Italy as Italian citizens. About 70 percent of the 260,000 German speakers chose German citizenship, and some 80,000 actually emigrated by 1945. That same year, those who had emigrated were allowed, with some exceptions, to return and apply for Italian citizenship.[11]

Environment and Production

Faller is a mountain village. At this altitude, 2,225 feet, the median temperature is fifty-one degrees Fahrenheit annually. In January the average is about thirty-two degrees, and in July it is about seventy degrees. The annual rainfall is over sixty inches, distributed over one hundred days. Rainfall evaporates rapidly and agricultural yields vary greatly from year to year.[12]

In Italy the size and type of farm as well as the land tenure conditions vary from region to region. The greatest difference is from north to south. In Faller, as in the north of Italy generally, there are many privately owned small farms of twelve acres. In addition, some land is rented on a cash basis by farmers. The northern system stands in contrast to the southern Italian agricultural arrangement of *mezzadria* (sharecropping), where farmers pay a percentage, usually one-half or more of their produce, for the use of the land.[13] Farming in Faller, as in agricultural zones throughout Italy, is labor intensive, and capital is scarce. The agricultural technology is of the sort referred to by Eric Wolf as "paleotechnic," that is, it consists mainly of human labor and simple tools such as the *zappa*, a heavy, wooden-handled hoe.[14]

Faller families practice subsistence farming combined with wage labor in factories in Feltre or Lamon. Farm production is mainly for family consumption and not for sale. Principal crops are maize and corn. Corn is used for fodder for livestock and for polenta, which, along with rice, serves as the staple dish in Faller and in the entire Veneto region. Other crops in Faller are potatoes, cauliflower, artichokes, and tomatoes. A variety of legumes are also grown, particularly beans, peas, and lentils. In the countryside people gather wild mushrooms, asparagus, and berries, and they hunt grouse, partridge, and pheasant. The latter are often served with polenta.

Over five hundred years old, the town of Faller is divided into three parts—Paliser, Villa, and Ramen. Paliser is the newest section, built since World War II. Villa is the main section of town, where the church and the small square are located. Past the piazza begins Ramen, the oldest part of town. Here ancestral homes mingle with modern construction. Like most Italian villages which have experienced heavy emigration and received immigrants' remittances since World War II, the original Alpine architectural configuration of Faller is being replaced with concrete block and stucco. In years past, regional identities in Italy were clearly indicated by differing architectural styles and construction materials. Today, however, wide use of relatively inexpensive concrete block and stucco throughout Italy give a similar appearance to villages of every region, and lines of demarcation are increasingly blurred in Italian architecture, as they are in most other expressive forms such as language, music, and dance.

Mass media and mass production have entered Faller, and in this village the change is radical, as it is throughout Italy. Everywhere in Faller tall slabs of timber lean against the sides of houses, ready to be fashioned for their renovation. Plastic coverings shake in the breeze over dark entrances about to be given new doors or windows. House roofs of commercial red tile replace the old terra-cotta tile. House interiors are simple, clean, and functional. There is usually a large kitchen area with stove and refrigerator, dining table and chairs, a sofa, one cabinet where wine and liquor bottles are stored, and perhaps another where cups, saucers, and small ceramic figurines are displayed. Floors are wooden and scrubbed by hand once a week. Walls are white and bare, except for a crucifix or religious pictures and occasionally some family photographs. In one house there was a photo of the owner's son playing an electric piano in a rock band.

As one would expect, population is declining in Faller. Six hundred people lived in the village at the turn of the century. Today there are only two hundred. The population decline, primarily an effect of emigration, is viewed by villagers as inevitable. Most of the young men have emigrated to Switzerland for jobs in construction or to Germany for jobs in factories.[15] Some have found wives abroad and become permanent residents in those countries. Since 1960 the trend has been for whole families to emigrate and make their way as a unity in the foreign land. They work hard and save money; after sufficient money is accumulated, some return to Faller, buy land, build a house, and are hired by the paper mill at Fonzazo or the foundry at Feltre. Every morning at 5:00 A.M., the returned immigrants leave Faller for work and travel one hour to the factory, where they toil for eight hours. Every afternoon, they return to work the village fields for the two or three hours of daylight remaining.[16] A factory job is preferred, for the villagers say it offers regular work and steady pay and does not subject man to the capricious conditions of nature. Fallerese regard this combination of factory and farm work as superior to either occupation by itself. The arrangement affords the family its food plus a bit of capital to be used for purchases of equipment and for luxury goods.

In the nineteenth century as today, highly skilled men from Faller went to different parts of Europe rather than across the Atlantic Ocean for work. Most immigrants were seasonal workers who stayed closer to home in the Austro-Hungarian Empire. They could do factory and farm work. A few had ventured forth and traveled to Brazil and Argentina to labor in the sugar fields. Most Italian immigrants to South America settled the land, while of the small fraction who came to the United States the majority settled in cities.

In the twentieth century until World War II, almost all unmarried men emigrated from Faller and remained away for as long as twenty years in order to make enough money to buy a house and a small parcel of farmland at home. If the young man was married, his wife rarely accompanied him to France, Belgium, Luxembourg, or the United States, where he labored in the coal mines. More frequently, the wife remained at home, raised children, and, with in-laws, worked the fields and cared for farm animals, rabbits, chickens, pigs, and cows. Small children would be cared for by grandmother until ready for first grade. Children as a rule went to school only for three years; as soon as they completed the third grade, they went to work in the fields and gradually took over the chores of old people. Not only did the economy force families to separate, but tragically, many mine workers contracted silicosis and died before the age of fifty, extinguishing their dreams of returning to plow the soil and enjoy the clean air in the rural village they remembered.

This pattern of what Douglas Holmes calls the ''discontinuous peasant-worker'' strategy has predominated in Faller and in the northeastern region of Italy since the nineteenth century. Opportunities for industrial employment in northern Europe attracted men from rural areas to work in those manufacturing centers for most of the year and then return to their households periodically to help with the planting and harvesting of farm products. Holmes distinguishes two other working patterns which operate less frequently in Faller. The ''continuous peasant-worker'' strategy allows the men to remain in the village and farm while maintaining a full-time, wage-earning job in a nearby factory. The third pattern is the ''passive peasant-worker'' strategy, which is also found in Faller.[17] The Italian pension system provides all people— housewives, doctors, government workers, farmers, laborers— with a continuous income after retirement. This enables those pensioners in the village to continue to work the land on a full-time basis.

Almost all men who did not emigrate were able to stay behind in the village because they owned land and cattle. They worked their farms, ploughed the fields of others with their horses, and cut and transported hay for neighbors. Most immigrants would have preferred to remain in Faller to be close to their families, to speak their native tongue, and to avoid the possible pain of rejection in foreign lands, where Italian laborers are often not well received. Today, however, most believe it is impossible to live in Faller as a farmer. Only pensioners seem able to get by. In this village, where the land does not yield easily and where cash is needed to buy new products, agriculture has become a supplementary occupation.

Young people shun the land and seek to finish high school or vocational school at Servo, Fonzazo, or Feltre, which equips them to become mechanics, draftsmen, and electricians. Before World War II, the only high school was at Fonzazo, a long journey down the mountain which had to be made on foot. Today, industrial training has expanded to allow the young to develop skills so that they may function in a technological market-place beyond the Dolomite community. Wage-labor economy is changing the appearance of Faller and deeply affecting its social relationships.

One villager's experience is a typical one.[18] Fiorentina's living room was once her father-in-law's stable. The second floor of her house was the hayloft. When her father-in-law died twenty-two years ago, his property was divided. Fiorentina's brother-in-law inherited his father's old house and Fiorentina got the stable and the surrounding piece of property. She and her son decided to remodel the stable to make it livable. As a first step they replaced the roof and made some outside repairs. The plan was to do other work as funds were available from Fiorentina's son's work in Switzerland as a bricklayer during the building season. With the money earned, they paid off the debts incurred in remodeling the stable. For ten years Fiorentina's son labored as a seasonal worker, working in the summer months in Switzerland and returning in the off-season from October to March to Faller to work on the house. Meanwhile, Fiorentina and her mother-in-law took care of the fields and the animals, and the building, although undergoing remodeling, was still used to house the animals.

When the stable renovation was completed, Fiorentina thought about the fact that she now had a house but no stable. She decided to build a new stable, but the local housing authority refused permission. Faller had now been placed in a tourist category and was no longer classified primarily as a farming community. No more stables could be built. Today Fiorentina's son and his family live in the stable converted into a new house and keep their cows in a rented stable.

Fiorentina's experience demonstrates the manner in which the combination of wage-labor economy and imported new concepts of what is suitable and beautiful has changed Faller. The combination has affected the village in both material and symbolic ways. The material changes are the most obvious. Architecture is visible. One can see a stable being transformed into a house, as in the case of Fiorentina's stable. The symbolic or ideological changes are less evident, but they are clearly represented there.

Material and symbolic forms of culture are interrelated and changes in one domain will result in changes in the other. Changes in the aesthetics of architecture and living space have consequences in actual changes in structures, such as the transformation of a stable into a house. The consequences of such material change, then, are seen in the way in which people interact, in the frequency and context of communication between people, and especially in artistic communication, such as story-telling.

The Storyteller in Italy

Clementina Slongo Todesco was one of eight children of Benvenuto Slongo, the town mayor, notary, folk veterinarian, and landowner. Benvenuto was considered the richest man in town because he owned over twenty head of cattle and many acres of land. As a child, Clementina would often go with her brothers and sisters through the dandelion fields into the woods to gather mushrooms. Her mother used these mushrooms for a tasty risotto made with rice and butter for the evening meal. Sometimes Clementina would help her father make sausage with veal and pork, a local dish for which he was renowned in the region. "Oh boy, when you fried a little of that sausage, the smell was sent all over town," Clementina remarked in an interview. The family was not poor. There was more than enough to eat. However, when Clementina was six years old, circumstances changed with the death of her mother. Two years later Clementina's father married a widow with a daughter near Clementina's age. The stepmother, Maria, or Yolla as she was called in the local dialect, was strict.

As she grew older, Clementina, like all mountain girls, came to be responsible for many chores. Up before dawn, she had *cafe orzo,* a mixture of two parts barley and one part coffee, for breakfast. Then Clementina was out in the bean, tomato, carrot, radish, and lettuce patches tending crops until sundown. She remembered that

> after two hours in the field, the stepmother came with a chest of
> bread and milk. In the afternoon she took us sometimes a little

fried salami or eggs and fried greens while we were hoeing or with the cows. At night there was lots of salty vegetable soup that was made in a big caldron. . . . We were so tired and sleepy. We had to be there on the corner of the field to work on the potatoes or corn or whatever it was and wait for the daylight. We never had enough rest. In the evening, one of my brothers went down to Fonzazo or Feltre to bring the supplies for the cheese house. Well, they came home late at night with the horses and were tired. They ate and went to bed because they had to get up early in the morning. So, I or my sisters had to wait for our brother, then take the horse to the fountain for water. The last one to go to bed went maybe eleven or midnight. And we were up at five A.M. It was like this every day of the year.

As part of her chores, Clementina learned to pile the earth up around the potato plants. Some days she would go into the woods to gather firewood. Other times she went to the stable to feed fodder to the cows or go with her brother who would take the *seivi*, two wooden pails hung together by a low-bending bow balanced on the back, to get water at the fountain.

In the summer Clementina had to climb the mountain to milk the cows that her father kept in a stable high above the town. With her brother she would bring the pails down to the cheese house. At the *caseificio* (dairy), the dairyman and his two assistants would pour the milk into large barrels, later to be processed into butter and cheese, as was the milk of every farmer in the village. Like other villagers Clementina would enter the quantity of milk she deposited in a large account book kept on the wooden counter of the dairy. Every fifteen days the dairyman would send a statement to Benvenuto and other farmers citing the quantity of milk still in reserve. In this Alpine hamlet the dairy served another function as a local bank. Whenever farmers had to pay taxes, they went to the dairy to withdraw their money.

At harvest time, hay was cut with a scythe. Men, women, and children worked together. As men cut the hay, women and children spread the stalks out to dry in the sun. The hay was turned over and over again to assure thorough drying; then, in the late afternoon, the *mea* (haystack) was made. During the summer months, entire families worked in the fields all day.[1] Sometimes women settled their infants snugly into woven baskets and carried them on their backs into the countryside to work the land. Clementina recalled an array of hearty women—reddish complexion, blue-green eyes, kerchiefs tied around chestnut hair—threshing and swooping rhythmically while cutting the hay. Work and song went together, and the pattern of the women's labors would be matched by music. Singing lightened the harvesting and made repetitive tasks less boring. Clementina remembered the women singing a traditional ballad called "La Invidosa Suocera":

Mama de la mia mama io vo a leto a riposar se mio marito viene mandatemi a chiamar.	Mother, dearest mother, I am going to take a nap; if my husband comes home, send him in to wake me.
A mezzanote in punto si senti bussar la porta la mama se nacorta che corse subito aprir.	At midnight exactly a knock was heard on the door; the mother had heard it and quickly ran to open it.
Mama de la mia mama dov'e le mi sorele dov'e le mie sorele le mie sorele dov'e?	Mother, dearest mother, where are my sisters; where are my sisters, my sisters where are they?
Le tue sorele e in camera a cucir e ricamar la tua sposina cara e a leto a riposar.	Your sisters are in the bedroom sewing and embroidering, and your dear little wife is in bed resting.
Mama de la mia mama presteme il vostro stile quel carteli d'argento che il cuore vo ferir.	Mother, dearest mother lend me your dagger, that silver knife that I want to pierce the heart with.
Il belo entra in camera con aria e con furor e con lo stile acuto le traforava il cuor.	The handsome young man enters the room, mad with rage, and the sharp dagger stabs her heart fiercely.

Marito mio marito	Husband, dearest husband,
cos'hai pensa di me?	what do you think of me
con tre bambini in cula	with three tiny children in the crib
che papa non sano chiamar.	who cannot yet talk?
Moglie di la mia moglie	Wife, dearest wife,
voresti tu guarir	if you want to be healed
trescento mila medici	three hundred thousand doctors
io ti fero venir.	I'll fetch for you.
O no, marito mio	Oh no, dearest husband,
non posso piu quarir	I can no longer be cured;
la pugnalata al cuore	the wound in my heart
la mia fara morir.	will make me die.
Vami chiamar d'un prete	Go call a priest;
che mi voglio confessar	I want to confess.
vami chiamar la mama	Go and call mother;
che voglio perdonar.	I want to ask her forgiveness.
Le undici son suonate	Eleven o'clock strikes;
a meza note sari gia morta	at midnight I will be dead.
diman sero sepolta	Tomorrow I will be buried;
si rivedremo in ciel.	we'll see each other in heaven.

On hot days families made polenta for lunch in the fields over a fireplace built of two or three rocks. It was the custom to organize work cooperatively along kinship lines. Groups of three or four families worked together rapidly to stack and store the hay before the rain came. At night after the harvest, men went to the village tavern, and young people lingered in the countryside to flirt and sing under the trees.

As years passed Clementina's family grew to fourteen. Washing had to be done twice a week, and Clementina shared this responsibility with her sisters. In the winter when it was her turn, Clementina stuffed the clothes into a potato sack, carried them down to the town fountain, and, with a small chunk of home-made soap, scrubbed while icicles formed on the edges of the garment. There was little talk as women toiled briskly at the fountain to complete the task, immersing chapped, bluish hands into the sheet of water, beating, twisting, and squeezing the soiled garments. For especially dirty clothes Clementina would add a cup of ashes to a tub of boiling water and soak the clothes overnight. The next morning they were taken to the fountain for scrubbing.

While Clementina's life was filled with many hard rural chores, she was not constrained, as were Faller girls from poorer families, to leave home to work as a domestic in a large city. Generally, domestics would send home almost all the salary they garnered through washing, cleaning, cooking, tending children, and sometimes serving as wet nurses. One woman remembers her experience as a domestic in the Ponte di Serra hotel in this way:

> The lady counted the potatoes she gave me at supper. Can you imagine! A young girl like I was, full of life and get-up-and-go, leaving the mountains for the city. I had such an appetite I could have eaten rocks. . . . The lady had two children; one had a spinal disease and was bandaged. He never wanted to eat. I had to force him to eat. Such patience I had to have because the child was nervous and kept kicking me as I forced the food into his mouth. My legs were always black-and-blue. And all night long I had to watch the eight-month-old baby who had whooping cough. . . . Early in the morning before seven A.M., I had to wash a chest full of underwear. At the fountain in freezing water, I had to wash all the clothes. No breakfast, not even a cup of coffee. I remember I was always hungry.[2]

Before mechanization had been introduced into farming, poor women from Faller and all over the Veneto went to Piedmont each year to spend weeks harvesting rice. Since Italy was and still is the largest producer of rice in Europe, these women, called *mondaie* (daily laborers), were indispensable in performing the exhausting jobs in the rice fields.[3]

Religion
While life in Faller was filled with daily farm work, heavy and urgent, there were moments of fun and play. Religious celebrations were extremely important in the lives of the people of the Veneto region. This area of Italy today is called *La Zona Bianca* (the white zone) because of the intense piety of its inhabitants and their devotion to the pope.

The Fallerese celebrated many religious holidays, the most important of which was the feast of Santa Filomena. This saint is a legendary figure believed to have been a martyred virgin of the third century. Occurring on the second Sunday in August, the holiday commemorates a miracle that is said to have happened in the nineteenth century. One night in 1833, according to local belief, the custodian of the sacristy could not sleep because he was thinking of the gravity of the plague which had struck the village. Suddenly, he heard a voice beckon, "Marco, Marco." Fearful, he asked, "Who calls me? What do you want?" The voice instructed, "Tell the villagers to make a vow and the plague will pass." In the morning the puzzled custodian reported his experience to the priest, who called a meeting of villagers to discuss what to do. They decided to set aside a special day each year in honor of Santa Filomena. The villagers built a special altar in the church and placed upon it a statue of the saint in a glass casket. Two days after this vow was made, as the story goes, the plague disappeared.

Today, everyone remembers this feast of late August as an occasion of great ritual and excitement. They recall that sometimes a full week was spent in preparing for the event. The little square in the center of the village was decorated with banners and Venetian balloons. Arches were made with moss and branches and hung all around the square. The festivities began about 9:00 A.M. with mass. A procession followed, and in accordance with the ancient vow, the statue of Santa Filomena was carried around town. Beginning at the church, the procession moved along the main road to the shrine, followed a tiny road up the hill which circled the town to the cemetery, and finally descended to return to the church. In honor of the saint, the villagers sang "Gesum Corona," "Virginum," "Veni Sponsa Christi" (Jesus Crowned; Blessed Virgin; Come, Bride of Christ), and other hymns to honor the saint.

A secular celebration followed the religious one. In the center of the square were rows of tables with fabulous assortments of watermelon, peaches, ice cream, strudel, and a local cake called *pinzeta*. There were also toys, like ceramic whistles and kites. All afternoon the community participated in races and games. Perhaps the most exciting of the adult games was called *albero della cuccagna,* the tree of plenty. Salami, cheese, and flasks of wine were suspended from a wheel on top of a tall sturdy pole greased with animal fat. Young men took turns trying to climb the greased pole, sometimes forming pyramids to boost a climber on his way. In this area, the man or boy who scaled the pole first had the honor of distributing the food to family and friends. The feast day ended with a return to the religious tone. Fallerese spent the evening visiting the cemetery to bring flowers to the graves of deceased loved ones and remained in the cemetery for a time looking at family pictures on the tombstones and informing their dead relatives about family events.

In the past men and women attended church in great numbers. In Faller men entered the church from a side door and sat in the front pews. Women entered from the back door and sat in the rear. Services were always well attended. Submission to ecclesiastical authority was regarded as the path to salvation. Not to submit would have been an expression of the sin of pride. Reverence for the teachings of the church and for "God's shepherd," the priest, was the center of village life. Springing from this religious core were the basic concepts which formed the cultural codes of the community: honesty and family unity. The people were devout. During Lent, when the church bells rang, people stopped working the fields and attended devotions. They made the stations of the cross and the novenas. Whenever they were without a priest for Sunday service, they traveled on foot to Fonzazo, Servo, or Sorriva.

The people of Faller were honed by suffering and stung by hunger and war. It left them with little patience for theories— political, social, or economic. Responding to political demonstrations in the large centers of Milan and Turin, one informant said:

> Don't come and talk to me of stupid things because I'll break the faces of those talkers, especially those young people who demonstrate. I'm talking about the truth now. They can talk about philosophy only after they've experienced what we have. There's no substance to what they say.[4]

The Stables

The stables offered the major place to socialize. During the cold months of winter it was the custom for villagers to gather in stables for warmth and companionship after supper. The stable was the symbol of wealth and power because it indicated ownership of cattle. A Faller proverb stresses the importance of wealth in the community; *La roba, marito, la goba,* rendered roughly, means that if a hunchback has money, she will find a husband. The older stables going back to the seventeenth century were built of pine timbers, while the later ones dating from the nineteenth century were made of stone. Stables were generally adjacent to the house and had two levels. The first floor was an open space with stalls along the walls for animals. The second level was for hay storage.

Clementina described her father's stable as the largest in town. She recalled there was room for five or six families, about thirty or thirty-five people. Every night from five to nine, November through March, she remembered sitting in the stable near her Grandmother Slongo and helping the old woman shell the beans and peel the potatoes for the next day's minestrone. Frequently, supper was eaten in the stable, for the fumes from the *camino* (fireplace), where cooking was done in the caldron, would not ventilate up through the chimney but would blow into the kitchen. Many times soup or a simpler *panecotto,* made of bread, oil, water, and butter, was prepared in the kitchen and carried to the stable to be eaten. People would sit on low stools and balance bowls of brimming soup on their laps. When the soup was too hot, the bowls were set in a pile of snow to cool. After supper Clementina might help her stepmother swaddle a younger brother or sister.

Most of the day in the winter, infants remained in the warm stable under the care of grandparents. It was not until they reached two or three years of age that they were allowed more freedom to play outdoors in the snow. Infants were fed a cornmeal and buttermilk mixture called *mussa* and cleaned with the unsoiled corners of underwear. Children were bathed in the stable, then covered with blankets and brought into the house to sleep. Mothers used a wooden bed warmer filled with lighted coal, a *monega,* which was placed under the covers of the child's bed. In the afternoon children napped in the stable on the hay stored in bins. If a baby were sick, the only thermometer in town could be borrowed from the dairy.

Standards of conduct appropriate to the home were observed in the stable. The stable was like a comfortable family room, where guests were greeted cordially and invited to pass the long winter evenings in the coziness of human companionship. A free zone, the stable functioned to mediate the intimate gestures of home life with the formal rituals of public interaction.

In Faller patrilocal marriage was the custom. The woman was carried like a bundle of logs, as one woman phrased it, and deposited in the house where she was ordered first to work, then to eat.[5] In the stable the young bride listened to the conversation of her in-laws and discovered what she did wrong, how she did not work properly, and how she was to operate differently. The critique continued for four or five years. "If the mother-in-law is sensitive and instructs the daughter-in-law properly, she gives her a belief in herself," one informant made clear.

In the stable women sat on tiny seats in a circle around an oil lamp. They brought chests filled with material and would sew, knit, and teach the girls how to embroider linens for their trousseaux. The central activity of the stable was the *filo,* the spinning of hemp on a spindle or spinning wheel. The hemp was grown in Faller, cut, and put into a tub of water to soften. Later it was combed with a special tool until it was ready to be spun on a distaff. After the hemp was spun, it was brought to a weaver in town, who wove the cloth on a hand loom into bed sheets, tablecloths, or suits of clothing. Some of the fabrics, like the sheets and pillowcases, were carried back to the stable to be embroidered in red thread with the head of the household's initials.

The stable was a communication center for villagers. As women worked they chatted about who was getting married, who was expecting a baby, who was sick, how to cook rabbit and pork, or how to season mountain lettuce. Behind the women sat the men, clustered in groups. They worked on winter tasks, such as repairing rakes and other farm implements or making wooden snow boots. They compared what they intended to plant in the spring and which crops to rotate the next season. Once in a while an occasional curse escaped from a frolicsome child who needed to be chastised. Interspersed among the others were the young people over sixteen years of age, shyly sitting a little apart, stealing furtive glances, flirting, the boy speaking softly of what he did in the fields that day, the girl quiet, sewing or mending. The stable was the opportunity for young men and women to meet, since all courting was done in the presence of parents. Eventually, a young man and woman were engaged. The traditional Faller term was *si parlano*, they are speaking. According to Clementina,

> they used to do that. The boys came from Sorriva, Zerzoi, Servo to Faller to see if the girls were interested in them . . . from one town to the other. And the boys from the same town were jealous because they thought these others from the outside would take the girls away. Like Zio Bepi said to another guy, "She wants you. She loves you, and you're making a mistake. She's the best girl in town, and you're letting a stranger come to take her away."
> . . . In front of everybody, Zio Bepi embarrassed him very bad. [She chuckled.] . . . Anyway, in the stables everybody is sitting right there in the stable, and the boy is bashful, and the girl feels ashamed. The boy doesn't have enough courage to ask the girl anything. He just tells her what he did during the day. And the girls were always sewing and making socks. I remember, once my sister was so nervous that even after she made a mistake while she was making these socks, she kept on going. [Laughter.] . . .
> Next morning she had to take everything apart to begin again.

The stable was also a medical center for villagers. Large bins lined the sides of the opposite walls of the stable where dry leaves, used to cover the floors of the cow stalls, were stored. During the evening, men and children sometimes napped here, for it was believed that if one had a cold he could be cured by lying on the leaves. Other folk cures were passed on in the stable. For pleurisy a glass was applied to the infected area to suction off the liquid formed in the lungs. Leaves and grated potatoes were used for abscesses, squash for toothaches, leaves from the nut tree to relieve arthritis. The local priest was thought to know something about medicine. He occasionally visited the patient in the stable and prescribed a cure. Doctors were used only in extreme circumstances, such as tuberculosis, pneumonia, difficult childbirths, and physical injuries.

In the stables villagers also exchanged narratives about popular religious beliefs and cures. These prescriptions were ways to avoid illness and misfortune. If the first person met on New

Year's Day was a woman, then bad luck was sure to follow. Once a young man met an old woman on New Year's Day just before going off to fight in World War I. Later it was reported he saw his own corpse, and finally his body was discovered by soldiers at Gorizia. On the evening of All Souls' Day, people stayed indoors because it was said that the souls of the dead wandered along the street in a procession toward the cemetery. It could be very dangerous to meet such a spirit, it was believed. As one story tells, on the eve of All Souls' Day a young man started off to see his girlfriend, and on the way, he encountered a line of ghosts with their thumbs lit as candles. Curious, the young man approached one ghost and pulled off the thumb light and took it home with him. For one year he suffered without light because of the theft. Finally, in desperation at the end of that time, he nervously rushed to the same spot, encountered the ghost, and returned the thumb light to its rightful owner.

Devil lore cycles were commonly heard in the stables. It is interesting that these tales were sometimes linked with historical events of official religion. Villagers report that before the Council of Trent in the sixteenth century herds of dogs ran through the town. People thought these restless canines were incarnations of the devil. Before the council it was believed that there were really evil spirits loose in the world; the bishops at Trent condemned these spirits to the sea and mountains, where they could no longer hurt people. Today one ninety-year-old woman in Faller claims to have seen the devil when she was a young girl. One late night she was in the stable tending a sick cow. Near the haystack she suddenly saw a beast with long back legs and short front legs, which she knew immediately was the devil. She ran from the stable to her home and swore never to venture out late at night again. Villagers tell another devil story that has to do with a woman who had only one child. One night immediately after she bore the child, she heard the door to her bedroom open but did not have the strength to open her eyes. Finally, when she managed to look around, she discovered her child dead in the cradle with a large slice of polenta on his chest. The infant's death was attributed to the devil.

Another type of personal narrative generated folklore about various members of the community. Clementina speaks about Zio Patrizio's father and mother:

> Patrizio's father was also a smart man. Not much schooling but he was the mayor of the village, and that man was thirty-five years old when he went to Servo to do his duty as mayor. And when he started back home, he never reached home, and they never found his body, and they never knew what happened to him or what. It was during the winter with quite high snow, and maybe it was the hungry wolf that devoured him, or somebody hit him and killed him and buried him. She never, never, never knew what happened to her husband. . . . She began to have toothaches. She went to the drugstore and he gave her a liquid. A few drops in the water and rinse your mouth twice a day. She was so worried, this poor widow. She forgot how much to take, and she took a full mouth of this water and rinsed her mouth, and all of her teeth came out the day after. Healthy . . . she was twenty-two years old. . . . I remember she used to take the chicory and take a little bowl and put it inside the mouth behind the tongue and swallow.

These rich narratives knitted the stable air with warmth, intimacy, and a communal sharing of human experience. The stable permitted a wide range of verbal behavior, wider than that afforded by the kitchen, living room, or tavern; at the same time it offered the safety of the domicile. Confidences could be shared, risks taken, failures and hopes made public, while comfort was expected from the group. Through preparing and eating food, nurturing children, courting, spinning, narrating, sleeping, relaxing, praying, playing games, teaching skills, planning work, and sharing aspirations, the stable was the context for this community, bound in isolation at two thousand feet, to affirm itself and the power of its traditions to sustain and interpret life. Everything that transpired in the stable was regulated by criteria that had been established by tradition, formed through shared social experiences over hundreds of years. Children learned how to interact in a group, becoming aware of what was expected of them in the outside world. Adults remembered, or were reminded of, their respective roles and what was appropriate action for carrying out their responsibilities. The stable was a form of folk theater for teaching the rules of proper conduct. At the same time the stable supplied the occasion for exploring the world beyond the mountain horizon and even beyond Italy. Returned immigrants and seasoned workers revealed opportunities for a new life in northern Europe or America in their narratives. Thus, the stable was both an instructional frame for discovering how to live in Faller and a compass by which to orient oneself to a world beyond the village.

In addition, the stable was a parlor, folk school, community hall, dining room, and dance hall. Often it was used for special celebrations. During harvest all the young people went to Clementina's father's stable to husk corn. After the work was completed the youngsters roasted chestnuts and drank wine spiced with cinnamon and cloves and filled the mountain air with songs and stories. In late winter on the last day of *Carnivale*, the villagers held a costume dance. Young men dressed up as young women, and women as men, and went singling about the town in groups, visiting the stables, Before the festive group arrived in the stable, a young boy dressed as an old lady swept the stable floor with a broom. Then the revellers paired up in this rite of reversal, entered one at a time, and began to dance the polka or waltz. At other times throughout the year, children played a game like forfeits in which someone had to give up a few buttons or pebbles if he or she failed a task like singing or reciting a tongue twister. They also played *sussurrava*, another forfeit game based on whispering. One played checkers, using for a table the opposite side of a *scegn*, a small backless chair supported by three legs which would usually serve as a milking seat or sewing stool. Always at the end of the evening the group recited the rosary and the "Litanie della Beata Virgine Maria" (Litany of the Blessed Virgin Mary).

Storytelling in the Stables

Nearly every night there was storytelling in the stables. Both men and women told stories. The most famous storyteller of Faller was Patrizio Zampieri, or Zio (uncle) Patrizio, as he was called in deference to his age. Well into his seventies when Clementina was a child, Patrizio was her next-door neighbor; he was married and had one child. He was quite poor even by village standards. He owned a few patches of land on which he could grow vegetables, but he had neither animals nor stable.

Clementina remembered that his family never seemed to have enough food. Every week Patrizio could go to the cheese works in the town square and gather the honeylike liquid remaining in the milk vats after the ricotta had been made. This distribution of whey was a form of charity the town council had established for the poor of the village. Clementina's family helped their neighbor by bringing him cheese and sausage as often as they could. Like almost all of the poor villagers who were pressed to leave Faller to work in the coal mines of France, Belgium, or Luxembourg, Patrizio could have emigrated, but he could not bring himself to leave home. He chose to remain and carve out an existence from the tiny plots of land, here and there, where he grew beans, corn, and potatoes and maintained a small vineyard. Sometimes he worked on civil projects as a member of a team constructing highways or cutting trees. The work was irregular, but it paid a bit, and the irregularity gave Patrizio the freedom he wanted to read and think and talk over his ideas with his neighbors. As Clementina remarked:

> He had something special. Not everybody was like him. . . . We children would all sit around my father like a little army. So Zio Patrizio would come and say, "Compadre Ventura, listen, I've got to tell you this." He always had something to say. He knew everything. . . . how many inhabitants were here and there . . . what this or that country was doing . . . what they produce . . . all this. It was just like school.

Every night Patrizio would visit the Slongos' stable, "hungry to know and talk." Patrizio had a wide range of interests and could talk persuasively on many topics. He engaged his listeners with the skill of a trained orator. At times he assumed the role of the teacher lecturing on the history of a foreign country, discussing the intricacies of political alliances or probing the Russian revolution, when, as he said, "they grabbed bishops, nuns, priests, and put them in prison and put horses in the churches and stole everything." Now and then Patrizio was a rebel, discoursing upon the paradoxes of the Bible and Catholic dogma, even though personal scriptual interpretation was forbidden to the layman by the church. At other times he took the part of a philosopher, wondering how such things as the development of the automobile would transform human life. In his most ritualistic role he was a poet. Clementina pictured him "sitting down with a pipe, one knee over the other, trying to be formal and to give the essence of the story as if it had happened right there." Clementina recalled that, when he was about to begin a story, everyone became very quiet. Then he would begin to talk, "giving stress to certain parts to make the story believable." His manner of narration was deliberate and realistic, his speaking so powerful that he was able to erase the boundary between fantasy and fact and cause his audience to suspend disbelief.

Clementina loved to listen to Zio Patrizio. She spent as much time as she could around him, and said she learned most of her tales from Patrizio in the stable. Here there was always a big terra-cotta jug of wine, for Patrizio was sure to wet his lips as the night wore on. There were aprons of apples, chestnuts, and sometimes a kind of deep-fried biscuit, *pasticcino,* to be passed around. Most of the children fell asleep but not Clementina. She recalled how she was riveted to her seat, staring at Patrizio as he spun out the thread of old-time stories, stories of talking cats and mountains of glass. When she was eight or nine years old, she discovered that she remembered "every word of the story, step by step." Zio Patrizio noticed this too. Late at night, after he finished telling a story, Zio Patrizio would challenge Clementina to repeat the story, and she would. When she woke up the next morning, she would continue thinking of the story and repeat it to herself. She loved to tell stories and found an eager audience in her younger brothers and sisters. She told the tales again and again as she watched the children in the kitchen or minded them while she tended cows in the field during the day.

World War I and Emigration

The magic of those tales exploded in the arena of World War I. During Clementina's sensitive years on the threshold of maturity, Austro-German tanks crossed over the fields of Faller and village life changed, becoming harsh and unpredictable. Clementina remembered vividly the suffering of people during the war. She was moved to give this account of her experiences.

I remember the war well. The Dolomites were full of soldiers, and they were bombing the whole area. The Germans had been fortified with arms and supplies for six years there. They were well fortified and the Italians were not. I get goose pimples when I think about it. When I went to Fonzazo, I saw the line of trucks. There weren't enough ambulances to take care of the wounded. They were taken away in trucks. Can you believe it, blood would run from those trucks onto the snow in the road. I would arrive in town where there was a hospital, and the poor men, the wounded, would stay there for three, four, or five nights. They would be fed there, lying in straw like beasts, bleeding, dirty, full of bugs. And in the winter their limbs would freeze. How those poor creatures suffered for four mountains that weren't worth anything. And the soldiers would always sing that song: "Noi qui in Trincea, mentre imboscati, mangiando, banchetando, cantando, e svitando, chi la vincera. La guerra e il teatro dei signori."[6] I've forgotten those things. They always made me cry.

She remembered starvation and cruelty.

Our poor village Faller. Ten thousand men came there, reinforcements, and almost as many horses. There was no more grass and water for them. And we civilians had to go up to the Val d'Eleniere, a mile up from the last home in Faller. We went there for the water. Keko Bepo, in dialect that's what we used to call the kaiser, Francesco Giuseppe [Franz Josef], king of Austria. We hated him; we sang songs about him. I don't remember them anymore. To tell the truth, all the poor women from age thirteen on no longer had a menstrual period—almost all of them. Everything stopped . . . no longer any blood . . . no longer anything. A beautiful blond, the wife of Tony, had blown up with malnutrition. Some of the old people wondered what was happening. They thought that maybe one of the Germans had hurt them. Instead it was starvation. And then something happened to boys and girls at the age of puberty. Their hands and feet swelled up, and then their skin cracked. And then, instead of blood flowing out of the skin, it was like water—a little pink.

The Germans were outside the houses. I remember there was a young girl, Mansuetta. She was twelve years old, a beautiful blond girl, tall. She grew so fast, and she was always weak. She sat on the steps in front of the office of German officials, where they also had a kitchen, you know. There was food for the Germans, and she begged for a little food, anything. So she went under the kitchen window where the Germans used to throw out garbage, potato peels and so on, and there they dumped a pail of hot water on her head. She began to scream and scream. And a little while later, she died.

The village turned into a battlefield:

> Those were bad times. The caravans of Germans took away sacks of bean, grain, cheese, salami, *speck* [bacon]—the Germans go crazy for pork. They took away everything—wine, whatever food they could take. Those things which they couldn't take away from Faller, they destroyed. They cut and hacked away at things, uncorked bottles of wine. The Germans announced that they wanted to go directly to Rome, ''Papa Krapir.'' They wanted to go to Rome to kill the pope. Well anyway, the first line of the German army tried to take everything with them, and when they climbed up Monte Grappa, we were like the third line of the army. We could see all of the smoke and the bombings from Faller, even at night. The windows of the houses had broken from the noise of cannon fire. Incredible. We used to go up to the third floor of our house to look at the bombings of Monte Grappa. My God, those were hard times. After the first line of the German army left, another line of replacements would arrive in Faller. They came in caravans. And they had to come over the mountains through Faller, because the bridges on the direct route to Primiero and Faller were blown up. So we knew that the Germans were coming to take everything. The villagers would take the little that remained and during the night carry that stuff to the stables—no lights, as if we were in a burial cavern—and we put our clothing, shoes, suits, food, beans, grain, salami, a little bit of everything and buried these things in the stable until the Germans left. Then we would dig up the food, look at it to see if it was still good, take a little to eat, then we buried it once again and covered it with horse and cow manure.

The extraordinary world of the fairy tale, a world split into two hemispheres of absolute good and evil, was suddenly grafted onto the familiar world of Faller. The raw brutality of the war singed the daily life of the Fallerese. From November 1917 to October 1918, the Austro-Germans occupied the village. The captain's headquarters was established on the third floor of Clementina's house. The fourteen people in the family, after cooking and making beds for the Germans, would give up their rooms to the officers and go to neighbors' houses to sleep. That year ninety people, about one-fourth of the village, died, either of starvation or the Spanish flu.

Clementina had three fast friends—John Todesco's cousin Giuseppina, Albina D'Allaboro, and Maria Slongo. They nicknamed themselves the four *ardite* (bold ones). They were shoved precipitously into adulthood at age fifteen as they helped bury the dead, for there were only women, old people, and children left in the village. The remaining men were either soldiers or, like John Todesco, about to be drafted into the Italian army. When the Austro-Germans came into Faller they conscripted all men up to sixty years of age into the German army. The Germans made them watchmen on the roads or had them cut wood. They watched the Italians closely and treated them like prisoners, giving them only boiled beets to eat.

> I remember my father had all his cows taken away except one. And at night after the Germans had gone to the front line, there was an incline going from the stable to the haystack. It was like a little road. We used to use that little road to carry the hay to the cows. And there were also two extra bedrooms in the haystack above the stable. At night, we took the cow from the stable and put her in one of the bedrooms in the haystack. We had a pail of water there and a little box in which to put the hay. We used to have to walk for two miles high up in the mountains to get the hay, which we used to feed the cow a little at a time. The cow understood. He saw the Germans carry off a different cow each day to be slaughtered for the soldiers. So a little at a time, the Germans had taken all the cows except one. That last cow understood this. She used to stare and stare and she seemed to comprehend everything. And we used to talk to the cow in the stable, "Don't make any noise. Shh! Don't moo." It was really funny. The cow never made a sound, even if she was hungry or thirsty. She was just happy to have someone there keeping her company.

Clementina's stepmother used to get milk from the one remaining cow. Then Clementina, in shoes made out of rags and a dress made of blue canvas the Austro-Germans had left behind, would go to Fonzazo to exchange a bottle of milk for a loaf of bread at the barracks. Because the bread was of low quality, the Germans would thicken it with sawdust. In their retreat the Austro-

Germans took every bit of food; then they let the horses roam free in the fields to stamp out the plants and bean shoots. Desperate for food, some Fallerese dug up dead, putrid horses and ate them.

The war ended in 1918. Four years later Clementina married a local boy, John Todesco. Clementina said their courtship had not been a completely traditional one. John preferred to court her in the privacy of the kitchen rather than the public arena of the stable. Clementina and John would sit on each side of the fireplace while she made bread with pumpkin and raisins. As Clementina's brothers and sisters came into the kitchen to get a jug of wine for the storyteller in the stable, John would offer pieces of chocolate to win their favor. John was serving in the army, and every Saturday he managed to receive permission to leave the military barracks to visit Clementina. After the marriage, they were the first couple in the village to address each other with tu (you), the personal form of address, and the first to go to Venice on their honeymoon. Clementina enjoyed the gossip of the old village ladies, recollecting what one elderly lady said: " 'They want to go to Venice for a honeymoon. If I had a young daughter who wanted to do that, I'd put her up the chimney.' [Laughter.]"

From the start John and Clementina were an adventurous pair. Their shared thirst for new experience was soon to result in their exodus from Faller. They had planned to immigrate to America, but because there was a quota of ten thousand on Italian immigration in 1922, John took the advice of a local lawyer and went to France, where there were fewer restrictions on entrance to the United States. For a while he worked in the mines, then moved to Luxembourg for a better-paying job. Fourteen months after leaving Faller, John borrowed four thousand lire from his father to pay for the transatlantic passage. He arrived first in Export, Pennsylvania, where he worked in the coal mines, then moved to Chicago as a bricklayer. Clementina was not to see John again until 1929, seven years after his departure.

Clementina remained in Faller to give birth to their daughter, Bruna, and to wait for John to return. During John's absence, as was the custom in Faller, Clementina left the home and stable of her birth and moved to that of her in-laws. John sent money earned in America to his father "the old-fashioned way" to help support the extended family. In her new home Clementina had to work very hard, "like a mule from sunup to sundown," on the farm. She devoted what little free time she had to playing and talking with her daughter. They had a special relationship. Bruna was an active child and would be off playing with her cousins Annetta and Marco. Clementina made Bruna's clothes and "kept her like a doll."

Clementina recalled the pig-raising contest she had with Zio Patrizio's wife and another neighbor. She and Bruna chose the runt of the litter. Treating the animal like a pet, Bruna would chase it around the square and skip alongside it on the dirt road. Every night they scrubbed the pig's back in the stable in a big basin of soap and water: "He just loved that, and I made it grow bigger and bigger." To the astonishment of the others, Clementina and Bruna won the contest.

All the while mother and daughter were immersed in the narrative traditions of the village. Raising a daughter alone in a poor village was a difficult task. In the stories Clementina found a way to see beyond the scarcity of food and material goods. Ruth Finnegan points out that

> the "best" poets are extraordinarily gifted, and many must have been drawn to poetry by their creative ability. In non-literate as in literate society, poetry is one medium through which an individual can, in a sense, free himself from the here and now, and through his creative genius, both re-interpret and rise above his environment.[7]

As she had listened so many years before in her father's stable as a wide-eyed little girl, Clementina now told stories to Bruna and to her nieces and nephews and other neighborhood children in the stable of her husband's family. She remarked, "There were no comic books, movies, or TV." Villagers made their own entertainment.

During these years another gifted storyteller entered Clementina's life. This was one of John Todesco's uncles, Giuseppe, or Zio Bepi, as he was affectionately called. Unlike the solitary figure Patrizio, who had died, Zio Bepi was charged with energy and buffoonery, a roistering spinner of yarns. Bepi was gregarious, full of jokes, a "wisecracker," as Clementina characterized him. He was a lovable master of ceremonies who, during weddings and other festive occasions such as baptisms, would spontaneously rise to his feet and recite a poem or verse in honor of the celebrants. Villagers were drawn to Zio Bepi. As he walked down the paths, he was always ready to deliver a proverb or a riddle, to forecast the weather, or engage in some friendly banter with neighbors in the town square. Everybody loved him, and he was a man whose talent was esteemed in the village. Cole and Wolf point out that in the neighboring village of Tret, most tokens of recognition are informal,

> granted by fellow villagers to the successful manager of a holding, to the individual with a cool head who can give reasonable advice, to the woman who raises a garden of beautiful vegetables, to the man who is continually successful at cards. Being informal, these tokens of esteem—and conversely their withdrawal—are based largely on individual performance.[8]

Like Patrizio, Bepi was an artist, a masterful teller of tales. Persuaded by an offer of roasted chestnuts or a Toscano cigar, a special gift usually reserved for holidays, Bepi would accept an invitation to perform at a stable. He told not only traditional tales of Faller, tales passed down orally from one generation to the next, but also personal experience stories. Linda Dégh points out that storytellers are usually experienced people who travel "through ninety-nine villages."[9] Bepi's personal narratives spanned the many and diverse experiences of his boyhood and adult working life. They chronicled his adventures as a shepherd's assistant in the Veneto region when he was a young man, as a foreman of railroad workers in Vicenza, as a miner in Belgium, Luxembourg, and France, and finally, toward the later years of his life, as a dairyman in Faller. Zio Bepi was always traveling and working abroad. He returned home twice a year for twenty to thirty days, for a vacation and to tend the cows. When he returned for a vacation, as his daughter said, he always had something to say about his adventures abroad: "De qua o'vist cossi; de la o' vist cola" (I saw something here and saw something there).[10] One of the lucky ones, he had not contracted silicosis and died, as had many of his townsmen who had gone to the mines in northern Europe. Bepi lived to be eighty-four years old.

Bepi differed from Patrizio in many ways. When Bepi told a story, everyone dropped what he was doing and joined in the storytelling, commenting and adding details. While Patrizio had been the soloist and had given formal performances before hushed assemblies, Bepi was a clown, and his wit sparked the dark interior of the stable. People in Faller today reminisce over Bepi's taking eight days to tell the story of the "Forty Assassins." Each night at the beginning of the evening, Bepi sat high up on a bench, puffing on his cigar, smoke circling his head like a conjurer's vapor, evoking characters out of thin air. He announced how much of the story he would tell that evening, from which event to which. Bepi so attracted people with his vibrant personality and dazzling tale-telling that he drew even the men who habitually relaxed at the pub. Parents promised that if children were well behaved, then Zio Bepi would come to the stable as a treat. On a typical evening all of the children nestled in the leaves in the bins, where it was warm and cozy. Bepi told his tales, keeping the children in suspense or sometimes careening off in digressions. His tales were instructive as well as amusing. He could answer questions or address objections from his audience. He loved to hear the little ones squeal and shout in glee as he assumed different roles and voices, mimed the part, or adopted a mock-heroic style for his narrative.

Zio Bepi, and before him Zio Patrizio, functioned as folk artists in the Faller community. They embodied in their narrative repertoire the brilliant discourse traditions of their native village. They are remembered by the Fallerese and Clementina as two distinct personalities, each of whom articulated a paradox of the folkloric experience in the stable. On the one hand, as narrators of ancient fictions expressed in märchen and legends, both tale-tellers legitimized tradition as the principal source of identity and action and heightened the community's awareness of itself as a cultural entity. On the other hand, as narrators of facts learned from travels and reading and expressed in personal experience stories, both pointed beyond traditional visions of the community towards new modes of seeing the world, shaped now by the forces of industrialization, urbanization, and immigration.

52

The Storyteller in America

Clementina revealed a characteristic belief of immigrants, one which is likely to have prompted over four million Italians to come to the United States between 1885 and 1914:

> In America when you work you earned money and could eat and drink what you wanted. And there was freedom . . . no wars . . . no soldiers. So I was a sort of rebel. I hated ugly and brutal things. I hate injustice and prejudice. So I said to myself, when I get married, I'm going to America.

Until 1929, when her husband returned to Faller as a United States citizen, Clementina maintained her life in Faller on the farm. After his arrival, John began repairing his father's house so that he and Clementina might have a comfortable place in which to stay when they visited Italy in the future. In the meantime the Fascists were conscripting men, and since John was a Democrat, he wanted to avoid the draft. So he abandoned work on the house, and as soon as he received an Italian passport and visa for Clementina and Bruna, they all left Faller. In June of 1930, they sailed for New York. When they arrived, they discovered that America was lacerated by the worst depression in its history. Undaunted, Clementina embraced her adopted country. She had been honed for survival during World War I. "No matter where you go, life's problems are an everyday thing for everybody," she said.

The world Clementina entered in New York was unlike the one she left behind in Faller. In 1930 America was already a fully industrialized country with an economic and social organization that was radically different from what she was used to in Faller.

In the village agricultural production had been primarily for family use, and a whole range of goods and services had been provided by the family. In the preindustrial era food production, for example, including the raising of crops and livestock and the cycle of preparing and conserving food, had not shifted away from the family to commercial enterprises.[1]

Work and leisure were integrated. In 1930, when Clementina and John traveled to America, the Fallerese were going to their stables every evening to work in warmth, enjoy the companionship of family and friends, and participate in storytelling. Almost overnight in the United States, the Fallerese had to become wage laborers, live in apartments in the city, and compete for jobs. Instead of growing food on their land, they sold their labor for cash to meet daily needs. Time, space, and energy had to be organized differently, and at the same time ways of relating to people had to change. In the American city with no stables to draw people together for mutual evenings of work, play, and tale-telling, traditional forms of communal relationship and verbal artistry deeply embedded in their character were abruptly challenged and transformed. Immigrants underwent an industrializing process, a process characterized as one in which

> a society of peasants, craftsmen, and versatile labourers become a society of modern industrial workers. . . . There was more to overcome than the change of employment or the new rhythm of work: there was a whole new culture to be absorbed and an old one to be traduced and spurned, there were new surroundings, often in a different part of the country, new relations with employers, and new uncertainties of livelihood, new friends and neighbors, new marriage patterns and behavior patterns of children within the family and without.[2]

A new calendar of living and working was established by the industrial marketplace. Intense periods of toil in the fields, punctuated by periods of rest, gave way to a certain regularity and discipline of cost-effective production in the factory. Traditional social customs jarred with profit-making patterns of industry. Agrarian and life cycles—planting, harvesting, weddings, funerals, births, baptisms, confirmations, and religious celebrations— were the bane of manufacturers.[3]

Although nearly everything in the industrial economy worked against it, some Italian ways of life continued for a time. The Italian neighborhood made this possible. "Little Italies" that sprouted in the urban centers of America allowed the bonds of custom, kinship, religion, and language to be transmitted and maintained. One ethnographer refers to Italian neighborhoods as "shock absorbers," because they enabled the uprooted immigrant to enjoy a period of apprenticeship in the social institutions of American society.[4] These urban enclaves provided the newcomer with *paesani* (fellow villagers) and relatives who had already deciphered the puzzling codes of the new culture. Lopreato argues that Italians may have been culturally inclined to live in a thickly settled neighborhood.[5] That *civilta* (culture and civility) is lacking in the countryside while present in the city and village has been a part of Italian thought for millennia. As Handlin and Moss point out, the village is the fixed point by which the villager knows his position in the world; it is the principle of order and structure in the universe.[6] However, the neighborhoods in New York where Italians settled did not make *civiltà* an easily attainable virtue. Italians lived for a time at a density of eleven hundred to the acre. There were places where over twelve hundred people lived in 120 rooms.[7] With such a vast change in scale from open fields and stable to city congestion and apartment living, the immigrants began their long process of adaptation.

In the 1930s, open-air vegetable markets and clothes racks crowded the streets and sidewalks of New York, and newly arrived immigrants swelled the stoops of tenements, speaking in their regional dialects. Clementina and John lived in a two-room apartment in a section of Manhattan where other Italians had settled. Although their intention was to continue on to Chicago, where John had been working as a bricklayer, they stayed in New York for eight years. During that time their second child, Benny, was born.

Clementina and John developed a close friendship with two other families in the neighborhood—one from the Veneto and the other from Piedmont. The women became *comare,* in a sense, sisters by adoption, because of the closeness they felt for one another. While their husbands found work as bricklayers, these women worked whenever they could as seamstresses in the garment district, riding the subway to Canal Street before sunrise to pick up their orders and returning in time to see children off to school. Clementina and her friends often picnicked in Central Park, and Clementina would tell stories to Bruna and the other children. Sometimes the families would go to Coney Island with the fraternal Club Italiana for a Sunday afternoon outing. After the children had romped on the beach, eaten popcorn, and indulged in the merry-go-round ride, Benny would fall asleep in Clementina's arms, and Bruna would beg a story.

Just as immigrants told stories in barracks when they went abroad to work in the mines of Germany, France, and Luxembourg, Clementina, the Italian immigrant in America, recounted the same tales she told in the stables of Faller.[8] In the winter, when it was too cold to play in the streets, Clementina would entertain her children with tales while she was in her kitchen cooking or sewing. Bruna trailed Clementina like a puppy, as eager to hear the tales as Clementina was to tell them. Sometimes Bruna and Benny would cry when they heard the stories, and Clementina would hug them and reassure them that it was just a tale; although she would offer to stop, they insisted she go on. She tried to tell stories which "fit their ages."

In 1938 Clementina and John left New York and moved to Michigan. Clementina wanted "to live among Americans, to learn English because I don't intend to go back to Italy." When they settled in Detroit, Bruna was sixteen years old and Benny was eight. They rented a three-bedroom house and planted a garden with cabbage and bean patches. John found work in construction, and Clementina worked at a Chrysler plant during World War II. Because of John's rheumatism and the cold winters in the Great Lakes region, John and Clementina began to look for a warmer location. In 1944, John was told there were job opportunities in the West, and later that year the family moved to Phoenix, Arizona, where John found work as a bricklayer. Bruna, who had in the meantime received her undergraduate degree from Wayne University, taught briefly in a Michigan public school, then joined her parents in Arizona. During her summer vacation in 1949, Bruna was on the first flight from Arizona to Italy to visit her cousins Annette and Marco and her grandmother. A few years later, Bruna married John Baroni and bore six children: Nancy, Mary, Laura, Ann, James, and Thomas. In 1961 Bruna succumbed to a lingering illness and died before she could finish everything she had planned, including publishing the stories that had enriched her childhood.

When Clementina and John were interviewed in 1977, they were gracious and charming. They were especially proud of their grandchildren and were eager to participate in their young lives. Clementina described what she wanted for them: "The best—and that means health and happiness first, then that they keep good company, that they have a family, that they are all good people and good workers, that they are good kids, even at school, that they always make high marks, that they are industrious, and that they find a person who loves them and will make them happy."

Clementina found it difficult to believe a book would be written about her. She discussed, among other things, her manner of storytelling. "It really came easy," she said. A story seemed to come all at once, full-blown, from her memory. Like her mentor, Patrizio, she could capture the lifeblood of a character in a few strokes. Like Bepi, her other great teacher, she could be dramatic, waving her hands and imitating the voice of an ogre or giant in pursuit of a young girl. In spinning the web of her stories, Clementina would forget the audience in front of her. She structured her tales with the traditional conventions of the märchen, repeating things three times for the most part—three tests, or three masked balls, or three brothers—usually beginning each tale of magic with the conflict between a tyrannical stepmother and a beautiful and abused young girl or boy.

The theme of the wicked stepmother, so pervasive in Clementina's märchen and in her personal experience stories, is a common one in Italian folklore and in European fairy tales in general. These tales developed in peasant societies over hundreds of years, and their themes reflect the historical, political, and economic circumstances of peasant society. The märchen give us a way in which to learn about and understand the cultural history of the people of the land, the tillers of the soil, those who produce mainly for family consumption, who divide labor by sex and age, and who organize society by domestic groups and kinship relationships. The theme of the cruel stepmother, concerned about her own blood progeny and indifferent and often abusive to step-children, tells us something about work, family, and the major concerns of the Italian peasant. When Clementina was growing up in Faller, life was hard. Men, women, and children worked long hours; food was often scarce. Infant mortality was high. Poor diets and illness claimed nearly 50 percent of the infants aged two or less. Women in Faller, weakened by hard labor and relentless childbirths, often died young, as did Clementina's mother. Death in childbirth was not uncommon, and women also succumbed to tuberculosis and pneumonia. Since an adult woman in the household was essential to the maintenance of the family, fathers of families with small children generally had no choice but to remarry soon after the death of a wife. Thus, children were often reared by a stepmother.

The condition of the stepmother in Faller, as in other Italian villages, was unenviable. She had to take on the responsibility of her new husband's children; matters were sometimes compli-cated when she herself had children from a previous marriage. Relationships of siblings linked only through the remarriage of their mother or father were often bitter. We have a typical ex-ample of this in Clementina's family. Clementina's stepmother came into a family of eight children, bringing one child of her own, who was six years old. She then gave birth to three addi-tional children of Clementina's father.

Most women in the village were overworked, undernourished, and burdened by the care of numerous children. Many had to manage their households alone because their husbands had emi-grated in search of work. Clementina, for example, was without her husband, John Todesco, for seven years. The stepmother, in her struggle for the survival of her large family, perhaps tended to favor her own children over those which she had acquired through marriage. Certainly, she was frequently accused of this favoritism, as we see from Clementina's personal experience sto-ries. Stepmothers, of course, varied individually, and some were no doubt kinder than others. However, even if a stepmother tried to be kind and fair, her position was difficult. All mothers had to try to extract as much work as possible from their children. By the time they reached six or seven years of age, little girls in most families generally were working long, hard hours every day. The stepmother was the logical person for children to blame for their hardships. While a child might be able to accept the heavy work load given to her by her own mother, she was unlikely to view the work given to her by a stepmother as a natural outcome of necessity. Clementina complained about her long work hours and about always being tired and hungry. She had no way of seeing this as the normal state of affairs for a child under the difficult circumstance of the agrarian family in Faller. For Clementina, traditional stories told of the life she left behind many years ago, particularly her relationship with her stepmother: "I was there in the story. I wanted to be Margherita or Barbarina and express with all my heart the trouble and suffering and injustice."

In the United States, Clementina Todesco became an American in many ways. She wore double-knit pantsuits in Phoenix and drove a Honda sedan. The foods she prepared were chiefly American dishes—steaks, potatoes, vegetables, ice cream for dessert. The polenta and spaghetti of the village, she explained, were prepared on special occasions and when requested by her grandchildren. In her final years she no longer remembered the stories she told to her daughter, perhaps because the people who needed to hear them were no longer there. Until her death in 1982 at the age of 79, she told other kinds of stories about life in Faller, about World War I, and about the challenges of settling in America.

In Faller today in contrast to the American scene, those stories which Zio Patrizio and Bepi told to Clementina continue to be told, though less regularly than before World War II, which was a turning point in European social and economic history. The children can still hear the stories of "Little Peter," "Barbarina," and "The Old Magician Sabino" on holidays such as the feasts of San Rocco or Santa Filomena and occasionally on Sundays around the kitchen table. Through Carolina and her husband, Pietro Todesco, brother of John, contact was made with five storytellers—all women, all over fifty years of age, one as old as eighty-nine— who told forty-one tales, twenty-one of which were variants of ten of the tales in Clementina's repertoire. A discussion of the structural features of these variants is found in the Annotations to the tales. Zio Patrizio and Bepi told stories for the whole town, while the women, like Clementina, considered storytelling as something one did modestly in the space of the family—

not as a communal ritual—unless called upon by a curious American. The women said that the stories were meant to entertain the children and occasionally to instruct them in the proper ways to behave. They enjoyed telling stories because it brought back the atmosphere of the past, when people were poorer but seemed closer. After World War II, with the introduction of gas and electric heating, the stables no longer served their traditional social function as secondary living rooms; storytelling moved into the kitchen, and some of the women of the community became principal narrators.

In the American urban industrial setting, an evolution of both social context and story content is evident in the tale-telling tradition. The evolution is a function of immigration, the shift in the physical and social context of the tale-telling event, the change in the social organization of work, and the interplay of the tale-teller as individual and bearer of tradition in the new society and culture. In Clementina's repertoire of tales, there is a shift from one narrative genre to another, from märchen and legend to personal experience stories, from fiction made believable by tradition and time to fact that changes each day as new experiences color and shape individual memories. The shift continues from a communal experience represented in traditional tales to an individual experience represented by personal memories. In this movement, tale-teller and tales are transformed. Clementina and her art moved through inevitable changes the moment she left her village and its stables. What emerged with Clementina in the new setting was a different way of communicating with others, still artistic, still startling in its power to evoke life, but no longer part of a traditional art.

Part II
Photographs

John, Clementina, Bruna, and Ben Todesco, New York, 1931

John Todesco (above left) in 1925, soon after arriving in New York

Clementina Todesco, 1925

Bruna Todesco, aged five

John and Clementina Todesco,
Phoenix, Arizona, 1960

Clementina Todesco and Bruna
Todesco Baroni, 1959

Bruna Todesco in 1941

The Todesco family, 1937

Clementina Todesco in 19

Cicilia DalZot and her daughter Stella
Trento

Mother of Fiorentina Slongo

Stella Trento

Filomena Slongo and her brother

Flora Moretto

Fiorentina Slongo and her grandchildren

Fiorentina Slongo

Cicilia DalZot

Piero and Carolina Todesco

Cicilia DalZot

Maria Trento at the spinning wheel

Unidentified villager with saw for
cutting firewood

Unidentified villager

Mariotti Pedrazzoli, translator of tales from Fallerese dialect to standard Italian

Faller landscape

View of Faller from Ramen

The town of Faller

A stable with adjacent house

View of Monte Velazza and Faller cemetery

Traditional Faller house

A typical stable

View of Faller from Paliser

Part III
Tales

Märchen

1. Barbarina and the Black Snake

In a summer home on top of a high mountain, during the grazing season for the cows, lived a father and his five daughters. The youngest of the five daughters was called Barbarina, and she was the prettiest, most amiable, and loveliest one of them all. Each of the five girls had different chores to perform every day, and the oldest one and the youngest one had their chores about the house and in the garden outside. The other three girls helped their father in the grazing pastures and were responsible for getting the cows milked and in their stables at night. The girls' mother had died when little Barbarina was yet a very young child, so the four older sisters had acted as little mothers to their baby sister, and they loved her very dearly indeed.

One hot day, the oldest daughter was out in the garden behind the house picking vegetables for the supper table. She had on a large straw hat to protect her from the hot sun and was humming merrily at her task as she quickly filled up her basket with good-looking vegetables. Barbarina was within the house, setting the table and keeping an eye on the foods which were cooking. She too was humming happily while she worked. Suddenly she heard a shriek from her sister in the garden, and the next moment her sister opened the door and came running in as if the devil were chasing her. She was speechless with fear, and all she could do was point toward the garden, where in her excitement she had left her straw hat. The frightened girl ran upstairs to her room, and Barbarina heard her lock the door. Very much perplexed at all these surprising actions, she decided she would go out into the garden herself and investigate the cause for her sister's strange behavior. Courageously she walked out to where she could see her sister's straw hat lying in the grass. When she reached it, she drew her breath sharply, for what she saw was an enormous serpent slowly creeping into the hat and coiling itself inside. Its head was large and ugly, and its poisonous tongue was sticking out toward her in a terrifying manner. But Barbarina cried out, "Well, you have your nerve getting into my sister's hat and scaring her the way you did. You ought to be ashamed of yourself." She indignantly asked the great snake to get out of the straw hat, but the serpent did not move. Instead, it was looking out of its snake eyes in a very human, sad way which touched the girl very much. "Please, won't you leave the hat and let me get some lettuce for our supper tonight?"

"No," he answered the girl, who was very much surprised at hearing him talk. "I cannot come out of this hat."

"But why can't you?" she asked. "Won't you tell me?"

"Well, if you really wish to know, I will tell you," replied the snake, watching the girl with humble and love-filled eyes. He had fallen deeply in love with her. So he told her his story. "I was a young man not long ago and the son of a wealthy count. But I was motherless, and my aunt, my father's sister, came to our home with her daughter to supervise the house. Soon after I had finished my twenty-first year, my aunt began insisting that I marry her daughter. I did not love her; I really hated her, for she was as ugly and as hateful as her mother. I always dreamed of a beautiful, sweet, lovable girl as my bride, a girl like you. So when I insisted that I would never marry her daughter, being half a witch, she was able to turn me into the ugly snake you see now. She said,"If you will not become my daughter's husband, you will become the husband of no other woman." She said that no one would ever kiss such an ugly serpent, and it would be only in this way that the enchantment could be broken. I was only able to talk to you after you had spoken to me. So you see that to be able to become the youth that I was before, no one but you can set me free." Barbarina had been listening to this sad story with great interest and her soft heart had been touched deeply by the tale of the poor snake. She haltingly asked him, "Then you wish me to kiss you?"

"Yes, very much, I promise you that you will not become poisoned, but that you will give me my liberty. If you are willing to kiss me upon my mouth to set me free, will you also be willing to complete my happiness by doing one more great favor after the kiss?"

She was so kindhearted that she promised sincerely that she would help him all she could, without thinking what the favor might be.

"Then kiss me!" he said.

Slowly, but without fear, Barbarina came closer to the snake. She knelt down in front of the straw hat, and bending her sweet face close to that of the serpent's, courageously she kissed him upon his mouth. With a great, deep sigh the snake said, "Oh, thank you from the bottom of my heart, lovely girl, and now tell me your name."

"My name is Barbarina," replied the girl. "But what is the other favor you wish me to do so that you can become a human being once more?"

"My little Barbarina, the greatest task before you now is that of following me, for my life belongs to you. I did not mention that I can only receive back my human form after I have returned to my father's home with the girl who has kissed me. I have been wandering over this earth, looking for a girl like you, ever since my aunt cursed me into this form, and now I shall become the happiest man on earth if you will sacrifice yourself and follow me to my home. Will you do this, Barbarina?"

"I will do all in my power to gain your happiness back for you, dear snake," replied Barbarina, "and I will follow you to the end of the earth if necessary. But what is your name?"

"My name, Barbarina, is Sandrino. But let me explain to you how you must follow me. Until I reach my father's home, I shall have to crawl like a snake between high grasses so that passersby won't see me and kill me. You must always walk on the main road and call to me now and then so that I shall know that you are still following me. Always follow the widest roads, and if you come to a crossroad, always take the one on your right. You must never talk to anyone but me. Do you still agree to follow me, Barbarina?"

"I will be with you as soon as I tell my sister that I am leaving . . . ," but the snake cried out, "You cannot do that, Barbarina, for if you do, our plan will not succeed. They will think you crazy and will kill me at once." Understanding this well, without another pause Barbarina said, "Then I am ready to go, Sandrino."

Together they started out on the long and arduous journey back to the snake's home. The day was very hot for it was in mid-July, and soon Barbarina was tired and thirsty. When she knew that no one was near, she called out to the snake, "Sandrino, where are you?"

"I'm here, Barbarina; follow me!"

"I am very tired. Cannot we rest awhile?"

"Let us go on, Barbarina, until it gets dark enough so that I will not be seen. Then we will drink and rest."

So on they went steadily until night came. When they were near a brook, Sandrino called out, "Barbarina, let us stop here for the night." Soon they were settled on the soft grass beneath a tree by the brook. Barbarina was very tired and gratefully fell asleep at once while Sandrino guarded her all night. Early in the morning he woke Barbarina, and after eating some berries from the nearby bushes, they started on their tedious journey once more. This day was even hotter than the one before, and Barbarina became thirsty very early. About midday she met a woman who was carrying two pails of fresh, cool water. The woman, seeing the tired, dust-smeared girl, called out to her, "You poor child, don't you want some water?" Without thinking Barbarina cried out happily, "Oh, thank you, kind woman, I need it very much," and taking one of the pails, she drank to her heart's content. The woman engaged her in conversation, asking her questions about where she came from and where she was going. Suddenly it dawned on Barbarina that she never should have talked, and with muttered excuses she rushed off down the road. The surprised woman only nodded her head and walked on in the opposite direction.

Barbarina ran and ran to catch up with Sandrino, and she called and called to him, but she received no answer. She walked on desperately all day long, heartbroken at what she had done. She was desperate at the thought that her Sandrino would now never gain back his lost human form. She repented and repented, but this did not bring back Sandrino. She could never find her way home, and she knew no one in this part of the country. So she went on and on, always hoping that Sandrino would answer one of her calls. Toward evening, when she could not see the road clearly, she mistook one of the many paths branching off from it as the main road and soon found herself within a forest. She was at her wits' end with fear and sadness, when in the distance she saw a dim light gleaming through the foliage. Even though she was very much frightened as to what it might be, nevertheless she wanted to find out. Softly and quietly she crept up closer and closer to the light. She realized that it was a little campfire, but she could not at once see anyone about it. Then, as she got accustomed to the scene before her, she saw that a figure was bent over the fire. It was that of a hermit, clad in ragged monk's clothing and so ancient that his beard reached to his waist and his shaggy eyebrows half covered his eyes. After seeing the long cross at the end of the rosary around his waist and being assured that he was a hermit, she went up to him and called out, "O good hermit, will you help me?" The startled old man looked up and said, "Who is that talking?"

"It is only I, good father, a young girl who has become lost in this forest. I strayed from the main road while searching for my lost love. Can you help me find the way back to him?"

"I would be very happy," said the old hermit, "if I could aid you in any way. But I do not know where your lost love is. All I can do for you is to send you on to my brother who is older than I am and perhaps can help you in your trouble. Here is a little nut which I will give you. It will be of great service to you someday when you are in trouble, but you must not open it until you need its help most desperately."

Barbarina thanked him heartily, and then, because she was so hungry, she asked him if she could eat with him and rest herself in his crude hut. The old hermit gladly gave the girl his whole meal, which consisted only of a roll of roasted herbs and grasses. She ate it hungrily and thought it delicious, and she was very grateful for the good water and food and for the hard stone bed spread with leaves and moss that the aged man prepared for her.

The following morning the old hermit bade the girl good-bye and with his blessing she departed toward the hut of his older brother in the hope that this one could help her find Sandrino. She walked all day through the forest, until again at night she saw in the distance another light. She ran to it and beheld the same scene that she had observed the night before, only this hermit was much older. He had a beard which came down to his knees, and his shaggy unruly eyebrows almost completely covered his eyes. She went up to him, and after he recognized that she was only a young girl, he listened to her story.

This hermit told Barbarina the same story the first brother had recited. He said that she should go on to his brother, who he was sure could give her the information she wanted. Meanwhile she ate his poor meal and rested in his hut overnight. In the morning he gave her a chestnut and told her that this was the only thing he could give her which would help her when she was in trouble; but he warned her to open the chestnut only when she really needed it. With grateful thanks she went on her way.

Once more she walked all day through the dense forest and toward evening arrived, weary and hungry, at the little house where the third brother lived near the edge of the forest. This old hermit was the most ancient of the three, for his beard came down to the ground, and you could hardly see his features through the dense growth of white hair on his face. Barbarina explained her troubles to the kind old man and anxiously asked him if he could help her. The hermit told the girl that she should stop worrying for he would indeed help her. He knew Sandrino, where he lived, and what had happened to him. The happy Barbarina breathlessly asked him to tell her, and the hermit replied, "After you left him for a drink of water from the woman you met on the road, Sandrino had to keep walking on and on, though his heart was breaking with the disappointment that you had not kept your promise. But he hoped and hoped all that day that you would catch up with him. And then you got lost. You were lucky that you turned into the woods on this side of the road, for thus you found my brothers and me. Sandrino arrived home that night. Because you kissed him, you broke the enchantment, and he no longer had to wander through the world. His wicked aunt had to give him back his human form, though she was overjoyed that Sandrino had not been able to bring back with him the girl who had kissed him when he had been a snake. Sandrino has been roaming the countryside for two days looking for you, my child, but because you broke your promise to him he will not be able to recognize you until you have been punished for your sin.''

Barbarina was disappointed at this, but she assured the kind hermit that she would do all in her power in order to be able to become Sandrino's own once more. The old hermit told the girl that the wicked aunt was even now scheming with Sandrino's father and her own ugly daughter as to when they would make Sandrino marry his cousin. "O father, what can I do, what can I do?" begged the poor girl, and the holy man told her. He said that the wicked aunt had sent the housemaid away. She did not wish to have any girl prettier than her daughter in the house so that Sandrino could not see how really ugly the daughter was. The hermit said that the aunt would hire only someone more ugly than her daughter, and so here was Barbarina's chance. The old man told her that he could help make her ugly enough so that, when she went to the mansion of the count, Sandrino's father, she would be taken in as a servant by the wicked aunt. Therefore, the hermit produced from his cloak the skin of an old duck, which was very yellow and goose-pimply. Placing this on Barbarina's face, he pressed it around the contours so that it actually looked as though the girl herself had such an ugly skin. It made her very, very repelling to the eye.

Next the old hermit told Barbarina that in his hut, which was larger than those of his brothers, there was a pure white stallion. "You will find need of him in the future, my child," he told her and then proceeded to give her a large walnut, which he told her she should open only when she was in dire need of help. "You are always welcome to come here to my poor abode, my child," said the kind hermit, "and it is not far from my place to that where Sandrino lives. You need walk only a half mile to reach his home. And no matter what cruel things may happen to you under the rule of the wicked aunt, remember that it is only for a short time that you will have to endure your punishment for not having kept your promise. Now I shall tell you which way to go. When you arrive at the palace of Sandrino's father, apply for a servant's position, and then work hard and diligently until you will be rewarded. Do not lose the ring Sandrino gave to you, but do not let anyone see it until the proper time. Goodbye for now; may God keep you. Do not forget to come and see me often.''

After having been directed to Sandrino's home, Barbarina set forth full of eager excitement and anticipation to see Sandrino once more, this time in human form. She would work, oh so hard, she promised herself. Very soon she was miraculously standing outside tall iron gates, through which she caught sight of a magnificent white mansion with beautiful flowers all around and tall trees at its sides. Taking a deep breath to give her courage, she opened the iron gates and timidly walked toward the stately mansion. She knocked softly, and the wicked aunt answered the door because the servant had been sent away. Upon seeing the ugly girl in front of her, she cried, ''What are you doing on my doorstep, you ugly, ugly creature? Get out of my sight at once.''

''I only wish to ask you for a servant's position, and I'll do any kind of work, even the scullery maid's, just so I can make my living,'' replied the frightened girl.

When the wicked aunt heard the ugly girl's request, an evil glint came into her eyes, and she said, ''You poor girl, of course you may come in. I have just the position for you, because my previous servant left last week.'' And she ushered Barbarina inside the beautiful house. The aunt had decided that this ugly girl would be just the person to have about the house. She gave the girl the dirtiest, most tattered clothes she could find and told her that she was to do all the household chores from the very top to the bottom of the house every day. ''In this way,'' she thought, ''Sandrino will meet her many times during the day, and through seeing her ugliness, he will appreciate the better looks of my daughter.''

As for Barbarina, she was very happy that she had been given the opportunity to work in Sandrino's home and complete her punishment. The words of the kind old hermit still rang in her ears. She would yet get Sandrino at all costs. She did not give herself away when she first saw what a handsome young man Sandrino actually was in human form, for the yellow skin hid her blushing face. She worked hard and diligently, even though at times she was so tired she could hardly move. She had to do all kinds of chores, even to the hitching of the horses to the best coach and the shining of everyone's shoes in the house. But she was faithfully carrying out her punishment and waiting for the day when she would finally be able to identify herself to Sandrino as his lost Barbarina. She kept the ring that Sandrino had given to her as her identification hidden in her bosom, so that no one ever ever suspected that she was anything else but a very ugly, homeless girl.

Sandrino had been a very unhappy young man since his liberation from the snake form, for he could not be happy with the thought of Barbarina going through his mind all day, wondering where she was at the moment and if she was still living. He had roamed the countryside for many miles around, over and over again, but no trace of her could he find. He felt desperate, for he knew that his father and his wicked aunt were planning the date for the wedding between his cousin and himself. In failing to bring home the girl who had kissed him, he had not redeemed the final part of the enchantment and thus was under obligation to marry the ugly girl whom he despised. While he could hardly bear to look at his cousin, his wicked aunt had done something even more unpleasant. She had hired the ugliest girl he had ever seen, so that his aunt's daughter would appear preferable in comparison. "Life is miserable," he thought. His good, kind nature was slowly becoming mean and unsatisfied, and his love for his father was fast disappearing because of the older man's actions.

One day the aunt approached Sandrino and told him that soon the celebration of the engagement between the cousins would be announced. "I think it only proper that you bring your future wife to some dances and balls in the evening," she told him, "and show the world that you love her and are going to make her your wife!" Sandrino was even more miserable than before at the idea that he would not only have to look at the daughter himself but would have to exhibit her to the people of the world, who would wonder how he could ever bear to have her near him. He sighed deeply and told his aunt that he would take his cousin out as she wished. That evening the daughter made hurried preparations to dress in her most beautiful clothes, for her future husband was taking her to a ball.

Barbarina watched all the commotion while her heart ached. She was so sorry for Sandrino, and she doubted if she could hold out much longer under the hard labor and the lashing tongue of the wicked aunt. She felt some jealousy, too, that Sandrino would dance with his ugly cousin all that evening while her heart was breaking with sorrow. All this time she was very busy getting the coach and the horses ready for the two supposed lovers, scurrying about from one horse to another and putting everything in shape. Sandrino came out some time before his cousin so that he could check on the hitching, and when he saw the ugly servant his anger flamed up. "Must I see ugliness all the rest of my life?" he exclaimed as he seized his riding whip and beat the poor servant mercilessly. Poor Barbarina did not cry out and make a scene, but rushing into the house as soon as she could escape, she fled to her own small attic room. There she prayed God to forgive Sandrino's evil temper.

Then she heard the coach leave down the road, and a great feeling of longing and desperation came over her. She so wanted to let Sandrino know that she was still alive and loving him as much as he loved her. She felt troubled and rebellious against the hardships she was bearing. She longed and longed so hard to go to that ball that night that the temptation to open one of the nuts the three hermits had given her came over her. She took the first small nut out of its hiding place and decided that she was in enough trouble to warrant visiting the oldest kind hermit to ask him what she should do. She sneaked out of the house in the dark and set out at a run toward the hermit's hut. She arrived panting and out of breath and found the hermit ready to help her in what she wished to do. She told him how very much she wanted to go to the ball, but because she did not have the proper clothes, and since she could not let herself be recognized, she dared not go. The old hermit told her that she could open the first small nut that his brother had given her and that he would give her the white stallion he kept in his hut to take her to the ball. Barbarina looked at him in surprise, but she opened the nut as she had been directed. To her utter amazement the most lovely, most breathtaking, shimmering gown fell at her feet. It was nightblue in color with sparkling silver stars all over it. But this was not all. Shoes, stockings, gloves, purse, underclothes, and all the other things that would complete the ensemble came out with the dress.

Barbarina was speechless with delight. The hermit told her to hurry and prepare herself, and after removing the ugly skin, he led her into his hut to dress. Meanwhile, he went to prepare the stallion. Soon Barbarina came forth, like a star in the night, shining brightly and looking very magnificent. The hermit helped her mount the pure white stallion, which also had silver stars in his mane and on the saddle. He told her that she was not to tell anyone who she was and that she must be sure to leave before Sandrino did, so that she could get home and meet the coach at the mansion door in the form of the ugly servant girl once more. She promised and departed, the most beautiful and happiest girl in the whole world.

When Barbarina entered the ballroom alone that night, everyone's gaze fell upon her and was held by her shimmering loveliness. When Sandrino saw the beautiful maiden he turned pale, for she resembled his lost Barbarina very much. Of course he thought she must be a great lady, and it never occurred to him that it could be anyone else. He went up to her, as all the other men on the dance floor did, and asked her for a dance. He felt he was in heaven as he glided smoothly over the floor with this lovely creature in his arms. He asked her where she came from, and Barbarina gave a puzzling answer. "I come from over the shoreside, where my master beats me for my ugliness." Sandrino laughed at this, thinking that she was teasing him; nevertheless, she told him no other place that she came from. He tried all evening to dance with her once more, but all her dances were taken. Finally, it was time for her to leave, and she left just as mysteriously as she had arrived.

Barbarina arrived at the hermit's hut and left the stallion there. Then she rushed to the mansion and sneaked to her room without having been seen. In her attic room she removed her beautiful gown and accessories and donned her dirty tattered rags once more. She was just in time because, just as she was ready, she heard the sound of the approaching coach and hurried down to meet it.

When Sandrino and his cousin arrived home that night, the ugly servant maid was there at the door to help them alight and to put the horses away. Sandrino shoved the servant girl impolitely out of his way and went to his room, where all night he dreamt of the lovely girl he had danced with who so resembled his lost Barbarina. The cousin went to her room very much disappointed in her first evening out, for after that beautiful girl came, Sandrino did not pay the slightest attention to her. Her whole evening had been spent just sitting and being stared at for her ugliness.

The next evening the aunt made Sandrino take his cousin, and wife-to-be, to another ball. Once more Barbarina was able to sneak out of the house and to the hermit's hut where she opened the chestnut that the second old hermit had given her. Another gown fell out, this one even more stunning than the first, for this had half-moons all over it, and the accessories were even more beautiful. The hermit removed the ugly skin and got the stallion ready. And then Barbarina was off once more to dazzle the men at the ball again. Sandrino was so impatient that he struck at the servant girl again—but he never connected what the lovely lady said at the ball with what he did to his ugly servant maid. And Barbarina could not tell him. Her punishment was this suffering that she must endure from him.

That night Sandrino dreamt of Barbarina and saw her as even more beautiful than the lovely lady, for he would dress her to surpass the beauty of any other woman—if only he could find her. But he was sure by this time that he had lost her forever, and it was this certainty that made him accept without further rebellion the wishes of his wicked aunt. He thought there was nothing else to live for if he could not have Barbarina with him, so he no longer cared.

The aunt made Sandrino take her daughter to another ball on the third night, and Barbarina also planned to go to this one. She felt it was her last hope, for she had no other nuts to open after the last walnut and did not know how long her punishment would last. The third night Barbarina was truly a dream. Her gown was golden and shimmering; there were many suns of gold on it. Everywhere she went light radiated from her, and one just held his breath at the sight of her beauty. Try hard as he could, Sandrino could not get her to tell her name or where she came from, only those few words about coming from where a master beat her. He kept believing that she was playing with him and felt grieved at her nonchalance. He tried to follow her out that night, but she was fast and elusive. He caught sight of her riding away on a pure white stallion and, calling his cousin, he set out on a chase in the coach. Barbarina had to make her stallion run very fast, for she could hear the noise of the coach following her. The hermit helped her put on the skin, and then, running all the way to the mansion, she barely made the necessary change before the coach arrived.

Sandrino had given up the pursuit when he realized that he did not know which road the lady had taken at the crossroads. Very much disappointed and discouraged, he returned to his home. The next day the aunt told him that he and his cousin would have to announce their engagement now and that a gala party would be held in their honor the following night. Barbarina was set to work to make all of the preparations, and she went to bed very tired indeed that night. She was coming to the end of her hopes; she realized that right after the announcement of the engagement the marriage would take place, as was the custom in those days.

The next night Barbarina was very busy serving everyone, and she saw the repelled looks that the guests gave her when they beheld her ugliness. Sandrino had tried hard to persuade his aunt to send the ugly girl away, but she had had her own reasons for keeping her and making her serve at the table. The guests could see that by comparison her daughter was pretty.

Soon after this party, the wicked aunt announced that her daughter would be married to Sandrino the following week, and more preparations and hard work had to be endured by Barbarina. Finally the eventful day arrived, and with a broken heart Barbarina had to watch the boy she loved so much be married to the ugliest girl she had ever seen. That night she called the new wife to her attic room and told her she had something very interesting to show her. The curious bride went, and Barbarina showed her the beautiful gown and accessories which she had worn to the first ball.

"Where did you get this gown?" furiously asked the new wife after she had recognized it as the one the lovely lady had worn the first night of the ball. "Give it to me. I want it very, very much."

"It was given to me," honestly replied Barbarina, "and I will give it to you only if you will do something for me.''

"I'll do anything you ask, just as long as you give me this gown,'' said the new wife. She thought that if she wore the gown she would appear just as beautiful as the lovely lady, and thus her husband would love her truly.

"I want you to let me sleep with your husband tonight!'' said Barbarina.

The new wife was struck dumb, but her willful wish for the gown and the plan that came to her mind led her to say, "Yes, I will let you sleep with my husband tonight. I will lose nothing by it.'' She felt secure in her plan because she was going to give Sandrino a sleeping potion and thus would get her gown.

That night in Sandrino's room Barbarina called and called to him, but he was fast asleep and could not be awakened. All night she called and prayed to him but with no success. Early the next morning the new wife came and told her to leave. Barbarina told her that she had another gown that had been given to her, which was even lovelier than the first one. If she would consent to let her sleep once more with her husband, she would give her this one too. The greedy wife said that she wanted it, and after Barbarina had shown it to her, she agreed that again she would allow her to sleep with her husband. But she gave Sandrino another sleeping potion, and again he slept all through the night. Barbarina was unable to awaken him. She was by now almost desperate, and it was only after showing the new wife the third and most beautiful gown that she let her once again, and for the last time, sleep with her husband. But again Sandrino was given the sleeping potion so that he did not awaken during the night. Barbarina was at the end of her endurance. When early morning arrived and the new wife came into the room to sleep with her husband, so that he would not guess when he awoke that she had not slept with him during the night, she sent Barbarina away and told her not to disturb them until it was time to bring them their coffee. Dejected and heartbroken, Barbarina left the room.

The sleeping potion was wearing off by this time, for the wife had given Sandrino a lesser dose than on the preceding nights. He was still sleeping, though, and dreaming of Barbarina. He called out her name and besought her to come back to him. He cursed his wife over and over and over again in his sleep and swore that he hated her so much he could hardly look at her. His dream was so intense that his actions were violent and his words against his wife harsh indeed.

The young wife had never realized how thoroughly he disliked her, and she was intensely taken aback to hear all his curses against her. But what hurt more deeply than anything else was that he already loved someone else. No matter how hard she would try to make him love her, he would never, never do so when he had someone more beautiful than she on his mind and in his heart. In desperation she shook him hard, and this jostled him out of his drugged sleep. When he saw her next to him, the expression on his face was one of horror and disgust. He moved away from her, showing how repelled he was by the sight of her. This was too much for the young wife. With a broken heart she ran to the window which overlooked the river that flowed beneath one side of the mansion, and, with a great sob that broke from her with a gasping sound, she threw herself with all her might from the open window—down, down into the dark waters, which swallowed her into their depths.

Sandrino was shocked at the sight of this, but in his innermost soul he was happy—happy that now he would never have to see her ugly face again. He was free and could go out and search for Barbarina to his heart's content. He was working himself up into a happy state of mind when the servant maid entered the room with the coffee that the young wife had ordered to be brought at this time. When he saw the ugly girl, Sandrino winced and angrily told her to leave his sight. But Barbarina was determined to try her last plan before she gave up and thus was not frightened away by the angry tone. "Why, where is the mistress?" she asked. "I have brought the coffee that she ordered."

On being reminded of his wife, who was now drowned in the river and would be seen no more, he laughed loudly and hysterically and cried out, "She's drowned, do you hear? She jumped out of the window when I showed her that I didn't care for her. Now I can try to find my Barbarina!"

"Won't you have some coffee, sir?" asked Barbarina, and with trembling fingers she offered him a cup of coffee within

TALES

which she had placed the ring that Sandrino had given her when he was still a snake, and which he had told her she was to show to no one except to him as an identification.

Sandrino took the cup of coffee offered to him and drank slowly, pondering all the things that had happened that morning. How would his wicked aunt take the news, he wondered. The coffee was good and hot, and it helped him get hold of himself— but what was that shining in the bottom of the cup? He looked more closely and received his second shock that morning. There on the bottom of the cup was the ring that he had given to Barbarina to show to him for identification. But how did it get in his coffee cup? How had the ugly servant maid come across it? And then it dawned on him that perhaps Barbarina had finally found his home and this was her way of letting him know that she was near. But when he lifted his eyes to dismiss the ugly servant maid, there in front of him was his beloved Barbarina. She was in dirty, tattered clothes and in one hand she held an ugly-looking yellow skin. With a start he recognized that his loved Barbarina was both the beautiful lady he had seen at the ball and the hideous servant maid that he had beaten so often for her ugliness. But all he could realize now was that his Barbarina was there in front of him, alive and well and just as beautiful as he remembered her to have been. Barbarina was smiling through her happy tears at him, for her punishment had come to an end when the new wife had drowned herself. The aunt had lost her wicked powers, though she still did not know this, nor that her daughter was dead.

Sandrino held open his arms and Barbarina ran joyously into them. They both cried with happiness at having found each other at last, and soon they were able to talk about the adventures they had experienced in getting together once more. Barbarina explained all the trials she had gone through as a punishment for having broken the promise she had made. Then Sandrino begged her forgiveness for having beaten her and for not having realized at the ball that, when she said she came from over the shoreline where her master beat her, she had meant him. They forgave each other happily, and taking her finger, he slipped the ring upon it and set forth to tell his father the good news. And then they remembered that they must go to the wicked aunt and tell her that her ugly daughter had killed herself.

Sandrino did this. From the great shock that she had lost not only her daughter but also her power as a witch, the wicked old woman dropped dead at Sandrino's feet. Then he went to his father and told him all that had occurred. He explained patiently and truthfully all the evil things his aunt had done, and from the evidence offered, the father had to believe his son. He was introduced to Barbarina and had to agree that this girl would make a more desirable wife than the ugly, bad-tempered cousin. He begged his son's forgiveness for having doubted him, and the boy, so deeply in love that he felt he could be kind to everyone in the whole world, was happy to grant his forgiveness. Sandrino and Barbarina were married soon after. When the whole ugly story of the boy's suffering, the plot against him, and the cruelty of the aunt was made known, everyone was happy that the two evil women were dead. They adored Barbarina, for her ways and her loveliness attracted them all. And the two lovers lived happily in the lovely white mansion the rest of their lives.

2. The Cats under the Sea

There was once upon a time a widower who had an only daughter named Maria. He wished to give her a mother again, so he remarried and brought his new wife and her daughter Rosa to the house one day. But this time he had not found a good woman like his first wife. This woman was extremely partial with her good moods and would grant anything to her own daughter, who was about the same age as Maria, at the same time piling all the work on Maria. The poor girl was very wretched, especially after her father had left for a foreign place to work. She would often cry when she prayed to her own dead mother, and once when she had been cruelly scolded, she begged her mother to tell her whether she ought to die. "If you think it is better for me to end this miserable life, pray to the good Lord that he make me die and go with you," she said.

During the years that passed, there were many times when she wished sincerely that she could join her mother, but it seemed that God had other plans for her. She grew healthier and more beautiful every day, kinder and more understanding towards her mean stepmother and stepsister. Even when she was blamed for Rosa's mistakes, she was patient.

One night Maria dreamed that her mother came down from heaven to encourage her. In the dream she went to Maria's bed and told her, "Courage! Soon you will end your misery!"

The next morning Maria's stepmother ordered Maria to take the laundry to the river and to wash it spotlessly clean. She gave her only a very small amount of soap for all the clothes she was to wash. But Maria patiently obeyed. She went to the river, and though it was late autumn and very cold, she plunged garment after garment into the icy water and scrubbed with the soap with all her might.

And then a catastrophe happened. The soap slipped out of her hands into the river, and she could do nothing about it but watch it sink. She was frantic and began to cry softly. To her surprise she heard a voice ask her why she was crying. Maria had not seen anyone, and so when she turned her head, she was astonished to see a little old woman behind her. Maria told her sorry tale, and the old woman felt pity for her. Therefore she told Maria that, if she would follow her instructions carefully, she would be able to recover her soap.

"You must jump into the river," the little old woman said, "and when you drop to the bottom you will see a lovely palace. Knock at the door and you will be answered by very polite cats. Go now, and you will recover your soap."

Maria trusted old people, so she did as she had been told. True enough, there was a palace beneath the river, and Maria courageously knocked at the door. A kitten opened the door and bade her welcome. She entered and told him why she was there and who had sent her. Before he could let her have her soap, she must first go to the king of Catdom, the kitten told her. He told her of the many rooms that had to be crossed. In the first room she saw a little kitten making a large bed. She felt compassion for him and offered to help. She made the bed and then went on. In the next room was another little kitten sweeping with an enormous broom. She helped him too, as she did still another kitten that was mixing dough for bread. Then she opened the door to another room and entered. Here she found a kitten with a big knife and a great piece of meat to be cut up. He was having trouble because of his small size, and Maria did his work for him. In like manner she helped the kitten who was peeling potatoes and the one who was laying the dining room table.

The overjoyed kittens surrounded her and happily told her that they would let her meet their king. This they considered to be a great honor, and Maria followed them with joy. They entered a spacious room with rugs and draperies and a beautiful throne at the end of the room. On the throne was a great big cat, the king of Catdom. He was very much surprised to see a stranger in his home and inquired how Maria had gotten there. Together the kittens answered that Maria was the nicest girl they had ever met, telling the king how she had helped each one of them, and asking that he should grant her any wish she might have. Then she told them her story, how her stepmother had sent her to do the washing and how she had dropped the only piece of soap she had into the river. She told them about the old woman and what she had advised her to do, ending with, "So here I am, and I hope that you have found the soap for me."

The old cat quickly answered, "Why, yes! We have found your soap!" Thereupon Maria gently asked if she might have it back. The king replied, "Not yet. You must do something for me first."

"Why, yes, I'll do anything you say," she answered.

"You must follow my kittens and do all that they ask of you." So she followed the kittens, who took her to a large room where there was a great big closet containing many beautiful dresses for girls. There were also shoes, hats, gloves, stockings, everything to make a girl look well dressed and pretty. They told her to choose the ones she liked best and to dress herself in them.

Then they took her back to their king. He was well pleased and insisted that she stay for dinner with them, since she had done so much to help prepare it. Maria ate with great appetite, for she had never before eaten such delicious food. After this bounteous meal, they did not present her with the little piece of soap that she had dropped but with a very large square that would last her a long time. Maria was overjoyed, but before actually letting her depart, the old king cat said, 'Now listen to me, and remember all that I tell you, for it is of great importance. When you go out of this door, close your eyes, and do not turn around. During your climb to the top of the river, you will hear a donkey bray. Do not open your eyes or turn to see where the noise is coming from. After that bray, you will hear a rooster crow. This time open your eyes and you will see something that is waiting for you.''

Maria followed his instructions and did not turn around when she heard the donkey. But when she heard the rooster, she opened her eyes, and there she was above the water. Seeing a bright light, she looked into the water and reflected there was her image with a shining star upon its forehead. Extremely happy, she came out of the water, and to her great surprise she found that all her dirty, dingy clothes had been washed by someone and were the whitest that she had ever seen. But this was not all. She also saw a white pony attached to a lovely carriage. Her clothes were in it, and climbing into it, she was surprised to feel that the carriage was moving when she hadn't even pulled the reins. She was even more surprised when she realized that the pony was not taking her home but in a different direction, namely towards the large city adjoining her village. At the same time that she noticed the change of direction, she also saw that the pony had golden horseshoes instead of the iron ones she was accustomed to seeing on a horse.

Thus, confused about all these events, she forgot to pay attention to the pony and soon found herself in front of the royal palace. Everyone was surprised to see the shining star upon her forehead and to see her enter the grounds of the king's palace without permission. Like everyone else who saw her, the young and charming prince of the royal house was stupefied by her beauty. But he noticed that the horse had lost one of his shoes in the courtyard of the palace. He rushed down and picked up the horseshoe, thinking that the girl must be extremely rich, since she was beautiful and well dressed with such an expensive carriage and horse. Therefore, he called his guards and gave chase to Maria's carriage. The prince hoped to overtake her and get to know her, for he had fallen deeply in love with her at first sight.

Maria, meanwhile, arrived at her humble home. The horse stopped there as if he knew the place where she lived. The prince, hot on the chase, gave the signal to stop when he saw the girl's carriage in front of the house. The stepmother and her daughter, greatly excited at the sight of such wealth, rushed out to welcome their visitor. They did not recognize Maria at once, but when they did, they remained speechless. However, they quickly recovered, demanding to know how such a change had been made possible.

Maria answered them by saying, "Help me carry in this wash and then I will have time to tell you all about it." In the excitement of being told the strange news, they helped her, something they had never before done. Then honest Maria told them from the beginning what had befallen her. As she was about to come to the end of her story, a loud knock sounded at the door. Maria rushed to the door, thinking that it was someone inquiring about the carriage in front of the house. But when she opened the door, the carriage had disappeared, and instead of it, she found herself confronting the prince of the region. He had brought back the lost horseshoe and took this opportunity to make her acquaintance. He asked if he could enter and talk with her. When he inquired whether this was her house, she said it was. When he asked if the others were her mother and sister, she said that they were her stepmother and her stepsister.

As he realized that she was in a miserable home with a stepmother and a stepsister, and also seeing how beautiful she was, he bethought himself of not allowing her to remain there any longer. He realized that he was truly in love with her and began planning to make her his wife. The angry stepmother insisted that she was not going to let her daughter leave the house; after all, who did he think he was? She had not recognized the prince and therefore was greatly shocked when he answered that she must obey him. His word was law, he said, because "I am the prince of this land and my orders must be obeyed."

Having said these fateful words, he took the more than willing Maria in his arms and sped away with her and his guards. He took her to his palace, and after a few days, he gave a great feast in her honor and celebrated a beautiful wedding.

But let us return to the stepmother and the angry and envious sister. They had heard most of Maria's story, and the mother accordingly planned to have the same fate happen to her darling daughter. Therefore, she made Rosa rise at dawn, collect all the dirty clothes she could find, and set out for the river to do the washing. The sister did this because she was told to, but she also was very curious to see what would happen and promised her mother that she would do all that Maria had said she had done.

When Rosa reached the river, she began to wash industriously. Looking about her to see that none saw her, she purposely dropped into the river the large cake of soap Maria had brought home. Then she began to cry in loud false notes. The little old woman appeared in front of her and asked why she was crying. The girl told her a story similar to that of Maria, but the old woman recognized that Rosa was not sincere. She saw that she was only imitating what her good sister had done in order to obtain the happy results.

The old woman, who was a good fairy in disguise, told her to do the same thing that she had told Maria to do, for she was going to give her the same chance and see what she would do. If she could and would carry out the orders, she would help her become good. But if she did not and acted as she did at home, woe unto Rosa! Obediently, Rosa threw herself into the river, sank to the bottom, and then, sure enough, saw the cats' palace. Hurrying up to the door, she knocked very loud and rudely demanded of the little cat doorman to be allowed to see the king of Catdom. The doorman admitted her with misgivings, and she continued her way as Maria had described. She, too, passed the kitten that was making big beds, but she did not offer to help him. On the contrary, she said, "Beast, get out of my way, you clumsy thing." The kitten was offended, as were all the other kittens that she met while going from door to door trying to reach the king's room.

The kittens sent one of their number ahead of Rosa to warn the king what kind of girl she was. When Rosa appeared in front of the king, he did not welcome her as he had done Maria. He glared at her and harshly demanded what she meant by intruding into his kingdom. She told him almost as rudely that she had dropped her soap and that, directed by a little old woman from above, she had come to him to get it. She also told him that she knew he would see that she was dressed beautifully before going to the upper world again and that the kittens would invite her to a good dinner with them.

The king had mischief in his eyes when he said, "Why yes, that is just what we are going to do." Then he directed his attendants to take Rosa to the junk room where they jumped on her, tore the clothes from her, and dressed her in the old torn clothes that her stepsister had left behind. Rosa was furious, but they said that she had to wear torn clothes if she wished to become beautiful. Then the king called her to him and told her to obey him. In a way he felt sorry for this poor girl and thought he would give her a chance.

First he returned Rosa's old soap. Then he told her to go to the upper world, closing her eyes and not looking when a donkey brayed but opening them and looking when she heard a rooster crow. With these directions in mind, she went on her way. This time the rooster crowed first, and Rosa, thinking that she was being fooled, did not turn around, for she remembered that Maria had heard the donkey first. Consequently, when the donkey brayed, she opened her eyes and looked. To her surprise she felt something foreign on her forehead, and gazing into the water, she was greatly amazed and angered to see that she had a donkey's tail attached to her. Of course, she tried to take it off, but to her utter consternation she could not remove it. She pulled and pulled but to no avail. It would not come off. Ugly as she naturally was, you can imagine what this did to her appearance. She was almost unrecognizable. Deeply chagrined and beginning to blame her sister and mother, she looked around for the fine clothes and the carriage which she had expected to await her as had happened to Maria. But no carriage; no pony; her clothes were almost dirtier, dingier, and more ragged than before.

In a great rage she picked up the old clothes and started for home, thinking up mean things that she would say to her mother for having made her go on such a wild goose chase and for making her get to look so ugly. As Rosa was planning all kinds of revenge on her sister, she suddenly remembered that Maria was no longer at home, that she was now a princess, and the thought almost drove her mad. When she arrived home, her mother did not at first recognize her and, thinking that she was a beggar, chased her from the house. The girl cried out and asked her mother whether she would send her away after she had already brought such disgrace upon her. When the mother recognized her own dear daughter in such a terrible condition, she was frantic and was so angered at Maria, thinking that she had tricked them, that she planned to murder Maria for revenge.

She therefore went silently to the castle one dark night and hid under the window of the princess. But she was found by the watchman who was going his rounds to see that all was well. They convicted her almost at once, for they found a large sharp knife hidden in her robes, and she was sentenced to life imprisonment. As she was a cruel woman and had been very mean to Maria as a stepmother, Maria did not grieve too much, though her nature was such that she felt sorry even for this evil woman.

As for her stepsister, Maria and her husband, the prince, went to see her. Upon beholding her, they felt great compassion for her. After all, they thought, "She is yet a young girl, and it is only through the wrong teaching of her mother that she is so selfish and mean." So they had one of the best surgeons of the region operate on her and, though it left a mark for life, they succeeded in removing the donkey's tail. She was then put in a convent, where she became a very devoted nun. There she realized the evilness of her mother and often prayed for her soul. The mother, on the other hand, felt ill will towards all and always remained bitter and mean of spirit. Her nature would not change no matter how well she was treated. She was so mean and ugly in temper that she did not live long. She died of envy when she heard that her husband, Maria's father, had been called by the royal house to go and live with Maria. When he had been told all about his second wife's evil ways, he was shocked and grieved. Of course he could not get her out of prison, and in reality he did not wish to, so she died. Rosa became a good nun, Maria a beautiful, kind princess and later a queen, while her father became head gardener for the king and lived a long and happy life.

3. The Cherry Tree and the Pumpkin Vine

There once lived a very cruel stepmother. She was kind and loving to her own daughter but was a mean, hard, work-driving woman to her stepchild, the rightful member of the home in which they lived. The stepchild was a very good, kind girl with a heart of gold. She never dared answer back to any of the untruths her stepsister told about her and did the work of all three women without flinching. Yet the stepmother was dissatisfied with her. One day she spoke to her husband, the good girl's father, about her. She told him untruths about the girl—how she never obeyed her stepmother, how she answered back impertinently, how ugly her temper was, and many other things which were equally untrue. The mother was so jealous of the good girl that she convinced the father to have her sent away from home.

The heartbroken girl departed one morning and stopped off at her grandmother's to say good-bye. The old lady was very sorry, but because she herself was very destitute, she could offer no help to the stricken girl. Instead, she took out a little half-worn broom, a rope, and an old crust of hard bread. These she offered to the girl as the only things she could give to aid her. "They will come in use at some future time," she told the girl."So take them, for it is all an old woman like myself can offer."

The girl, much touched, thanked her grandmother and departed. She was planning to go to the faraway city and ask for housework. She would do anything which would give her an honest living, and if she made enough money to return to her hometown, she would help her grandmother live happily.

The girl was passing along a country lane when she came upon a poor woman who with loud moans was pulling a pail of water out of her well, using the long braids of her hair as a rope. The girl rushed to aid her and asked the woman why she had to do so hard a task with her hair. "Doesn't it hurt you?" asked the girl.

"Oh, my dear child," cried the woman, "it most certainly does. But I have a cruel husband; he will not buy me a rope with which I would be able to pull the water out of the well easily, but insists that I do it in this way. My head is forever sore from the pulling of my hair, and my eyes are beginning to hurt me too. Soon, I think I shall die." And the poor woman burst into tears, sobbing on the girl's shoulders.

"Oh, but you needn't hurt your head anymore," the girl told the surprised woman, "for with me I have a rope which my grandmother gave me. You may have it to pull buckets of water out of your well, instead of using your hair. Here, take it."

The woman was very grateful and, taking the girl with her into the house, fed her good bread and hot porridge. The girl was truly thankful, for she had been very hungry, and in this way she was able to save her crust of bread. Bidding the smiling woman good-bye, she went on her way again, refreshed with food and happy from having done a kind deed.

After walking many more miles along the same lane, she came upon a woman who was sitting on the doorstep of her home. Her hands were bandaged in rags, and she was crying as if her heart would break. Feeling moved to tears also, the girl ran up to the woman to find out what was the matter.

"Oh, my poor child," the woman cried. "How lucky you are not to have a husband. Mine is so cruel and merciless that he makes me clean the hot stove every day with my bare hands, and now they are so sore I cannot even touch them. He will not buy me a little whisk broom with which I could do the work so much more quickly and easily." And she commenced to wail once more. The girl felt great pity for the woman, but since she had no money with which to buy a whisk broom, she was about to depart when she remembered that her grandmother had given her a little broom. Taking it out quickly she gave it to the woman, who could hardly believe her eyes.

"You blessed child," she said. "I am very grateful to you and any time I can be of help to you, if you will let me know, I will do my very best."

Again the girl went on her way, very happy because of her good deed. Soon she found herself passing through a large garden. She hurried, for she did not want to be caught trespassing. But on her way she saw a cherry tree filled with so much fruit that it was pulling the limbs to earth and they were in danger of breaking. The tree looked so weary and tired that the girl had compassion for it. Going up to the tree, she shook some of the fruit off and placed sticks beneath some of the heavier branches to support them. When she was through, the tree gave a big sigh and said, "Bless you, my child. You have a truly kind heart. Now I can live again. If ever you need my help, just call upon me and I will be of such service to you as I can."

The girl went merrily on her way once more. But what did she see at the bend in the lane? A pumpkin vine which was carrying such heavy pumpkins that it would at any minute be torn from the flimsy support to which it was clinging. Rushing to it quickly, the girl took first one enormous pumpkin and then another off the vine and placed them on the ground. When she had finished her task, the vine also sighed as the cherry tree had done and said, "Bless you, my child, and thank you for your much-needed aid. If ever I can help you, let me know."

"I will," said the girl, and was about to start off again when the vine asked her where she was going. The girl explained her desire to go to the city to make her fortune because she had been sent away from home by her cruel stepmother and stepsister. The vine took pity on the girl, and, remembering some witches who lived nearby, it whispered to the girl to come closer so that she could hear something which was very important. She did so, and the vine cautiously told her that not far from here was the home of four witch sisters. "The eldest one is about to be married," said the vine, "and tonight they are celebrating her engagement. Under her bed she has a casket of money that her three other sisters gave to her for a wedding gift. They stole all that money, so there is no reason why you shouldn't have it when you need it so much more than they do. But listen carefully. They have a huge watchdog in front of their home that can be bribed not to bark if you will throw him some bread. Do you have enough to hold his attention until you have entered the house?"

"Yes, I have," whispered the girl in return, delighted at this wonderful news.

"Go tonight, then, and throw the bread to the dog and climb to the second floor. The first door you come to will open into the room of the eldest sister. The family will be busy celebrating, so that, if the dog doesn't bark, they will not hear you. The casket of gold is beneath the bed. Take it and run this way as fast as you can. Good luck."

That night the girl cautiously approached the house which the vine had told her was the home of the witches. True enough, in front there was a huge dog, to which the girl gave all the bread her grandmother had given her. The dog was gratified and did not bark when she entered the house. Up the stairs she softly ran, and, opening the first door, she pulled the casket out from under the bed. With it she hurried downstairs and out through the door without having been noticed. She ran all the way to the vine with the heavy casket, and it cried out to her, "They have discovered the loss and are preparing to give chase. So hurry, hurry to the cherry tree. It will hide you, and I will tell them that I have not seen you.''

When the angry witches came to the vine, they asked if it had seen anyone go by carrying a heavy casket. "No, I did not," said the vine. But wanting to look further, they hurried on to the cherry tree. Now the cherry tree had a large cavity on the side and in it had let the girl and the casket hide. When the witches asked, therefore, whether it had seen anyone go by, it said, "No, I haven't." But the witches kept looking far into the night until, finally discouraged, they gave up the search until the following day. When they had returned to their house, they scolded the dog for having let in the stranger and waited until morning to resume the search.

Meanwhile the cherry tree had let the girl out, and she had hurried on to the house of the woman to whom she had given the whisk broom. She asked the woman to hide her quickly and to tell the witches, if they came, that she had not seen her. The good woman did as she was told, and the witches, hearing that she had not seen anyone with a casket, started off in another direction to search. The girl took this chance to run to the house of the woman to whom she had given the rope. This good woman hid her also. And when the witches asked her whether she had seen anyone with a casket, she too said that she had not, and, upon searching, they could find no one in her home. At this point they gave up the money as lost and returned to their home very much disappointed, for the betrothed of the eldest sister had deserted her when he discovered that all her gold had been stolen.

The girl, meanwhile, had arrived safely at her grandmother's home and told her the exciting, thrilling story and the good news. The poor old woman, who had known only misery and suffering in her life, was overjoyed to find that they would not have to starve or go begging anymore. She and the girl lived on together very happily in the little hut.

Not long after, the stepmother heard that her stepdaughter was living very comfortably with her grandmother and went to see for herself. She was angered to see that it was all true and that the girl and her grandmother looked very healthy and well dressed and prosperous. She demanded an explanation, and the kindhearted girl could see nothing wrong in telling her how successful she had been. She explained every detail—from giving the rope to the first woman to giving the bread to the dog. With this good piece of news the mother hurried home to tell her daughter and induce her to do the same. The daughter agreed, and the mother gave the girl a new piece of rope, a large new brush, and a very big piece of bread. She told her to do everything that her stepsister had done and sent her on her way. Then she sat back and meditated on what she was going to do with all the money her good daughter would bring her. She was counting her chickens before they were hatched.

But let us follow the stepsister. She was getting angrier and angrier for having to do this silly thing, for she was getting tired and hungry. Of course she was not supposed to eat the bread, but when she reached the first woman's house and saw her pulling the heavy pail of water out of the well by means of the braids of her hair—for the rope had long ago worn out—the stepsister only taunted her instead of helping her. When the good woman had finally pulled the bucket of water up, she looked at the girl and saw that she was carrying a rope. "Oh, be a good child and sell me your rope," cried the woman. "My husband will not buy me one or let me go to market to get one."

"Oh, really," taunted the cruel girl. "If you think I'm going to give you my rope, you are very much mistaken." And with that she walked off, munching a piece of the huge loaf of bread that her mother had given her. The woman only looked at the girl and said, "How unlike the first good girl. I shall not give her help if she should need it."

The stepsister was cruel again when she came upon the weeping second woman who had worn her first whisk broom all out. The girl said, "Oh, what a funny sight you make, crying like that. I bet you would like this whisk broom. But I'm not going to give it to you." And with a wicked laugh she ran off. The poor woman was deeply hurt, and she too saw the difference between the first girl and this one. "I shall not give her help if she should need it," she vowed.

The stepsister had eaten half of her loaf by now and thought that she had better hurry on and reach the house by night. So she walked swiftly through the garden, not paying any attention to the suffering cherry tree, which was filled once more with fruit, or to the vine, which was pulled down by the weight of the pumpkins. They both cried out for her help, but she scornfully told them she did not need to help them, for she knew where the witches' house was and how to get in. So she went right by them and let them suffer. By night time she had arrived at the house, and again the witches were celebrating—this time the marriage of the second sister. She too had received a casket of gold from her sisters and had hidden it under her bed. The girl threw the large piece of good bread to the dog, who made no move to get at the girl when it had such good bread to eat. Stealthily, she climbed the stairs and entered the first door but found nothing under the bed in this room. She entered the second door, and here under the bed she found the casket she was looking for. Hurrying out with it, she began to run toward home. She passed the pumpkin vine and the cherry tree, who once more cried out for her help. "I'm in a hurry, you fools; help yourselves."

She came to the second woman's house, and being very tired and worn out, she begged her to hide her and let her rest. "I certainly will not, if you weren't kind enough to help me save my aching hands."

And the stepsister had to hurry on again with the heavy casket, for the witches had discovered the theft and were hot on her trail. This time everyone and everything they met told them that they had seen a girl go by with a casket and pointed out the direction in which she had gone.

The tired girl reached the first woman's house and besought her to hide her, but the other would have nothing to do with this cruel girl. Gasping hard, the stepsister had to drag on as best she could, for she could hear the witches hurrying to catch her. When they asked the second woman whether she had seen a girl with a casket, she told them to hurry for the girl could not be far away. When they asked the first woman the same question, she told them that the girl had just left her house and that they had better hurry or she would reach her home and then it would be too late to punish her.

At this news the witches ran even faster, and though the stepsister had a good start, she was so tired from carrying the heavy casket and full of fear of being caught that she moved very slowly.

Just one mile from her home she was caught! The witches swooped down on her and began to beat her miserably. "You will steal our gold, will you," they cried. "Well, we will show you the proper way of punishing wicked girls like you."

After they had beaten the girl almost senseless, they bent two saplings which grew close together and tied one leg of the girl to each tree. Then with a loud whoop, the witches let go. The saplings snapped back to their original positions with terrific force and with each of them went half of the stepsister. Now she was dead.

The witches took her to her home, and since it was very dark by now, they were not seen. They placed the split body of the daughter outside her mother's door and left.

You can imagine the horror of the mother when she opened the door early next morning hoping to see her daughter arrive with the casket. Instead, she saw her, dead and mutilated on the doorstep. A note had been left by the witches, stating that the first time the girl had escaped from them, but that she could not fool the witches twice, and so she had received her just punishment. The stepmother could do nothing to bring her daughter back to life, and it was no use blaming her stepdaughter, for that wouldn't make her own one come alive. Heartbroken and full of remorse that she had sent her daughter for gold, the mother also died.

The good girl and the grandmother came back to live in the home of the girl's father, and when they had explained the stepmother's true character, the father was very sorry that he had sent his daughter away. But she assured him that all was forgiven, and they lived happily ever after.

4. The Devil Gets Tricked

There once lived, in a quaint little town, a mother and her three daughters. The girls were from eighteen to twenty-one years of age, but even so, the mother would not allow them to have boy callers or to go to dances and public places. They always had to be with her if they went out, and when they remained at home, she locked them in their rooms.

One day when the town was celebrating a great feast day, the oldest girl felt rebellious and thought to herself that it was her right to go out that night. And so, when she came from vespers that evening, and a young man of the town slyly winked at her, she smiled back and nodded. The wink was a way of asking whether she would let him walk with her some way. The mother was busy with the other two girls and could not see that her daughter in front was busily whispering with the boy. When she finally did look for the girl, the boy had left. Quickly the mother and daughters went home.

When the evening came which had been agreed upon by the oldest girl and the boy, the girl pleaded a terrible headache and said she wished to go to bed instead of remaining up sewing. The mother took her to the bedroom and locked the door behind her before going downstairs again. The girl really had no headache at all, but in the few minutes she had talked with the boy, they had agreed that he would call for her that night. They would go to the neighboring town, where she wouldn't be recognized, to dance. He would bring a ladder, and she would get out through the window.

Now she proceeded to prepare herself for this escapade. She made herself her prettiest, and then, removing her shoes and opening the window, she sat on her bed to wait. Presently, she heard a slight rattling noise, and going quickly to the window, saw a ladder placed against it. Her heart beat faster, for she knew that she was doing something she shouldn't but she couldn't back out now. In a few seconds the young man was at her window, telling her to get out with the least noise she could. The girl was so excited she did not notice that the young man looked slightly different from what she had thought and she proceeded to get out of the window.

"Let me carry you down," he whispered, "for you might slip and hurt yourself or make some noise that would attract your mother's attention." So the girl did as she was told; but as soon as the young man had placed her on his shoulder to carry her down, he gave a fierce yell and flew high up in the sky. The terrified girl was speechless for a moment and then began to scream with all her might. Now she was sorry that she had obeyed her impulse to dance instead of obeying her mother. The people of the town rushed out to see what the noise was all about and, looking up, could see only a dark spot in the sky where the screams were coming from. They started talking about devils and how they take bad people away and were sorry for the person the devil had taken that night. For they were all certain that it had been a devil, as it truly had been. He had changed himself into the form of a young man to deceive the girl, and then, making the town boy change his mind about getting the girl, he went himself. The ladder had been imaginary, so no sign was left that night to show whom he had visited.

The mother and the two sisters had come out of their house, too, but they never suspected that it was their own sister who had been spirited away. Soon they all went back to their sewing, telling weird incidents that they had heard about. It was past midnight when the mother and the two sisters left their sewing, and since the oldest sister slept alone, they were careful not to disturb her because of her headache.

The next morning, when the mother called the girls, only two appeared, and the mother, going to her oldest girl's room, was deeply shocked when she saw the bed still made and the window open. She cried for the girls to come and see if it was true, and when they saw the room they knew that it was their sister who had been spirited away by the devil the preceding night. The mother was desperate, and the girls began to cry. They were sent to get the priest, but when he came, there was nothing he could do. He advised them to pray, but that was all he could say. The girls were very sorrowful for a number of days but then began to feel better. It was the mother, though, who pined and pined and whose hair began to get gray prematurely.

But let us see where the devil has taken the oldest sister. He flew over hills and vales and finally alighted atop a house in the midst of a forest. He took the frightened girl inside and told her not to be afraid. "You will be the mistress of my house, now, so I am giving you the keys to the different rooms. You may enter them all and see what they hold, but you must never enter this one." And he showed her the door he did not want her to open.

As the days passed and she saw that all she had to do was cook, sew, and clean for the devil, she began to get curious. "What could be in that room he doesn't want me to open?" she wondered. One day she could not bear her curiosity another minute, so she took the forbidden key and opened the door. A great wave of heat struck her face,and the carnation that the devil had given her to wear behind her ear wilted instantly. What she had seen had frightened her terribly, for she knew that the devil would find out she had opened the door and would punish her. She had beheld many suffering, writhing, screaming girls in the eternal fire. She had seen hell. Though she quickly closed the door, the telltale carnation was wilted, and try as she would to brighten and freshen it up, the flower would not revive. When the devil came home that night and saw her he said, "So you have disobeyed my commands, have you? I warned you that I would punish you severely if you opened that door. Now I shall make good my word." And taking her roughly by the arm, he dragged her to the forbidden door. Opening it wide, he pushed the shrieking girl into it, and she fell down, down to the flaming fire of hell.

But the second girl was getting angry at her mother for not allowing her to go to dances and to have a good time, so she, too, planned to sneak out one night. She pleaded that she did not feel well and waited by her window for the boy who had promised to come and take her dancing. But instead it was the devil again, and the second girl was fooled too. She was borne high above the town, and her screams brought the townspeople out again. The mother and the last sister rushed apprehensively to the second girl's bedroom and were confronted with the empty room and the open window.

The mother fainted and became severely ill. The third girl could do nothing to get her sisters back, but she cared for her mother diligently. And the mother was so afraid that she would lose this girl too that she would not allow her out of her sight for even a minute. After a time, the mother, who was very religious, was well enough to go to church. There she prayed and prayed for her daughters, but they did not return.

The second girl had been taken to the same house by the devil and had been given the same instructions which had been given her sister. The devil gave her a carnation to wear and told her that if she opened the forbidden door she would be punished. The second girl was fooled by the easy tasks she was given, and she became very much interested in knowing what was behind that forbidden door. One day she did the same thing her sister had done, and she, too, beheld hell fire and even saw her sister burning in it. Her carnation was wilted too, and when the devil returned that night, he punished her in the same way he had done all the other girls he had kidnapped. He threw her into the eternal fire with the others.

And now the devil wanted to get the youngest sister, but because she had never thought of disobeying her mother or going out dancing, he had no excuse to go and get her at her window. But one night after vespers had been said and the youngest daughter and the sad mother were on their way home, he joined them while in the form of a good friend of the family. The mother invited him in for some coffee, as was the custom, and he quickly accepted. While the mother was making coffee in the kitchen, he gagged the girl and quickly took her high in the sky and to his home. When the mother returned with the coffee and saw no man or daughter, she immediately knew what had happened. The shock made her drop the scalding coffee, and giving a heartbreaking scream, she fell to the floor in a dead faint. Her neighbor, hearing the scream, rushed to help her and had to cry with the mother in sympathy for the girls. The good woman nursed the mother, but it was apparent that she would not live for long. Her hair had turned completely white, and she looked very old and ill.

Now the younger girl was much smarter than the two older girls and thought to herself that she would do all that the devil told her to do in an effort to save her two sisters, if there was yet time. So she did not scream out or kick or scratch the devil, but let him carry her to his home. There he explained to her what she must do, and she sweetly answered that she would be glad to cook, sew, and clean the house for him. He was surprised at such submissiveness but was glad of it. Now he also gave her a carnation and told her not to open a certain door, and she, perceiving that probably the forbidden room had been what had caught her sisters, was determined not be fooled by the same trap. So day after day, she did as she had been bidden, and evening after evening when the devil came home, he saw that the carnation was fresh and bright.

Now the younger sister had looked through all the other doors and had seen that the devil had a wonderful collection of bedding. One day she asked him if he intended to pay her wages for her work, and he was so satisfied with her that he agreed. "What would you like to get?" he asked her.

"I will take my pay with sheets, towels, pillowcases, and bedspreads," she answered. He was quite satisfied with this and felt very well disposed towards the girl. Seeing this, she took the opportunity to ask him if he would let her go back and see her mother occasionally; then she would be able to carry some of the linen to her, as she very much needed it. The devil told her that she need not bother, for he would take the linen to the mother himself. The girl instructed him as to what he should say. She was playing the game marvelously, for she had a good deal of common sense. "Tell my mother that I am very happy here, and that I am getting very good wages from you. And please pretend that my sisters are all right too, for she is an old woman and is very ill; so have pity on her and at least say that they are well."

The devil liked the girl so well that he promised to pretend that he was a visitor from another town, and to say that he had seen all three sisters safe and sound, and that the youngest had sent him with the linen.

The girl was more than satisfied. But now to make the trick successful. Her chance came when he announced one day that he would be gone for some time. As soon as he had left, she took off the fresh carnation, wrapped her hair up in heavy material, and putting her transparent apron over her face, she cautiously opened the forbidden door. She had been smart enough to reason that if the devil had forbidden her to open this certain door, it was because it was his domain. It was hell! She had guessed what must have happened to her sisters. She had prayed fervently to the Blessed Virgin Mary for guidance and had been inspired to do what she was doing.

When she opened the door and was met with the terrible heat, she did not feel it very much, and her hair was not scorched at all because it was covered. Peering cautiously through the doorway, she saw the agonized girls in the pit of hell. But she also noticed what the other girls had not seen. There was a staircase leading down to it. Cautiously stepping upon the stairs she descended until she was almost down. She did not seem to feel the heat, and soon she could reach down and get hold of her oldest sister. She told the other sister that she would soon be down for her, too, but that she must have patience. Taking the exhausted first sister up the stairs, she rushed to her bedroom. The oldest sister was not burned, but she had suffered very much when she had been in the pit! She looked at her youngest sister and blessed her, but warned, "Now he will throw you into the pit."

"You must not worry about me, dear sister," the girl replied, "for I will be able to send you home, by him, without his knowing what he is doing." And telling her the plan she had formed— placing each girl in a chest in which she would lead the devil to think that she had placed the linen which he had promised to take to her mother—she told her sister what she had to do. "You must cry out in a seemingly faraway voice every time the devil wants to descend to earth to put the chest down to rest or to look into it; you must cry, 'I see you, I see you descending, go quickly and then come home again!' Soon he will reach the house and give our mother the chest with the news that we are all well and working in another town. He will leave quickly, for I shall tell him that I have need of him at home. Do not forget now." The oldest sister promised to remember. The youngest sister hid the oldest one until the devil's return.

When he entered his house, the girl told him she wished he would take the linen to her mother that day. When he agreed, she said, "Hurry back, won't you? I'll be watching at my window and shall see you go and come. You don't have to rest, so come back directly."

He said he would do this, flattered that she considered him so strong that he didn't have to put down the chest to rest. The girl placed her sister in the chest instead of the linen, and soon the devil was on his way, carrying the first sister to her home. There were little holes in the chest so she could breathe, and she was able to look down over the different towns and know when they arrived at her own. Once while he was flying, she felt him lowering himself toward a strange village, and remembering what her sister had told her, cried in a faint faraway voice, "I see you, I see you descending; go quickly and then come home again."

The devil was surprised that the youngest sister could still be seeing him, but not wishing to show that he was weak, he went all the way to the girl's home. There he hurriedly knocked at the door and, giving the overcome mother the good news of her daughters' safety, left the chest with the youngest girl's compliments and departed. The mother took the chest and, opening it, was surprised to see her first daughter. The girl explained all, and they both cried with joy that they would all be united once more. The youngest sister had told the oldest one not to worry about her, for she would get herself out somehow.

When the devil got home quickly that night, the youngest sister complimented him on his agility and strength. He glowed with pride and offered to take anything else she wished to her mother.

"I didn't put all of the linen in the first chest," she told him, "so won't you take another one tomorrow?" He said he would be gone on the morrow, but that he would do so on the following day. This satisfied the girl, because it would give her time to rescue her second sister. And so she did. She instructed her in the same way that she had the first, and on the following day the devil took the second chest of what he thought was linen to the mother.

Meanwhile, the youngest sister had made a large rag doll with a face that looked like herself. When she placed this doll in her bed, it looked very much like herself asleep. When the devil returned that night she praised him very highly again, and he, seeing that her carnation was always fresh and dainty, was proud that she was not as curious as all the other girls had been. So he felt like doing anything she asked just to receive her compliments.

A few days later she begged him to take the rest of the linen she had earned by working for him to her mother. "It will be the last chest I shall ask you to take, so please, won't you do it for me?" He agreed that he would.

On the following day she pleaded a headache and told him that the chest was not yet packed but would be outside her room when he came home. He agreed not to bother her if she was in bed. "You can see," she said, "if I'm asleep by looking through the keyhole; and if you see me in bed, don't disturb me."

The next day he came to the hall and saw the chest outside the girl's door. After looking through the keyhole and seeing the doll, whom he thought was the youngest sister, in the bed, he went on his way to the mother. He was seriously in a hurry this time, for he was worried about the girl. He did not want to lose such an efficient worker, so he left the chest at the door and flew back home. The mother and two sisters were overjoyed to see that the youngest one had been able to escape too and thanked her over and over for her intelligence in helping set the other two free.

When the devil returned home and discovered how he had been fooled, he was intensely angry; but because he had been fooled, he no longer had any power over the girls. They were safe from the devil forever after. They realized how much better it was to obey one's mother than to obey one's whims and impulses, so the girls became very good girls. And the mother, getting a little less severe, allowed them to have visitors at the house. In this way the girls met some fine boys, who fell in love with the girls and asked to marry them. The three sisters were all married on the same bright, sunny day, and they lived happily ever after.

5. The Ducks That Talked

In a village in Italy there once lived a family of four—a man, his daughter by his first wife, his second wife and her daughter by her first marriage. The stepmother's daughter was about the same age as the second husband's daughter, and during the first few years they all lived together, they got along fairly well. Then the husband found that, if he wanted his family to live comfortably, he must go to foreign parts to make his living; so he left the stepmother, her daughter, and his own daughter and departed to another country. All the letters that he received from his second wife were very satisfactory. She told him that the girls were growing up well and that they both helped her very much. She told him many more lies such as these, for she had, as soon as he had safely left, placed all the burden of the household chores and meal getting on her stepdaughter. She mistreated her sometimes, too, to show her, she claimed, that she must obey and always do as she was told. The stepmother and her own daughter had the best of everything: the best food; the new clothes and shoes, which they gave to the stepchild only after they had nearly worn them out; the most comfortable beds, chairs, and sleeping room. In fact the stepmother and her daughter lived in luxury, while all the drudgery was placed on the poor stepdaughter. She was made to do every kind of disagreeable task.

On a certain early spring day, the stepdaughter had been sent to the woods to get enough kindling to make fires for a week. The load would be a very heavy one, but she dared not return without it, for then her stepmother would beat her and send her back for more. Moreover, she was forbidden, once she left the village, to wear the only pair of clumsy shoes she owned, for her stepmother had told her that she would not get another pair for a long, long time. So every time she got outside of the village, she would take her shoes off and walk barefooted on the stony paths and dirt roads. Many times her feet were so sore from walking thus that she could barely get home. On these occasions her stepmother would tell her that her feet would eventually heal by themselves but that the shoes, if she wore them, would have to be sent to the shoemaker, and that would cost money.

On the day the stepmother had sent her stepdaughter to the forest for wood, the girl busily went about, stooping to pick up loose kindling wood. A pair of shoes tied by the strings were hung around her neck, and her feet were bare and blue from the cold. She was so scantily dressed for the early spring weather that she shivered from the cold. But even for all this, she was humming merrily and scurrying about, picking up first one piece of wood and then another and stacking it with the pile which she would eventually tie together.

It so happened that on this day the king of the region and his men were out hunting in this same forest and passed by the clearing in which the girl was picking wood. The sight of her stopped all the men, but they kept quiet at the king's command and watched the beautiful girl, for she was lovely to behold even though so poorly dressed. Upon beholding her long golden hair and her shapely figure, the men could not help admiring her. But neither they nor the king could understand why the girl was wearing her shoes around her neck instead of on her cold, blue feet. After ordering his men to go out of sight so she would not be frightened, the king went to her and began to talk to her. He did not tell her who he was but asked her why she was picking up wood on such a cold day. She explained that her stepmother had sent her out and that she had to collect a big load or she would be punished. Next he asked her why she wore her shoes around her neck instead of on her feet, and her answer took him by surprise. "My stepmother says that my feet will heal by themselves if I wear them out, but she would have to spend money to get the shoes repaired. So she lets me wear my shoes in the village so that the peasants won't think that she's not keeping me fully dressed." The king asked her about her father and was told that he worked in a foreign country and knew nothing of how her stepmother treated her.

The king was very much captivated by the girl's beauty, and as he talked with her, he discovered more and more the cruelty to which she unsuspectingly was subjected. He asked the questions so cleverly that the girl answered as though he was only a hunter or a mere peasant. He felt great pity for her and knew that he loved her. During their discussion, he gave her a gold coin and told her that he wanted her to buy a pair of good shoes and to wear them all the time, no matter whether she was within or outside the village. Later, even though she insisted that she could not take it, he gave her another coin to buy herself some proper clothes.

By this time he was so much in love that he did not dare leave the girl without some assurance that he would find her again. He asked her where she lived and how to get there. Then he took off his ring and told the surprised girl that he wanted her to wear it only when he told her to do so. By now the girl had become very curious as to who the youth might be and asked him outright who he was, for that was her way with the humble folk of her village. The young man told her that he was emperor of that region. At this information the girl gasped and fell to her knees in awe. She began to stutter apologies for having talked in such a forward manner to the king, but he pulled her to her feet and assured her that he had enjoyed her conversation very much. The poor girl was so frightened in his majesty's presence that she could not say one sentence that made sense. At first she insisted that she could not keep the ring. When the king told her that he loved her and that he planned to make her his wife, she accepted the ring.

"I shall return to my palace, and then, when I am ready for you, I shall come to get you. Only then are you to put the ring on." With this the king bid the girl good-bye, and, calling his men, he galloped away to his palace to make ready for his bride-to-be's reception.

The girl, half stunned with happiness, wandered home as in a dream with the two pieces of gold and the ring well hidden on her person. She told her stepmother that a man had given her the two gold pieces so she could get shoes and clothes, but she did not explain that he was the king and that he had promised to come and get her, for she hardly believed this would happen. The cruel stepmother laughed happily at the sight of the shining gold and assured the girl that she would find a better use for the gold than clothes and shoes for her. The poor girl suffered in silence the refusal to make her comfortable, though she felt good all over when she felt the ring that the king had given her on a string around her neck under her ragged dress.

One day, when the girl had given up hope that the king would ever really come and put her out of her misery, there was a knock at the door, and her stepmother, always curious about visitors, saved her from the chore of opening the door. This time it was not a gossiping neighbor but a handsome man who was at the door, and the girl recognized the king. Behind him were his men, and the stepmother was completely taken by surprise when he asked to see her stepdaughter. She asked him who he was, and when he told her he was the king, she gasped. Bowing low, she let him in. He explained to the stepmother, after he had smiled reassuringly at the girl, that he wished to marry her stepdaughter, whom he had met in the forest not long ago. He told her that he wanted the girl's measurements and that in a week the wedding carriages would come to take them all away to the palace. He assured the stepmother that she would come to live at the palace too, and the girl, hearing this, thought that finally her stepmother would be satisfied. No mention of the stepsister had been made by the girl, and now the stepmother was rendered so speechless by the king's news that she, too, forgot to mention her daughter. The king did not know there was another girl in the house. She was not present at the moment, so after getting the girl's measurements, he left, still thinking that the girl he loved, who was beautiful and good, was the only one the stepmother had.

When the king left, the stepmother said nothing to the frightened girl, who expected an outburst of rage from the cruel woman. Instead, the stepmother schemed in favor of her own daughter and decided that she would let everything run it proper course until the very day that the king would come to take his sweetheart away. Then she would have her way.

Finally the end of the week was at hand, and the wicked stepmother was hoping that her plans would work out successfully. At the time that the king had mentioned, the many wedding carriages in which his friends rode—as was the custom during those days—arrived at the girl's home. Since the stepmother had told her own daughter to hide in her room until they were ready to start, this girl was not observed by the king. He told the stepmother and the beautiful stepdaughter that, because of custom, they would have to ride in the last carriage while he would ride in the first one. He told the stepmother that his future bride was in her care until they reached the palace, and she assured him that she would indeed take good care of her.

When all had entered their designated carriages and the drivers were ready to strike their whips, the stepsister sneaked out of the house and quickly ran into the last carriage, while her mother held the door open and then closed it at once. The lovely stepdaughter, dressed in the beautiful clothes that the king had brought for her, was very busy and excited, smoothing down a ruffle here and a pleat there, and lovingly turning on her finger the ring that the king had given her, for now she was permitted to wear it. She had not seen anything amiss in her stepsister's entrance, and she was too happy to suspect any treachery on her stepmother's part.

The long string of carriages only had been on the road for a short time when the bride-to-be became very thirsty. She did not wish to seem childish before her stepmother, so she did not say anything until she could stand it no longer. Then she meekly said that they must stop the carriage somewhere and get some water because she was so thirsty that she felt as though she would die if she did not drink. The cruel stepmother told her that she should be ashamed of herself, a grown-up girl so babyish as to want a drink of water while she was on her way to get married.

"Wait until we get there, can't you?" said the stepmother.

"I've waited as long as I can," gasped the poor girl, and at this the sly stepmother took out a bottle of sparkling, inviting water and showed it to the thirsty girl. "I have some water here that I brought along in case of such an emergency as this," said the stepmother, "but I shall not give you any unless you give me the ring you have upon your finger." You see, the evil stepmother's plan was working out. Before they left home she had given the girl some food in which she had put a drug which made her very thirsty. She had schemed that by luring and bribing her with the bottle of water, which also had some of the thirst-making drug in it, she could get the ring and all the marriage clothes. Then she had decided that in some way she would kill her and would then make her own daughter appear as the bride-to-be. Thus far her evil scheme was working perfectly, for the desperate girl was so thirsty that she took off the ring and handed it to her stepmother, who gave it to her daughter to put on. She let the girl take only a small sip of water to wet her mouth and refresh her temporarily. Instead, it made the girl even more thirsty, and she begged her stepmother for more.

"If you give me the wedding dress that you have on, I will let you drink even more than you had the last time," promised the stepmother, and the poor girl wanted water so much that she gave up her wedding gown. She was feeling terribly ill by now and did not care what was going on about her. Her head drooped, and she felt nauseated and faint. She let her stepmother take off her gown without any struggle and did not care when she saw the woman put the dress on her daughter's lap. Now the girl was dressed only in her beautiful underclothes, and the next step in the plan of the cruel woman was to get these too. Of course the water the girl had been permitted to drink the second time made her even more thirsty, and now she asked for more.

"If you give me all your underthings, I will give you the whole bottle of this good water," bribed the stepmother.

By now the girl was so ill that she could hardly hold herself up. Seeing this, the woman and the stepsister wrenched the rest of the clothes off the beautiful girl and she was left naked. The wedding

122

carriages had come to the bridge over which they must cross to arrive at the king's palace. Seeing the river that flowed beneath this bridge, the evil stepmother cried out happily that they would throw the half-unconscious girl out the door and let her drown in the river. Together the two women opened the carriage door and shoved the poor girl over the rail. Down, down she dropped and hit the water with a loud splash. "Surely," the evil woman thought, "she is dead by now." Then the stepmother quickly proceeded to dress her daughter in the beautiful wedding clothes of the drowned girl. The mother arranged her daughter's hair in the style of the stepdaughter's, and after placing the veil and the last flower, her daughter did resemble the murdered girl a bit.

The carriages had arrived at the palace door by this time, and everyone was dismounting and hurrying to help the bride-to-be and her stepmother from the last carriage. In the confusion, the king did not notice the girl much, and it was only as they were walking up the aisle of the church to get blessed by the priest that he realized the great change in his bride-to-be. He permitted the ceremony of the blessing to proceed, but when they returned to his palace to begin the festivities of his engagement, he called the stepmother to him and told her that his bride-to-be had changed very much and that she no longer looked the same as when he had seen her at her home.

"O your majesty," said the stepmother bowing. "Nothing is wrong with my stepdaughter except that she had a very wretched trip here. She has been sick and faint all the way, and last night she had a very terrible dream. She was telling it to me on the way here, and the remembrance frightened her so that she became paler and paler, until she was changed as you see her now. I'm sure she will get over it in due time and be just as beautiful as she always has been."

The king was not satisfied with this answer but had to accept it as a possibility. That night when all the guests and his bride-to-be had retired to their assigned suites, he went to his window and wondered and wondered what had really happened to his beautiful girl. He felt that he had been tricked, for no one could change so markedly in just a few hours. He promised himself that he would look up a noted physician before he would marry the girl and get his opinion on whether anyone could become so changed by a dream. Very sad, he remained at his window all night and was still there early the next morning when he saw the duck girl go by with her dozen ducks, taking them to the river's edge to swim about and find their food.

Returning to the fate of the beautiful girl, we find that as soon as she struck the cold water she was so shocked that she immediately regained consciousness and felt well once more. Fortunately she had landed near the bank of the river, so with a few kicks and strokes she succeeded in getting to dry land. But she was in a terrible predicament. She had no clothes! Being very timid and God-fearing, she did not dare let herself be seen while she went out to try and find someone to whom she could tell her story. She remained hidden in the bushes all afternoon and all night, worrying and thinking about her king and the trick that her stepmother was playing on him. She must try to save him, she knew, but how, when she had no clothes? Early the next morning she saw a dozen ducks, trailed by a young girl, come down to the riverbank. She had let her long, beautiful hair out so that it would partially cover her, and now she was running her fingers through it as was her habit. She did not realize it but grain was falling from her hair, and the hungry ducks ran to her hiding place to eat of the good grain. The poor girl was horrified, for now she would be discovered. And she cowed there in shame when the other girl, who was about her own age, came to see where the ducks were getting all the grain. Of course she was very much surprised to see the lovely girl in such a condition and asked her what had happened. In the meantime she took off her own dress and gave it the bashful girl. Encouraged by this kindness, the poor girl in sobs told the duck girl her woeful tale. When she was through, the duck girl jumped up and told her they must return at once to the palace, because preparations had already been made for the wedding feast. She assured the girl that she would get in touch with the king and tell him now he was being tricked. Gathering her ducks about her she began singing:

Gri, gri, gri,	Gri, gri, gri,
La Bella mi 'an passi.	The beautiful one has fed me.
La è bella come un fuor,	She is as beautiful as a flower,
La è la sposa del Imperator.	And she is the wife of the king.

To the great surprise of the beautiful girl, the ducks took up the melody too and began singing "gri, gri, gri" all together. When the duck girl was close to the palace, she noticed that the king was still at his window with a very moody expression on his handsome face. She paraded the ducks under his window, and when he heard what they were saying, he ordered the girl to wait for him. He rushed out to her and breathlessly asked her what she knew about the beautiful girl and his wife-to-be. The duck girl told him how she had discovered a beautiful girl with golden hair, hidden behind bushes at the riverbank. She said that she had been thrown out of the last wedding carriage by her cruel stepmother, after the woman made her remove the promise ring and her wedding clothes for her own daughter, about whom the beautiful girl forgot to tell. The king was delighted with this discovery, but he told the duck girl that he would not tell the two evil women that they were discovered. He would play a trick on them too, and she—the duck girl—must help him. She agreed happily, for she wanted to see the beautiful girl win back her king.

The king told the duck girl that he would get the old clothes in which he had first seen the beautiful girl. When he had brought her the wedding gowns, he had insisted on taking her old clothes as a remembrance of their first meeting. "Take them to her, and have her put them on," said the king. "Then hide her in your rooms, and, when I give the signal, allow her to come down the main stairs into the dining room in which all my guests and fellow hunters, the stepmother, and the faking girl will be. Leave the rest to me. Now go and tell her that all will be well, and give her my love."

The duck girl took the clothes which the king had given her and hurried back to the beautiful girl. She told her the plan, and the girl was once more happy because she would have her lover back. The duck girl took the beautiful girl to her own small house, and there she bathed, fed, and helped clothe her. She brushed the girl's hair until it shone like sunshine, and she looked as beautiful as she had the very day the king had first glimpsed her in the forest. She was barefoot and had her shoes hung around her shoulders, just as the king had ordered. When the beautiful girl was all ready, the duck girl sneaked her into the room at the head of the grand staircase. There they waited for the king's signal, which would come just when the herald announced the bride-to-be.

Meanwhile, the preparations for the feast and the presentation of the bride-to-be to the court were in progress. In her daughter's room the stepmother was trying her best to get the girl to look as beautiful as she could. She painted her; she combed her; she dressed her exquisitely; but even with all this, she was not half as lovely as the beautiful girl in her old clothes. The king had not been in once to see them that morning, and the mother was a little bit worried, although she remembered that the king had given his promise to marry the girl that had his ring, and that a king cannot break so great a promise. She was sure that with the other girl out of the way—dead—the king would have no choice but to marry her daughter, hoping that she would grow more beautiful after they were married. When the time for them to descend to the dining hall came, they went ahead without fear. They found their designated seats of honor in the hall and sat there waiting to be presented. Soon all the guests, the court members, the king's fellow hunters, and the princes and princesses invited from other countries were present. At this point the bugler gave a resounding bugle call, and the herald, stepping out on the grand staircase, announced, "Your majesties, members of the court, ladies and gentlemen—the bride-to-be of our king!"

At this everyone turned to watch the king receive the young woman, seated with her supposed stepmother in the seats of honor. But to their surprise, the king was not even looking that way. He was watching the staircase with a smile upon his lips; and when everyone turned to see what he was looking at, they saw a barefooted, ill-clothed, beautiful girl with golden, shining hair and with a pair of worn-out shoes hung about her shoulders. They gasped in surprise and turned for an explanation from the king, who has holding his arms to receive the beautiful girl. They turned to see what had happened to the two women, who they thought were the honored ones, and saw that guards were holding them. Then the king spoke, and they all listened wonderingly as the mystery unfolded.

"You see the beautiful girl here by my side?" asked the king. "She is the girl I had fallen in love with, and there in the guards' care you see the cruel stepmother, who tried to convince me that her own ugly daughter was the girl I had fallen in love with and promised to marry. She pretended that her looks had changed merely by having dreamed of a frightening occurrence. You can all see how guilty they both look, and they deserve severe punishment. If more proof is requested, I can ask my fellow hunters, who were out with me the day I met this lovely girl by my side, if they recognize her as the girl I promised to marry or if it was this ugly one with her mother who we saw that day.'' The hunters all cried together that they had seen the barefoot girl that day, not the ugly one.

With this assurance the king went on. "This cruel stepmother made my wife-to-be go out into the forest clad only in the torn clothes you see her in. She made her go barefoot, because she claimed that feet could get well by themselves, while shoes would have to be sent to the shoemaker, and money would have to be spent. Not satisfied with that, she also made this poor girl wear the oldest and most worn-out dresses they had in their possession, so that she would look uglier than her stepsister. Her stepmother did not feed her properly either and made her do every chore in the house while she and her daughter did nothing. And the most cruel thing of all. She schemed to kill my bride-to-be, and after taking all her clothes by force, she threw her into the river as the wedding carriages were crossing the bridge so that she would drown. Miraculously she was able to get to shore, where my duck girl found her and brought her back to me. Now she is back where she belongs. Do not these women deserve just punishment?''

"Yes, yes," cried everyone.

"Burn them alive," cried some.

"Drag them through the city," cried others.

"The stake! The stake!" shouted everyone then.

And taking the matter into their own hands, they went out and made two hugh piles of wood in the plaza. They took the evil, screaming women and stripped them as these women had stripped the beautiful girl. Pouring oil over the dry wood, they set it burning, and after tying each to a stake so neither could escape, they threw them into a blazing pile to burn alive. Thus were the evil women rewarded.

The marriage guests left guards to take care of the punished women while they all went back into the palace to celebrate the engagement of the true lovers. The beautiful girl was dressed in lovely clothes and was prepared for the marriage ceremony that took place at once. Everyone was very gay and happy, and the joyous couple was very handsome to behold. The duck girl was rewarded and became the new queen's maid. The king sent word to his young wife's father that he could return to his own country now, for he would live with them in the palace. After the king had explained the wickedness of the second wife and her daughter, the father agreed that their punishment was deserved and just. The king, the queen, and her father dwelt happily together in the palace as long as they lived.

6. The Forty-One Robbers

There once lived a poor miller's helper who had twelve children. He and his wife were very poor indeed, and it was all they could do to keep themselves alive. The poor man not only helped the miller when he was needed but went out to pick up wood to sell and offered his services to the farmers of that district just for food as his pay. This poor man had a childless brother who was a shoemaker and who was comparatively well off. He was very stingy and mean, though, and had a wife who was even worse in her selfishness and distrust. They would not part with a piece of leather except for their own good. Even if the children of his brother died, the shoemaker would not lift a finger to help out.

One day the poor man and his wife found themselves without any food at all in the house and no prospects of getting any for some time. The children suffered from hunger, and their poor mother was heartbroken to see them so. She sent them to bed and told them that by falling asleep as fast as they could, they would soon forget that they were hungry. She promised to have something for them in the morning; so the children were pacified. She told her husband, when he asked her why she had promised them food when they didn't have any, that she had hidden some yellow cornmeal for just such a situation as this, and she would make the children cornmeal mush in the morning.

Then she sent her husband out into the forest, even though it was almost dark, to look for wood and pine needles so he could sell them the following day and make some money to get some more cornmeal. The discouraged but determined man took his donkey and a couple of sacks and started out through the forest to look for wood. He went deep into the woods in the hope of finding more. After he had filled his two sacks with wood and pine needles, he was preparing to return home. But suddenly heard a loud noise and then men talking. Frightened, he hid his donkey in some bushes and quickly climbed a tree.

Just a few paces away he saw that, where he thought there had been a large boulder of solid rock, a door had opened and out of it were coming many men. He counted them all because they came out one at a time. Suddenly, one of them cried out, "Are we all here?" And the men answered, "Yes, captain!" Forty men had come out, and the leader made forty-one. The fascinated man in the tree watched as they began to march away. He heard the captain cry out to the door, "Scermon, close!" And to the surprise of the poor man, the door closed. Soon all the band had gone, and the man breathed freely once more. He realized that this must be the hideout of the band of robbers he had seen depart and wondered how much loot and stolen goods were inside. He descended the tree and approached the rock. He was not afraid to enter the hideout because the captain had asked if all were present and they had answered yes. So the poor man cried out the words he had heard the captain call to the door—"Open, Scermon"—and the rock opened. Once inside he said, "Scermon, close," and the door swung back into place.

The sight that met his eyes was amazing. He was in a beautifully furnished dining room on the table of which were left the remains of the supper the robbers must have just finished. He gulped hungrily at the sight of so much leftover food and thought of his own children at home, starving because they had nothing but cornmeal and not much of that. But looking about, he decided that this was not the only room in the hideout. He saw a door which led into a hall from which, as he continued his search, he found that many bedrooms led, each one belonging to one of the robbers, he imagined. At the end of the hall there was another room, and when he entered this one, he was astounded at what he saw. Chests, trunks, baskets of gold and silver money, and bags of jewels and paper money stood about. Suits of clothes, shoes, stockings, shirts, and many other pieces of clothing were hung about. And the room was full of every kind of bounty he could imagine.

He thought very deeply and finally convinced himself that he would not be committing any sin if he were to take some of the money the robbers did not need. "After all," he pondered, "they took this money from the rich, and they would never return it. They will never use it for a good purpose, and I, who need it more than they, have a right to it." With this he began to fill with silver pieces an empty sack he found on the ground. When he had filled this, he filled another sack with smaller change. Then he stuffed his pockets with paper bills and wrapped some more in his handkerchief. The sacks were heavy to carry, but he managed to drag them to the door. There he paused to rest, and when he saw the food on the dining room table, it was too much for him. He felt that he must sit down and eat something or he would not be strong enough to get home. He ate hungrily and drank some of the delicious wines on the table, but was very careful not to drink too much.

When he was ready to go, he cried out to the door, "Scermon, open," and the rock door opened in answer to his command. Taking up the sacks and the bundle of bills, he ran out of the cave. When he was safely outside, he cried, "Scermon, close," and the door swung shut. He ran to his donkey and hid the bundle of paper money in one of the sacks of wood and pine needles. The other sack of pine needles, roots and wood he emptied, and placed the two heavy sacks of silver and small change in it. The donkey had a heavy load, but the poor man helped him on the heavier side. Giving fearful glances behind him lest the robbers return before he had made good his escape, he finally left the forest in the middle of the night when all were asleep.

Cautiously he went to his own hut. He knocked softly, and his wife, who had been waiting for him, came to the door at once. "Quickly, quickly," cried the poor man, "open the door wide for we are both coming in. Be very quiet, wife, and do not cry out at what you are about to see." With this warning the speechless wife let him in, even though she was certain that he must have become crazy to shove the donkey inside the hut. Once inside he locked and barred the doors and windows, and then, covering them up so that no light would shine through, he proceeded to take the sacks off the donkey's back and show his wife what was in them. She gasped in astonishment and asked her husband where he had gotten so much money. He said he would explain later, but now they must quickly hide their riches. He placed the bills in an iron casket which he buried in the garden. Then he dug a hole in the kitchen floor where he planned to bury the silver and change. But the curious wife wanted to know how much they had. Her impatient husband said, "What difference does it make? You don't know how to count anyway. So don't waste time." But the wife was insistent and told him that she wanted to measure it, at least and see how many pecks they had. Her husband was very tired and agreed to let her have it her way. For the time being, however, she hid the money in the floor, intending the next morning for her husband to find out how much they had. She left out some change so she could get good food for the children in the morning, and then, though her tired husband went to sleep, she remained up until dawn guarding their treasure.

When morning came, she left for the village. There she could buy all the good food for her children that they had always lacked. She arrived back home before they had yet awakened and prepared a delicious breakfast for them. They ate ravenously and asked no questions. After breakfast they left the house to go out and play, or work in the fields, or help the miller. The wife took the opportunity to go across the way to her sister-in-law's house to ask her if she could borrow a peck measure. The distrustful woman hesitated to grant the request, though she knew very well she would get the measure back. But she was curious and wondered why her poor sister-in-law wanted a peck measure when she never had enough of anything to measure by the peck. So the sly woman, planning to find out what it was that her poor relative was going to measure, spread shoemaker's glue all over the bottom of the inside of the peck measure, so that a sample of anything measured would stick to it.

The poor woman suspected nothing and with all good faith went home to measure the money her husband had found. Again the man locked and barred all the doors and windows, and the two of them crouched on the kitchen floor and measured their money. When they discovered that they had enough to last them the rest of their lives, they were very happy. The woman forgot to look carefully inside the measure to see that no coins were left. If she had, she would have seen two silver pieces and a few small coins sticking to the glue. After measuring the money, the husband buried it and smoothed the dirt over it carefully so that no suspicious marks remained. Then he went to rest once more, and the wife returned the peck measure. As soon as the poor man's wife had left, the curious sister-in-law looked over the peck inside and out. Of course she discovered the money that remained stuck on the bottom. When her husband came home that night from his workshop, she showed him the coins inside the measure and told him that his brother must have stolen a great deal of money if he needed a peck measure to find out how much he had. She convinced her husband that he must go and demand an explanation from his poor brother as to how he had gotten the money. "Tell him that you will give him up to the police if he doesn't tell you where he got it," the wife told her shoemaker husband. And under his wife's urging, he went.

The poor wife was busy preparing an appetizing meal for her children when the shoemaker brother knocked at the door. Since her husband was still resting from his tiring experience, she greeted her brother-in-law and told him to be seated, but he only murmured gruffly that he would stand. "Well, well, and where did you get all this good food to eat? How did you make the money to get it when you never even have enough to buy potatoes with? Your husband must have sold a great deal of wood. How did he do it?" asked the shoemaker. All this questioning befuddled the honest woman, and she did not know how to answer. She stuttered out something that made no sense, and from her attitude the shoemaker came to the conclusion that his wife had been right and that his brother must have stolen the money. Next he accused her husband of being a thief, and the poor woman did not know what to say. Her husband had awakened, though, and heard most of the conversation. Now he came out and told his brother that of course he could never have made so much money just from selling wood but had gotten it from a source which did not make him a thief. Then he explained his whole exciting adventure to his brother, who promised, "I will not give you up to the police if you tell me how to get a lot of money too."

Upon learning how easily his brother had made so much money, the greedy shoemaker demanded to be told how to get into the robbers' cave and told his brother and sister-in-law that he would start out with two donkeys that same night. His brother reminded him, though, that he should not drink any of the fine wines and other beverages that the robbers might have left on the table. He might become intoxicated and forget the very important words which would open and close the mighty stone door to the robbers' den. The brother scoffed at the poor man and told him that he would do as he pleased and would get home in perfect health—with twice as much money as he had. His good brother wished him luck but renewed his warning.

The anxious, greedy shoemaker hurried home to his wife and ordered her to pack some food for him while he went to get his two donkeys ready for the trip through the forest that night. He explained to his wife how his brother had gotten a great deal of money, and she too, being very selfish, agreed that he should take two donkeys. The man was ready before dark and impatiently waited until it was a good time to enter the forest. Following his brother's directions, he soon found the tree into which his brother had climbed when he heard the noise that the robbers made. Hiding and tying his donkeys behind some bushes, the shoemaker climbed the tree and waited. Soon he saw the massive door of the cave open, and forty men and the captain came forth. The same question was asked, the same answer given that his brother had heard. They were all accounted for. He heard the captain say, "Scermon, close," and saw the door swing back into the rock.

Then the men marched away and the shoemaker came down from the screening tree. He ran to the door and cried, "Scermon, open," and the door swung open at his command. He entered and saw about him the richness and lavishness of the cave of the robbers that his brother had described. But he did not stop to look around all the rooms. He headed immediately for the last room and smiled greedily when he saw all the gold and silver and paper money that was about. He picked up a heavy sack of gold money and went to the door. He cried the commanding word and it opened. He went to his first donkey and loaded the sack of gold money on his back. Rushing back again, he picked up a sack of silver money and loaded that on the same donkey. The weight of both sacks was very great, and the poor donkey bowed low from the burden. The shoemaker was not satisfied with only one sack of gold and one of silver but felt that he must load up his second donkey too. So he rushed back twice again and loaded his second donkey with gold coins, two sacks of paper money, and smaller change. Now that he had gotten so far he felt that he needed some compensation for all his hard work of hauling the very heavy sacks to his donkeys' backs. He went back again, and this time he carefully looked over the dining room table; it was full of everything good to eat and of very many different kinds of delicious wines and beverages. He sat down with a satisfied grin and began eating and drinking to his heart's content. Soon he was filled with food, but his greediness prompted him to drink some of the very good wine and whiskey and then still more. When he felt that he could hold no more, he began to try to get away before the robbers returned and discovered him. He thought he could drag himself out if he could get the door open; but when he tried to think of the magic word which would open the latchless and knobless door, he could not for the world remember what it was. He called many words, but never the right one. At his wits' end, he tried to get up and push the door open, but he only succeeded in falling hard on the ground and going sound asleep where he had fallen.

By this time the robbers were returning from their looting expedition and were hurrying faster than usual because they were late. They rushed to the cave and the captain called out the magic word. The door opened a little, but the shoemaker's body inside prevented it from opening altogether. The robbers were surprised at this and all heaved together to push the door open. Once inside they saw the drunk, sleeping shoemaker and pounced upon him with glee; now they thought they had found the man who had stolen their money. The captain sent some of his men out to scout around and see if they could find anything on which the man might have hidden any more money. While some men went out to find the donkeys, the others poured cold water on the shoemaker and with the aid of kicks and beating roused him from his drunken stupor quickly enough. They accused him of the theft of their wealth. When the robbers discovered that still more money was missing, and when their companions returned leading the two half-dead donkeys laden with the sacks full of money, the band was so angry that they beat the shoemaker until he was almost dead. Then they sliced him in two and, unloading the donkeys, placed one half of the dead shoemaker on one donkey and the other half on the other. They headed the donkeys towards the village from which they were sure the man had come and slapped them until the frightened and tired donkeys ran all the way home.

When the shoemaker's wife heard the donkeys braying outside in the yard, she rushed out to see how her husband had made out. She saw the donkeys but no husband, and going up to one of the animals, she looked with curiosity into the sack on his back with the expectation of seeing a lot of money. To her horror she discovered that it was half of a human being, and when she looked into the other sack and she saw the same thing, she realized with dread that it must be her husband. Screaming wildly, she ran to her poor brother-in-law's house to blame him for her husband's death. Her screams awakened the poor man and his wife, who opened the door and let the half-crazy woman in. She told them what she had found in the sacks on the donkeys and told the poor man that he must have given her husband the wrong directions because the robbers had found him and killed him. He rushed to see his dead brother's body and then smelled it. The odor of liquor was strong, and calling the sobbing widow to the corpse, the poor brother made her smell it. He told her that he had warned her husband that, because he loved his wine so, he should not drink too much of the beverages he would find on the robbers' table. Apparently, he had done as he pleased and that is why he had been caught. "It is not my fault and you cannot blame me, for if you went to the police you would be in the crime as much as I would be." The woman had to admit this, and therefore she besought her brother-in-law and sister-in-law to help her bury her husband without anyone's discovering what he had been up to. Together they succeeded in sewing together the parts of the man's body and dressing him as befitted the dead. Then they pulled the sheet that covered him over his face as was the custom in that village when a person died.

The next morning the bereaved wife went about the town crying that her husband had died of a stroke during the night and that now she was a poor widow. The villagers went to the house to pay their respects, but because of the sheet over the dead man's face, they did not see that he was all sewn up. The next day was the time for burial, but the wife sobbingly asked the priest to let her place her husband in his coffin, so she could see him for the last time. He let her, and in this way no one saw the dead man's countenance. The coffin was locked by the shoemaker's wife and the burial held. When the widow returned from the cemetery, her brother-in-law and sister-in-law took her to live with them; then she would not tell of the money that they had hidden away in the house. The shoemaker's wife had to work hard, though, for there was much to do in a home which housed fifteen people; from then on she no longer had a chance to show her greediness and selfishness because her brother-in-law was the head of the house and in charge of all the money. He ruled the family justly and wisely and raised twelve fine and honest children. They never went hungry again, and the poor miller's helper sincerely believed that God would forgive him because his children had needed the money more than the robbers.

7. The Gourd of Blood

In a little town in the northern part of Italy, there once lived two brothers. The older one was wicked and selfish, while the younger one was honest and sincere. They were of moderate wealth, and when their father died, the older son divided the land as he pleased. That is, he pleased himself first and left the poor land for his younger brother. He kept the town house and the richest land and sent his brother to live in a hut situated in the fields far from the town.

As for their mother, the older son decided that she would live a certain amount of time with him and his wife and the rest of the time with the younger brother. He was so selfish that he would not allow her to remain in the more comfortable town house all the time. His wife was as mean as he and would not allow the younger brother to escape without having to give some support to his mother.

Since the poor mother was mistreated and made unwelcome at her older son's house and since the younger boy was extremely poor because of the bad land he had inherited, she asked them if they would help her support herself. She said that, if they would only buy her a little round stove and a sack of chestnuts, she would go out on the road and sell them roasted. In this way she would make enough money to support herself without bothering her sons; so they provided the stove and the chestnuts.

Of course she had to go to the house of her older son to sleep. After her hard day's work, for she was old and tired quickly, she went thankfully to bed. She seemed in perfect health, even though she was old. But on the following morning she was found dead in her bed.

The selfish older son and his wife were angry that the old woman had died, for it meant that they would have to spend money to bury her. All day long they thought of how to get rid of her body without incurring expense. Finally they came to a dreadful conclusion, but one which to them seemed very wise and not wicked at all. They planned to put the old woman at her usual place in the road, appearing to sell her roasted chestnuts. Accordingly, towards evening, when they knew the hay wagons would go by drawn by large teams, they placed the poor old woman in the middle of the road, propped her up in her chair, and made her look as she usually had looked.

There was a turn in the road before one came upon the old woman, and just as her body had been placed by her son and his wife, a rapidly driven wagon came around the curve. The old driver was not able to stop his swiftly moving horses in time to avert hitting the unprotected woman. And so she was run down and, as the poor stricken driver thought, dragged by his horses to a terrible death.

Hearing the screaming of the brakes as they were applied, the neighing of frightened horses, and the shouts of a flustered man, the old woman's son and his wife rushed out with feigned surprise on their faces. They pretended that they did not know the old woman was in the road and blamed the frantic driver for her death. They told him, though, that since there was no one else who saw the tragedy, if he would take care of the old woman and bury her, they would not report him to the law. They left him responsible for everything pertaining to the burial and quickly closed the door, satisfied with the success of their cruel trick. Now they would not have to spend unnecessary money on a funeral.

As that night was the night when the mother was to go to her younger son's house, this son, when he saw that she was not coming, set forth to town to see what had gone wrong. He arrived at his brother's place in time to see the old driver of the horses pick up the mangled form of a woman. When he asked what had happened, the frightened man showed him the body. He explained in a shaking voice, "This poor old woman must have been deaf, for she did not hear the noise that my heavy wagon makes on the ground. She did not get out of the way, and when I turned the curve, I was going so fast I was unable to stop in time to save her." Meanwhile, the young son looked at the body and realized that it was his own mother who had met this awful death. He shouted, "This is my mother, man, what have you done?" He began to sob loudly, for he loved his mother truly, and it had always hurt him that he could not help her more because he was so poor.

The old man, seeing that it was this boy's mother who, as he thought, had been killed and realizing that the son was grieving instead of beating him, threw himself at the boy's feet and begged for mercy. He asked the son to pardon him for what he had done and said to him, "Since no one can bring the dead back to life, do not report me, for surely if you do I will be given life imprisonment, if I am not killed at once. I will give you all that I have if you will spare my life so that I can support my family."

The boy agreed, and he received the four-horse team and the wagon full of hay, the old man's wholesale shop full of everything, and all the money that he had on him. With the money the younger son gave his mother a beautiful burial, and the rest of the merchandise he took with him to his rude hut in the faraway fields.

Though he grieved for his mother's death, he knew that she had been old and wouldn't have lived much longer anyway. He thought that she would be happy if she realized that through her death she had given him life, so to speak. For now with the food-stuff that he sold from the store of the old man, he made money and could have enough to eat. He was no longer poor, and thinking that now he could support a wife, he planned to get one.

Meanwhile, the older brother and his wife had been waiting for days for a visit from the old driver. They thought he would return to beseech them not to tell the police. They thought they could get money out of him by threatening to expose him. They were therefore surprised when no one came to see them. So they decided to go and see the young brother to tell him that his mother had died. They would tell him that they had spent a lot of money burying her and that he should give them half of the expense. They were deeply surprised when they arrived at the brother's home to find him brushing handsome horses which were attached to a large and well-built wagon. When they entered his hut, they were still further shocked to see that he had now acquired some comforts and that he had a great quantity of food and drink. They immediately asked him how he could have gotten possession of all this food and of the horses and wagon. They threatened to report him if he didn't tell them the whole truth.

He honestly told them the circumstances by means of which he had obtained the different possessions. When the older brother heard this startling news, he became very jealous. But before he could utter a sound, the younger brother kindly told him that he would split his possessions with him since his mother would have wished it. The greedy older brother replied, "You will give me only half, will you? Do you know that if it wasn't for me, you wouldn't have one scrap of these possessions?"

"What do you mean?" asked the younger brother.

"You fool, it was I who put our mother in the middle of the road, for she had died that morning; and by causing the old man to run over her we saved the expense of burying her by frightening him into doing so."

"So that was why my mother wasn't coming that night. That is why I came to see what was wrong and met the old man in the road. I wondered why she was so cold and ill-smelling when I picked her up, and the idea came to me that you might have played such a trick as this. But I did not want to bring trouble upon you if my ideas proved true, so I did as the man told me, and accepted his offer in return for my silence," said the younger brother. "And so I buried her and awaited your visit so I could give you half of what I gained," he continued. "And now you don't want half, but all, I suppose."

As the younger brother spoke on, it dawned on him suddenly what a monster his brother was. He became so angry that he took his whip and started beating him, screaming, "You were not satisfied that she had died, poor woman, but must go and plan this terrible plot as well."

With that he chased both his brother and his brother's wife from his land. But when his older brother got home, he planned a revenge. He plotted to kill his brother so that he would never be able to report him and his wife to the police.

The younger brother took his brother's anger into consideration and realized that he naturally would try to kill him. So he made a dummy stuffed with hay and placed it in his bed. He put a large nightcap on it, and it looked just like him asleep. He went to hide in the horses' stable, which was on the other side of his hut. In this way he could observe anything that went on.

His hunch proved correct, for about midnight he heard the door open and saw his brother's form silhouetted against the moonshine outside. He had painted his face so he would not be recognized and began to step carefully towards the bed. He held a long, sharp knife in his hand, and approaching the outlined form of his supposed brother in bed, he thrust the knife again and again into the dummy. He ran quickly to the door, whispering to himself, "That was an easy job, he didn't even make a sound." He planned to come again in the morning, letting people see that he was visiting the hut. In this way they would know he had not killed his brother, since he would find him stabbed.

But imagine his shock on the following morning when upon his arrival he saw a very healthy young man busy watering his animals. On seeing this, he quickly turned back and began to think of a better way to make his brother die. He planned with his wife to invite him to their house and tell him that they would accept his offer of giving them half of what he had received from the old man. Then the wife would pour some coffee for them all, and when he was not looking, she would pour some sleeping potion into his coffee. They would then tie him up inside a sack and carry him to the river, where they would tie heavy rocks about his feet and thus drown him.

The younger brother, having already experienced one trick, was prepared for more unfair play when he received their invitation, but he went anyway. When he was about to drink the coffee, he smelled a peculiar odor in it and, taking a little sip, tasted the sleeping potion. He watched for an opportunity, and when both were not looking, he threw the rest of the coffee into the ashes on the hearth. But he should not even have sipped it, for it was enough to make him extremely drowsy. He leaned against the table feeling a little dizzy, and the others, observing this, ran to him and gagged him. They tied his hands and feet and then put him in the sack they had prepared for the occasion. Stealthily they began carrying him towards the river, but since it was a long way from town and the younger brother was heavy, they often had to put down their load and rest. The small amount of sleeping potion that he had taken soon wore off, and the younger brother awoke in the sack and realized what he was in for. He could make no noise for his mouth was tightly gagged, but nevertheless he struggled until finally he bit through the handkerchief and freed his mouth. He knew that to cry out would only tend to make the two conspirators hasten his death, so he was quiet for a little time longer. And then they all heard the jingling of cowbells and the yells of the herdsman. The wicked brother and his wife were frightened, and, laying down the sack at the side of the road, they ran a little further on and hid.

Now the younger brother had recognized the voice of the oncoming man, for he had met him many times going by his own hut. He knew that it was the half-crazy boy who took care of the herd of the late count of that region, and he remembered further that this poor herdboy was always wishing he could marry the king's daughter. The boy was coming nearer and nearer, and when he finally turned the bend in the road, for the roads in that mountainous region were never straight, the younger brother had outlined his whole plan of escape.

The younger brother began crying in a plaintive voice, "I won't marry the king's daughter, I won't. I don't see why I must do something I don't want to do. I won't marry the king's daughter.'' He kept this chant going until the herdboy on passing him overheard it and rushed to the sack. ''Hey, there, what did you say?'' he asked. The younger brother told him.

''Well, I certainly do,'' cried the overjoyed boy. ''I'll give you all the land the count left me besides my house and this herd of cattle if you will let me get into that sack. I will be very thankful to you.'' The other agreed without a minute's hesitation. He said to the boy, ''Untie the sack, and get in as soon as I have gotten out, for the men may arrive any time now to see whether I have changed my mind about marrying the king's daughter. And when they do come,'' the younger brother told him when he had gotten him in the sack without the other having seen who had come out of it, ''you begin to say that you have changed your mind and that you'll marry her now.''

''Thank you very much,'' cried the other joyously. ''I'll do that very thing, kind sir.''

And so the younger brother escaped into the bushes. He hated doing this to the boy, but he concluded that the boy was half-crazy anyway and that it would have been a loss of a more valuable life if he himself had been drowned instead. He had work to do.

By now the whole herd had gone by on the road, and the older brother and his wife, who had seen nothing of what had gone, quickly came out from their hiding place and, picking up the sack, hurried on their way. The boy inside began saying that he had reconsidered their proposition and that he had decided that he would marry the king's daughter after all. The two looked at each other and the wife whispered, ''He must have gone crazy from the effect of the sleeping powders,'' and laughed. They did not rest anymore until they reached the river. Here they told the man in the sack—the younger brother as they supposed—that he had better say his last prayer for this was his end. The crazy boy did not comprehend but kept insisting that they could let him out now, for he would marry the king's daughter. The other two tied stones about his feet, and counting three, they threw him into the deep river.

''At long last I have put an end to my meddling brother,'' sighed the wicked older brother. He felt no remorse at all; neither did his wife. They were that wicked.

Meanwhile the younger brother had arrived at the home of the nitwit who had been drowned. Taking a pen and pencil he forged a letter telling that he had committed suicide and that he had left all his land, his house, and herd of cattle to the younger brother. He signed it with the name of the crazy boy and took it to a court. They were sorry the poor boy had committed suicide, but they said with a little laugh that they guessed the reason was that the boy had not been able to marry the king's daughter. And so all this property became the younger brother's very own. He was rich now, and he thought this fact would be enough to punish his older brother by making him envious.

The older brother and his wife had returned home now, secure in the thought that the younger brother would bother them no more. They would wait a little while so that the disappearance of the younger brother would get around, and then they could go and take over everything that he possessed. But meanwhile, the younger brother, now having a large house and two barns and many cows, was all set up to get married. He wooed and courted the most beautiful girl of the adjoining town, whom he had always loved but never dared approach because of his poverty. She loved him too, especially after his sudden good luck, so she agreed to a quick marriage.

The older brother was getting impatient about the silence there was in reference to his brother's disappearance, so he decided to go and see for himself. When he arrived at the rude hut, he did not find his brother. Of course he expected this, but he went further on to the next house, which happened to be the large one that the younger brother was now living in with his wife, to inquire about the whereabouts of the brother. He would pretend that he knew nothing about the disappearance. When he got to the house and knocked, you may well imagine what a shock the wicked man received when the door was opened by no one else than his own young brother. He stood there gasping while the younger brother coolly looked on and asked, "How did you know I live here now? If no one else knows, at least you do, that I'm supposed to be dead by now. Eh, brother?"

The other was angered beyond control and cried to be told how he was still alive.

"Come right in," said the other, "and I will tell you what you have done and what has happened to me."

They sat down and the younger brother looked accusingly at his older brother.

"You are a murderer," he said, "for you would not only have killed me but many more besides me to satisfy your terrible greed for richness. I was smarter than you, and so you have murdered the crazy boy that owned this land and house instead. But he left a will leaving all he had to me because I was his neighbor and he had no relatives. I am rich now, as you can see, and I am also married to the most beautiful girl from the adjoining town."

While the older brother was listening to all this, he was slowly turning from a deep red to a greenish hue, and when the young man got through, the older brother gasped out, "Do you think you will get away with this? If you do not give me part of your inheritance I will kill you yet."

The younger brother agreed, and said, "I will do that. I have two barns, an old one and one that has just been finished. I also have a large herd of beautiful cattle. This is what I will do. Tonight when the cattle come home, I will let you keep all the ones that go into the new barn together with the barn, and I will keep all the ones that go into the old barn and the old barn. Agreed?"

The greedy brother said yes immediately, for he was captured by the thought of the new barn and the cows that would go into it. He did not doubt that all of them would prefer the new barn to the old. But when night time came and the cows started coming home and he and his younger brother were eagerly watching the progress of the cattle towards the barns, the older brother's ego was deflated. He saw all the cows except a poor thin stray one enter the old barn. He turned with fury towards the younger brother and yelled, "You have tricked me. Only one cow has gone into the new barn, and what good is a new barn without cows in it?"

"You must abide by your agreement," the younger man retorted, "and next time you receive such a proposition remember that cows always go to their accustomed place before going to a new one. And by the way, your cow happens to be blind too." With this last retort, he went into his house and shut his brother out.

The angered brother rushed home to tell his wife what had happened. He was terribly chagrined that his brother had fooled him and decided that this time he would surely kill him. When he told his wife all that had happened she advised him to send another man in his place, since every time he tried to kill his brother he failed. And so the older brother followed his wife's advice. He forced a man who was in debt to him to do as he told him, which was that that night he must go to the younger brother's new house and kill him in his bed. Because the man needed the money that the other offered him for his silence, for his poor family, he agreed to do it.

That night, though, the younger brother killed a sheep and, after shearing it, skinned it. He made a gourd out of the skin and filled this with the blood from the dead sheep. He told his wife he was sure that that night his brother would try to kill him. "But I'm going to fool him again," he told his young wife. "You must help me, though, by sleeping in my bed tonight, wearing my nightcap and with this bag of blood in your bosom. He will stab me I'm sure, only he will really stab the gourd of blood, and when he sees all the blood come out, he will feel sure that he has killed me. You won't be harmed because the gourd is large enough so that the knife will not be able to go all the way through." She agreed to do this and also to pretend that she was dead until she heard him praying by her side. At that time she would slowly come back to life, seemingly, and would tell him and anyone else who was in the room at the time that she had just been about to receive a casket of gold, if only her husband waited a little longer to pray for her return. And so they were all set. The younger brother hid in the room and waited.

Sure enough, at about midnight he heard the door open downstairs and an occasional creak as the hired murderer came upstairs. The door of the bedroom opened and a man with a knife came in. He went quickly to the bed and thrust his knife through what he thought was the heart of the younger brother. As a great spurt of blood flew into his face, he was satisfied that he had killed his victim. But as he was going towards the door, the younger brother threw himself on the man and cried, "What have you done, you killer. You have murdered my wife."

The poor frightened man begged the young brother to listen to him and he related the true story of why he was doing such a terrible deed. The younger brother believed him, but said that the confession could not bring his wife back to life and furthermore that he would go and get his older brother and show him what he had done. The younger brother put on a great scene of hate and tears when he reached his brother's house and told him to return with him and see what a great crime he was responsible for.

The older brother had not meant to have the girl killed and was really frightened now that both the man and the brother could charge him with murder. So he went along, begging his brother's forgiveness for all he had done and telling him that he had not realized what he was doing. The young brother kept a stony silence and only gave him a few looks that almost withered the older brother.

When they reached the bedroom, they saw the girl on the bed with blood running all over the covers and down to the floor. The younger brother threw himself at the bedside and began to cry and pray to the Virgin to give him back his poor innocent wife. Upon hearing that, the girl began to stir, much to the horror of both the other men. They watched and listened entranced.

"Oh, why did you not wait to call me back to life," plaintively cried the girl. "I was just about to receive the most beautiful casket full of gold. Only a little while longer and I could have brought that back with me."

The older brother, on hearing this, quickly came over to the bed and asked if this was true. "Do you mean that, if my brother had waited a little longer to pray for your return from the dead, you would have been able to bring back a bag of gold?"

"Oh I'm sure I could have," said the instructed girl.

The older brother rushed out of the house and ran all the way home. His greed was making him do a terrible thing, but he thought it didn't matter, for if his brother's wife had come back to life, so would his wife come back when he prayed. Only he would wait a little longer, so that she would be able to bring back the casket of gold from the land of the dead.

When he reached home, he found his wife still sleeping in bed and, getting a sharp knife, pierced her heart and killed her. He waited what he thought was a longer time than his brother had waited and then went to the bedside and began to pray to the Virgin to let his wife come back from the dead with the casket of gold. He prayed and prayed, but his wife did not stir. He was a bit alarmed at this and thought maybe he wasn't praying right. At that moment the other two men arrived to see why he had run off as he had. When they entered the room, they saw the dead woman lying on the bed and her husband praying. When the younger brother saw this, his eyes filled with hate and a little bit of pity too, for his brother in his greed for gold had taken him at his word and, thinking that a dead woman could actually come back to life, had really killed his wife.

"You fool, you greedy, selfish fiend," cried the younger brother. "Your wife will never come back to life again, for you have killed her. I played a trick on you about my wife, to see if you would really take me at my word. My wife had a gourd full of blood in her bosom, and that is what your man stabbed when he thought he had killed her. When you heard her words, your greed overtook your better judgment, and now see what your reward is—a dead wife and you her murderer. I hate you, even though you are my brother." The two men left and returned disgusted to their homes.

The older brother, realizing what a terrible deed he had done, went completely crazy. He stared at his dead wife, whom he had loved, for they were both of a kind, and in desperation stabbed himself, too.

When the police found them on the following day, the whole story of the older brother's hate came out, and the village people were glad that the wicked man and woman had finally died.

The younger brother inherited, by the law of the land, all his brother's property, so that now he was a rich and happy young man. He felt sorry for the poor man who had been made to attempt to kill him, so he gave him the town house and insured that man's family against poverty for the rest of their lives.

The younger brother and his beautiful wife lived happily in their lovely home and often told the tale of the gourd of blood and how God will punish all who are selfish and greedy.

8. Margherita

Margherita, while yet a young girl, lost her mother by death. Because she was so young, her father thought that he would be doing a wise thing to bring another woman into the house to act as mother to his daughter. He therefore married a woman of another town. On the surface, this woman looked like a very fine and motherly type, but Margherita soon found out how very unlike her dear mother this woman was. The new wife also had a daughter from her previous marriage, and this girl was literally a devil in human form. She would do anything to make Margherita angry or to cause her to be blamed for something she had never done. Yet the stepmother was so very cruel herself that Margherita always had more courage to tell news and other incidents to her stepsister, rather than to her stepmother. Margherita led this life for a number of years and was hated more and more by the two newcomers. Since the men of that town had to go to different countries to make their living, Margherita's father had also gone, so that as time went on she was dominated more than ever by her stepmother and stepsister.

One bright, sunny day she went out with the sheep that they owned. Now Margherita was a very beautiful girl and also had a very sweet and charming singing voice. This day she took the sheep quite a distance into the pastures; after finding a shady nook and a rock upon which to sit, she took out her knitting and began to knit rapidly. She soon began to sing, and her lovely voice carried far in the clear sweet breeze. The day was ideal for hunting, the king and his men had thought, for they had gone out early in the morning and were just now returning from a very successful hunt. They had to pass through the pasture to get to the city, and while passing near where Margherita sat, the king happened to hear her singing. He was thrilled by the voice at once, and ordering his men to keep on going, he came around the bushes that were shading Margherita and watched her unobserved. She was a lovely picture to behold, with her rich brown hair gleaming in the sunlight that filtered through the leaves and with a lovely expression of peace and kindness on her face. The king, falling in love with her on the spot, greatly startled her by calling out to her and praising her singing.

"Don't be startled, little lady," said the king, whom she did not recognize since she had never seen him. "I was attracted by your singing and came hither to see to whom such a lovely voice belonged. I like your singing very much. Who are you, and what is your name; please tell me all about yourself."

The girl was frightened at first, but the king was so kind and gentle that soon she had told him of all her suffering at the hands of her cruel stepmother. She told him that she was Margherita from the next town below the pasture and that her father was away and could do nothing to help her because her stepmother constantly told him lies about her. She also described the house she lived in and what she did. But she failed to mention that she also had a stepsister, for she had forgotten her in her interest in the king. The king in turn was shocked at what she told, but his love grew deeper while listening to her tragic story. He resolved to visit her on the morrow and to make the stepmother allow him to take Margherita to his palace until she grew up. He had made up his mind that he wanted to make Margherita his own. He told her that he would come and see her on the morrow if she would allow him, for he wanted to speak with her stepmother. The girl told him that he might do so, but that she was not sure what kind of a reception he would receive at the hands of her stepmother. But he was insistent and left her with the promise of seeing her again on the following day.

The happy girl went home in a joyous mood that night, and coming upon her stepsister before entering the house, she could not keep her glad news from her. Margherita had no one else to tell her girlish ideas to, and so, even though her stepsister was so mean at times, she was the only one to whom Margherita could talk freely. She began her story and was stopped often by the sneering remarks of unbelief from the stepsister. Margherita was too happy to notice. She kept on as though in a dream and told her stepsister that she had left the king man with his promise that he would return on the morrow. The stepmother came out then and, seeing Margherita sitting quietly on the steps doing nothing, was infuriated.

"You lazy, shiftless girl, why aren't you doing something instead of wasting precious time daydreaming? Come in here this minute and go and wash these fish I bought at the market today, in the river that flows through the forest. And hurry back, too; you have to prepare supper tonight," the angry woman cried. "And don't you dare drop even one little fish in the water either, or else you'll never live to see daylight again" was the final threat.

Poor Margherita jumped to her feet before her stepmother had uttered two words, for she knew what would happen if she didn't do just as her stepmother told her when she was so angry. By the time her stepmother had finished her threat, Margherita was down the stairs and on her way with the fish in a basket on her arm. The stepmother, with an altogether changed expression, went over to her daughter and asked her what the two of them had been talking about on the porch. She had heard something about a young man having spoken to Margherita while she was out with the sheep.

"Tell me all about it, dear," she asked her daughter. The girl willingly did so in an effort to make more trouble for her stepsister, whom she hated because Margherita was so much more lovely and beautiful than she. When the stepmother had heard the seemingly incredible story, she jumped to her feet, saying that she believed it because Margherita had never yet told a lie and wouldn't know how to tell one anyway.

"Don't you see what this means?" she cried excitedly. "If I fix you up so that you seem to be Margherita and do away with her altogether, you may have an opportunity of marrying this young man of wealth. You tell me she did not mention anything about having told him that she had a stepsister. All the better. He'll have to believe that you are Margherita." And with these words she took her daughter by the hand and quickly ran into the house. She washed and scrubbed and combed the girl, took Margherita's best dress that she had finished the day before, and after dressing her own daughter in it, stood back to see the result. "You'll do very well, indeed," she said "but now take off all these things so that, when Margherita arrives, she will not guess what we are up to."

Meanwhile, Margherita had hurried to the far-off river by the forest's edge. She placed her basket of fish securely on a pile of rocks that was near and, taking one at a time, washed them carefully so that she would not lose one of them. She had done them all except the last one, which was the biggest and heaviest. Taking him tightly in her two hands, she was about to wash him, when to her utter amazement she heard a voice say, "Please Margherita, don't hold me so tight, it hurts." And though she could hardly believe it, she realized that it was the fish that had spoken to her. She was dumbfounded, but the fish continued. "If you will let me return to my own water and set me free, you will be greatly rewarded someday. I know that if you go home without a fish, your stepmother will be very angry with you, but you must let me go anyway. I have a soul, too, and I want to live just as much as you do. Won't you have pity on me and throw me back into the river? You will never, never regret it, Margherita." The kindhearted girl could not resist his pleading, and with a little laugh she said, "You poor fish, of course I will throw you back. My stepmother cannot do much but beat me, and I won't mind that too much because I will remember that I have helped you."

With this she threw the fish back into the water. But he quickly came to the top again, and before she could leave, he said very earnestly, "Little Margherita, remember carefully what I am about to tell you. You will be punished severely for having allowed me to escape, but if ever you should need help of any kind, you must return to this identical spot and call me. You must call, 'O, Tenchina of the high sea, this is the hour that you must come and help me.' Don't forget me, Margherita, call when you are in need." Before she could answer he was gone.

Picking up the remainder of the fish, she hurriedly set out for home. It was dark by now, and she was afraid of what her stepmother would say at seeing that supper was not yet prepared. But she bravely ran on. When her stepmother saw her coming so late, and particularly when she discovered the largest fish was missing, she was fury itself.

"Why you miserable, clumsy toad," she yelled at the frightened girl, who had never before seen her so angry, "I'll keep my promise yet about not letting you see daylight again." And throwing the fishes into the house, she took Margherita by the arm and dragged her towards the forest once more. The stepmother had seized the excuse of the missing fish to pretend that she had sufficient cause to be infuriated and to do away with

Margherita. She had put a fork into her apron pocket and had hidden a rope beneath the apron.

When they had penetrated the forest almost to its very heart, the wicked, cruel woman commanded Margherita to undress. The shivering, frightened girl did what she was told and looked with horrified eyes at the mad woman. First, the stepmother took out her rope and beat Margherita unmercifully, then she tied the half-fainting girl to a tree, took out the fork, and proceeded to pry out Margherita's beautiful eyes. The poor girl fainted and could not cry out. The wicked stepmother gave an ugly laugh and told the unhearing girl that she would preserve the eyes so that she would be sure that Margherita would never see again. "Now my daughter will marry your rich young man when he comes tomorrow," were her parting words.

When she got home she did as she had said. She placed the eyes in a solution of preserving water in a jar and kept them with her in her room. The stepsister did not bother to ask how her mother had done away with Margherita but was in a flurry about the young man who would visit them. For the first time since they had come to live in the house, they cleaned it up themselves, for Margherita had done this before. When they had finished, they went to bed and waited for day.

The next morning the king was preparing for his visit. He had ordered some new dresses and shoes for a young lady, and with this package under his arm, he entered his carriage and went on his way to Margherita's home. The two scheming women were all ready for him; the stepsister looking very nice for her, but very ugly compared to the beauty of innocent Margherita. When the king arrived at their door and knocked, the stepmother answered and welcomed him in her best manner. He was puzzled at this, for he had expected to be met with a barrage of ugly words and with the statement that he could not see Margherita. He had been prepared for this sort of welcome, but not for this honey-smooth, oily kind of reception. But he entered anyway, feeling that something was wrong but not knowing what it was. And then to his horror he quickly found out. The stepmother asked him what he wished, and he told her politely that he wished to make Margherita his wife when she was a few years older, but that in the meanwhile he wished to take her to his home to be educated as befitted the future wife of a king. When the step-mother heard he was the king, she almost fell over, but she calmly continued and asked him when he wanted to take Margherita away.

"Today, if possible," said the expectant, happy king. He had not thought that she would allow him to take her so easily. But his happiness soon came to an end, for when the stepmother called Margherita and the stepsister appeared, he knew at once that he was being tricked. He said as much, that the girl could not possibly be Margherita; but the stepmother said that this was the only girl she had and that it was truly Margherita. She threatened him with the words which most counted with a king. "You have given your promise to marry Margherita. This is Margherita, and a king cannot break his promise. You must take her and me with her, for I am her mother, to your palace, and keep your word about teaching her as befits the future wife of a king." The bewildered young king had to accept this, for it was true that a king could not break a promise once given. Very crestfallen and unhappily thinking about what could have happened to the real Margherita, he escorted the stepmother and her daughter to his carriage. It was still early, so no one saw them leave. They arrived at the beautiful palace and were given rooms and gardens and servants, and the stepsister began to be trained as befitted the future wife of a king. But the king was very sad and always kept thinking of his Margherita, his own true love.

But what had happened to Margherita? Had she died by the cruel treatment given her by the half-mad stepmother? She suffered torturous pain during the whole night and had fainted many times. But in the early morning, she thought surely she would die. She felt the cold tongue of a dog licking her blood-smeared feet. He was whining and running back and forth, barking for his master to come to him. Finally she heard footsteps and the gasp of a shocked man. The man ran over to the girl and cried, "You poor child, whatever has happened to you? Who has done this monstrous thing to you?" Margherita fainted again, partly from shame at her state and partly from her burning pain. When she came to, she was lying on the ground with the man's coat around her and a cool handkerchief tied about her burning eye sockets.

When the man saw that she had come to, he asked her to tell him how this had happened to her, so that he could report the criminal to the law. But Margherita became very much frightened at the mention of the law, for she was still afraid of her stepmother and dared not reveal who had mutilated her. She therefore told the kind man that she did not remember and asked him not to mention it again. She thanked him for all he had done, but asked him to let her lie there and die. She would be of no use anymore, she said. The man felt great pity for her and said, "Don't say that, poor child. I am going to take you home to my wife and daughter. My daughter has always wished for a sister, and she will be very happy, I know, to take care of you like a sister."

With that the man carefully picked her up, carried her through the forest towards the opposite side of her village, and soon was at his own house on the outskirts of the forest. He took her into his cottage and told her story to his wife and his daughter, who was about sixteen years old, the same age as poor Margherita. They, too, were very sorry for her and, placing her in bed, proceeded to nurse her back to health.

The grateful Margherita could not thank them enough, and with this new kind of treatment—kindness, gentleness, plenty of good food, and love—she soon recovered and was able to walk about and help with the sewing and bedmaking. But she could never see again, and because of this, she felt herself a burden to the kind family. She voiced this feeling one night to her dear "sister," as the hunter's daughter wished Margherita to call her, and the girl put Margherita at ease on the subject. "You must not even think that you are a burden, Margherita dear," she said, "for we all love you very much, and I would be very unhappy if I didn't have you with me. Making me happy as you do is sufficient reason why you should remain with us as long as you and I live. Now please do not mention leaving me again. Will you promise?" Margherita only too gladly promised and endeavored to make her sister as happy as was within her means. Even if she was blind, she could still be kind. And so two years passed this way, Margherita living the happiest life she had known since her own dear mother had died.

It was again a bright, sunny day like the one two years before when she had been out with the sheep and had met the charming young man. She and her sister decided to go through the forest and enjoy the fragrance of the flowers and pick some for their mother.

Margherita called the sister many times when she thought she had found some different flowers, for she went about gently touching them to determine which kind they were by their shape. The sister watching poor Margherita who could not see the beauty of the flowers anymore, felt a great wave of pity engulf her, and before she thought, she cried out, "O Margherita, how I wish someone could help you to see again." Seeing the strange expression that came over Margherita's face when she said those words made the sister gasp with sorrow for having hurt her feelings, as she believed she had. She rushed to her to beg for forgiveness, but Margherita spoke. "O dear sister, thank you for saying what you did. You have reminded me of something I should have done when I first got well. I never told you, did I, about the fish I dropped in the water to set free because he could talk? He begged me to let him go, and I felt pity for him, so I did. He told me to call him when I needed him most and he would come. I have forgotten, but now I shall call him."

The sister thought that poor Margherita had gone crazy and was upset with worry and sorrow. But she was determined to play the game as Margherita directed.

"Are we by the little river that runs through the forest?" Margherita asked. When she was told that they were, she directed her sister to a certain mound of stones by the river's edge. She described the rocks carefully and told her sister to look for them as they walked along. When the sister thought that they were by the rocks, she told Margherita, sho began to shiver with anticipation. "Do not laugh at what I shall do, dear sister," Margherita said, "for I believe that the fish will help me as he promised." And then she began to call the fish in the way that he had told her to. But nothing happened. Margherita asked the girl to keep looking for a fish coming through the water toward them. But her friend told her that she could not see any fish on the water at all. Margherita was a little frightened by now, afraid that perhaps after all the fish would never come.

But she did not give up hope right away. She asked her sister to lead her a little further along the river's edge, because maybe they weren't by the group of little rocks where the fish had told her she was to meet him. They went a little further on, and then Margherita called the fish again, "O Tenchina of the high sea, it is time that you come to help me." Again they both waited expectantly, but again nothing happened. Poor Margherita was very near tears. But she still believed and so tried again. And the third time success was hers. From a long way off, Margherita's adopted sister had caught sight of a shining fish, swiftly jumping wave after wave, getting closer and closer, and always headed directly towards the two girls waiting on the bank.

Soon the fish had reached the side of the river. He looked up at Margherita and asked in a sad voice, "O little Margherita, why did you forget me? Why have you waited so long to call me? You are almost too late, but if you do all that I tell you, we may yet be in time." All this was a little puzzling to the two girls, but they believed the fish with all their hearts. He knew all that had happened to Margherita, for it had been in his power to know it, and this was why he had warned that they did not have too much time. The stepsister was soon to complete the required tutoring to become the wife of the king, and if they did not do something quickly, they would be too late to bring Margherita back to what was rightfully her life and future. So the fish told them to wait for him there at the edge of the water and said that he would return very soon.

The girls were excited and incredulous that the fish could actually help Margherita win back her lost love. Soon the fish came back, and under one fin he was holding a basket full of the most delicious looking fresh figs that one had ever seen. Both girls were very much surprised to see them because they were so much out of season at that time. The fish said to the sister of Margherita, "You must take this basket of fresh figs and walk to the city with it. Go with it immediately beneath the future queen's window and cry, 'Fresh figs for sale, fresh figs for sale; buy some before they are all gone.' This will bring the stepsister to the window, for she loves fresh figs more than any other fruit. When she asks you what you want for them, you must answer, 'One eye, if you please!' Of course she will call you ridiculous, but you must insist. Finally she will want the figs so much that she will take an eye out of the jar in which her mother is preserving two eyes. They are Margherita's eyes, and she shall have them back. Now go, and do all that I said.''

The girl was more than happy to be able to help Margherita, especially if it was possible to make her see again. So she took the basket of fresh figs and hurried to the city. She quickly went beneath the stepsister's window and began to cry, ''Fresh figs for sale, fresh figs for sale; buy some before they are all gone!''

The stepsister, who was busily sewing on her wedding gown at the time, heard the girl, and because she liked fresh figs so much, immediately put her head out of the window and cried, ''What do you want for them, girl?''

''One eye, if you please,'' said Margherita's sister. The other laughed at her and told her to stop fooling with her. But when she saw that the girl actually wanted an eye for them, she remembered Margherita's eye in the bottle which her mother always kept in her bedroom. She took out an eye and hurriedly returned to the peddler. The girl gave her all of her fresh figs when she was given the eye in return. The stepsister asked the girl if she would have any more figs tomorrow, and the good girl said that perhaps she would and that she would return. With this she calmly left, but when she was out of the stepsister's sight, she happily ran all the way to the river's side, where the fish and Margherita were waiting for her.

The fish asked for the eye and then told her to wait, for she would go back again that day with some fresh strawberries, which were also out of season then and which the stepsister liked a great deal too. He went away but soon came back with a beautiful basket full of luscious, red strawberries. And again the good sister went quickly beneath the stepsister's window and began to cry, ''Fresh strawberries for sale, fresh strawberries for sale; buy some before they are all gone.'' Now the stepsister had just finished the fresh figs, and they had awakened in her a yearning for fresh strawberries. So when she heard the good sister cry her wares, she immediately put her head out the window and told her she would buy them all. ''What do you want for them?'' she asked.

''One eye if you please,'' said the good sister as she had done before. So the stepsister went hurriedly to her mother's chamber again and took the other eye. She gave it to the peddler. Then she had a dog killed for eyes which she could substitute for Margherita's, so that her mother would not notice that she had used them to buy herself some fresh fruits.

The good sister ran back to the river's edge faster than ever, for now she had her beloved Margherita's other eye, and if the fish meant to help them, Margherita would be able to see again. When she arrived at the water's edge, there were the fish and Margherita awaiting her. The fish was very happy that the stepsister had given the eyes with such little trouble and immediately called Margherita to him. "Stoop down near me, Margherita," he said, "and lift your eyelids." She did as she was told, and soon she felt one eye and then the other eye settle into their sockets. The fish smoothed her eyelids with his cool wet fins and said, "You may open your eyes now, Margherita, and see once more. At least I have been able to help you this far." Margherita was trembling with fear lest she would not be able to see when she opened her eyes.

But she bravely did as the fish told her, and to her utter joy she could see again. When she beheld her good sister and the fish, she began to cry. She hugged her sister to her and thanked the fish with all her heart. She turned one way and then the other; she looked up into the blue, unclouded sky and down on the running water and green earth and thanked God over and over for his mercifulness and kindness to her. But the fish would accept no thanks. "My work is not yet finished," he told her. "You will soon see me in another shape by means of which I will complete my thanks to you for letting me go back to the water when I asked you."

Then to the girls' utter amazement the fish was gone and a little old woman was standing by their side. "Let us go now, Margherita," said the old woman, "for we must hurry if we wish to be on time to save the king from marrying the evil stepsister." The old woman explained to Margherita that the young man who had stopped to talk to her that sunny day when she was out tending the sheep was really the king of the city. She told the surprised girl that her stepsister had told her mother all that Margherita had related to her and said that the reason for the stepmother's wanting to do away with Margherita was so the stepsister could marry the young man herself. And so the old woman told her how it had come about that she had been found in the forest in the terrible state she had been in and that the fish had waited and waited for a long time for Margherita to come and ask for his help. "The king knew that the stepsister could not be you, but he had given his word that he would make her his future wife, and the stepmother compelled him to keep his promise. That is why they are living in the castle now. The stepsister has been tutored for two years, and the king wishes he could make it for a longer time, for he does not want to marry her," the old woman told the incredulous Margherita.

At this point the old woman turned to the good sister and said, "You must return to your home and leave Margherita in my care, for we will be very busy for a while. When we have finished our plans, we will call for you, and Margherita will repay you as she wishes for your kindness and loyalty. Good-bye for now, and do not say anything of our whereabouts. Your mother and father will understand when you explain what has happened to Margherita. But do not tell anyone else."

And with this the old woman and Margherita turned and began walking towards the city in which the king had his lovely palace and where he was waiting, very much discouraged, for his wedding day. He had often thought of his true love, Margherita, and was certain that the stepmother and the stepsister were tricking him. But he had no proof and so had to endure the pain of thinking what could have happened to the real Margherita, and of being able to do nothing toward finding out.

But let us return to the little old woman and the happy—now seeing—Margherita. When the two had arrived within the grounds of the king's property and not far from the palace itself, they stopped. It was evening by now, and the palace had been closed. No one was around the grounds at this time, so that the old woman remarked, "We are lucky tonight, Margherita, for I will be able to do my work without being seen." Then moving over to a lovely spot, she motioned with her hand, and to Margherita's bewilderment there arose before her the most beautiful, elegant, dreamlike palace she had ever hoped to see in her wildest imagination. It was ten times bigger than the king's and had many more windows, balconies, and decorations than his. A lovely lawn surrounded the palace, and rare, beautiful flowers could be seen in little nooks and in the magnificent garden at the back. There were two doormen at attention by the arched doorway, and when the old woman, holding Margherita by the hand, walked up to it, they immediately bowed and opened the beautifully carved door with ceremony.

But if Margherita had thought the palace elegant on the outside, it was still more so within—high, decorated rooms with the moonlight streaming through the windows and lavishly decorated reception and dance halls equipped with furniture and pictures and expensive articles of the most beautiful colors and forms. It was beyond any dream a mortal could ever have conceived. Soft white bear rugs were strewn about the floors, and Margherita's tired feet sank joyfully into them.

The little old woman smiled at seeing the wondering, incredulous look on Margherita's face, and taking her by the hand again, she led her up the winding staircase to the floor above. Here again words fail to describe the beauty. The old woman opened a door into a bedroom, saying that this room would be Margherita's and that she had given it to her because the window looked out toward that of the king. In the morning when he arose and opened his window, she would have a chance to see his great astonishment without being seen and to observe how he took it. The old woman instructed Margherita in all that she was to do and then left her, telling her to put on one of the prettiest gowns in the closet and then to come below for their supper. Margherita was enthralled when she opened her clothes closet. The gowns were all so beautiful, and she looked through many but could hardly choose the one she wanted. Soon she was ready, and she looked very lovely indeed. The little, oddly dressed woman was waiting for her at the foot of the stairs, and when she looked up and saw Margherita coming down the stairs, a look of satisfaction crossed her face.

Together they entered the majestic dining room. The table was wonderful to behold, for it was set with gleaming silverware and shining silver goblets and serving plates. There were many servants about, all ready to do anything they were asked to do. Margherita was stupefied, but since she was hungry, she ate very heartily of the delicious food.

"Tomorrow when you arise," the little old woman told Margherita, "go quickly to the window, but keep hidden behind the curtains, and watch the king. Soon his messenger will arrive below and present to you a very indignant-sounding letter from the king. He will want to have you report to him personally how you came to be in this palace. You will answer the messenger in a superior manner, saying, 'You tell the king that I have nothing to see him about, for I belong here. Tell him that it is he who should see me, for it is I who have things to say.' The messenger will then return, and he will have been so captivated by your beauty that, in telling the king about it, he will make him wish to see you more than anything else in the world."

And so it happened. Margherita went to sleep in her soft, comfortable bed, where she was awakened the following morning by the songs of birds. She quickly went to the window and saw the king's window open. The king looked out and took some deep, happy breaths, for the morning was very beautiful. But to his great astonishment he found that his view was obstructed by a magnificent palace. He swallowed and stared, and then rushed downstairs and summoned his messenger. All that the little old woman had predicted came true. The messenger came to Margherita, and she answered him as she had been instructed. The messenger was captivated by Margherita's beauty and hurried back to the palace of the king with the news. The poor king was shocked, but would not yield.

The following morning when he again opened his window, he looked towards the castle to see if he could catch sight of Margherita. What he saw made him catch his breath. Margherita, by the little old woman's directions, was leaning on the window sill looking out into the sunny world.

She looked vaguely familiar to him, but he could not place her. He saw how beautiful she was and fell deeply in love. Down the great stairway he rushed, and, summoning his messenger, he ordered him to get the beautifully woven rug that hung in the king's most beautiful room. "Get it studded with pearls immediately, and then take it with my compliments to the grand lady in the magnificent palace. Hurry!" The poor, surprised messenger did as he had been ordered, but when he took the expensive gift to Margherita, the messenger received this reply. "Tell your king that he can give this rag to the scullery maids, for it is fit only for them." She had been told to say this by the old woman, and the messenger had to be satisfied with it. The king was indignant when told what had happened, but was more determined than ever to get the enchanting lady into his home to see her. So he ordered a great banquet to be made ready for the next evening and sent an invitation to Margherita and the little old woman.

This time the old woman told Margherita that they could go. "The time has come when all will be told," she said to the girl. They prepared themselves the next evening, and when the king's most beautiful carriage and horses arrived to take Margherita to the palace, they were ready. The king had ordered thick, soft rugs to be laid from the door of her palace to his, for he imagined her to be the richest and most beautiful personage in the world. Radiant as she was with happiness at seeing her lover once more and knowing that soon he would know who she was, she looked most beautiful. When they had arrived at the palace and had been given the places of honor at the table, the guests began to eat. But they could not refrain from looking towards the new-comer and talking about the new palace and how beautiful she herself was. Of course the stepmother and the stepsister were there, but they did not recognize Margherita, thinking that she was dead. They were intensely jealous but had to cover it up by being nice to her. The king could not keep his eyes off Margherita, and he showed by every sign how captivated he was by her. Soon the meal was over. The guests sighed in deep contentment, and one suggested that each of them tell a story about himself or herself. When they came to Margherita, from whom they wanted most to hear, they were disappointed to have her report that she had nothing to say.

"Then your grandmother must have something to say about you," they said, for they had taken the little old woman as Margherita's grandmother. When they addressed her, she glanced up and gave them all a long, thoughtful look.

"Yes, I have something to say," she replied and, turning toward the king, commenced telling him the life of a certain little girl called Margherita. He started and turned pale, but, giving him a reassuring glance, she continued. She told the group how Margherita's mother had died and how the father had married again, how cruel the stepmother and stepsister had been to the little one, and what the stepmother had done to get rid of her so that her own daughter could win the young man. At this point the evil mother and daughter were at their wits' end as to what to do, for they knew very well who the little old woman was talking about. There was no way to escape, though, for two of Margherita's servants were behind their chairs with a hand on the shoulders of both mother and daughter.

The little old woman continued her story, and by this time the king was giving the stepmother and stepsister such dark looks that they easily could have died if looks could have killed. When the little old woman came to the end of her story she said, "I brought Margherita near to the palace to live so that she would have just such a chance as this banquet in which to let her story be known. I built an imaginary palace so that the king would be attracted and so that the truth would come out. This beautiful girl by my side is the long-suffering Margherita, and the two grinning woman, whom my servants are holding in their chairs, are the evil stepmother and stepsister. They deserved to be punished severely."

Then turning to the king, who assured her that they would be punished, she said, "I now give Margherita to you, for I know how you both love each other. Take care of her, and may your happiness be eternal and your kindness and understanding last until you die. I leave you my blessings!" With this she was gone. Her work had been completed. All present realized at once the truth of all that the old woman had said, and in their anger they asked for immediate punishment of the cowering, guilty women. Taking them to the public square, they ordered two stakes to be set up. Then they tarred the two, and, tying them to the stakes, burned them alive.

Soon after, the king married the happy Margherita, and at her suggestion they went to see the good people who had taken care of her when she had been in such misery. They took the good people back to the king's palace, for the imaginary one that the old woman had created had disappeared just as mysteriously as the old woman herself.

They were all very happy and lived long and merry. They were always kind and merciful. The people loved their king very

much, and their pride in the beautiful Margherita was wonderful
to behold. Margherita's father had heard nothing of what had
happened, for he had been away in foreign parts. When he came
home and was told all about the cruelties of his wife and stepdaughter, he was glad they had been burned, and he came to live
in the palace with his daughter.

The little fish had kept his promise. He had repaid Margherita
well for her faith in him. But to this day, Margherita believes that
the fish and the little old woman were really her mother, who
came down from heaven to help her.

9. The Old Magician Sabino

Once upon a time there lived on the outskirts of a small village a
widow and her only son, Vincenso, who was called Cenco for
short. Every day she sent him to the government forest not far
away to get wood for their fire, for they were poor people and did
not have any of their own. The boy would sometimes bring the
wood home to keep his mother and himself warm, but more often
he would take the wood he had found to the village bakery, where
he would get bread in return for the wood.

One day Cenco felt very ambitious, and thought that he would
get more wood than he had ever gotten before. So he told his
mother to pack him some lunch because he would probably
remain away all day. The mother gave him a large piece of bread
and a piece of fresh cheese. She also gave him a long line with
which to tie his wood up.

Cenco set out at a quick pace and was soon deep in the woods.
He walked for hours until he was finally in the very heart of the
forest. He thought that in this way he would be able to find much
more wood on his return towards home. He had begun to collect
good dry wood when, from behind some bushes, he thought he
heard the sound of snoring. Thinking it came from an animal, he
was a little frightened at first, but decided that he would investigate anyway. Thinking that if it were an animal it would jump at
him, he climbed a tall pine tree and looked down over the bushes.
He did not see any animals, but he did see an enormous, tall man
with a great long white beard over his chest who was sleeping
soundly and snoring frightfully.

164

Cenco thought that only a hermit would live so far in the forest and have such a long beard, so he took courage and began to descend the tree to go and see him. On the way down, though, he passed a bird's nest and saw in it a cuckoo eating the eggs. He grabbed the bird and put it in his large vest pocket, thinking that he would take it home to his mother. He finished his descent and approached the stranger. But upon reaching him, to his great horror he saw that he was awakening and that he had opened two great eyes that were as red as fire. He turned to run, but felt himself caught by the ankle by strong, ponderous hands.

"Please let me go, sir," cried Cenco. "I thought you were a hermit or I would not have disturbed you. Please let me go on my way."

"Oh, no, my little friend," said the old man who was really the wicked magician Sabino, known far and wide for his fierceness, strength, and wickedness. "I'm not a hermit. I'm a great magician." The old magician went on to explain to Cenco that he was very happy that he had met him, for he needed a young man like him to help him do his work. "I'm getting old now and need some help," he concluded.

The frightened youth asked what he, a mere boy, could do to aid him. The old magician answered that he had a home in the forest, a cave, and that he needed help to run it.

"I have left my house to come and gather wood here in the heart of the forest," the old magician went on, "but seeing what a good day it was for a nap I fell asleep under this bush." He ordered the boy to help him, and Cenco was greatly shocked to see that with two blows of the ax by Sabino a large tree would fall.

Cenco was so frightened that he just stared and began to do some fast thinking as to how he could escape. Finally, he thought he would outwit the old magician by some clever action on his part. So with a quavering but determined voice, he told the magician that he was cutting the tree the hard way. "You take too long by your method," said the boy. "The way I do it," we get lots of trees felled at once."

Sabino was surprised to hear this from the boy, for he thought that no one could outdo him in anything. So he asked him how he did it and was told that if he took a long rope like the one Cenco was carrying and tied a number of trees together at once, and then if both of them pulled real hard, they could uproot the trees and get the benefit of the roots too. The old man was delighted to have found this smart boy to help him, but he thought that he could not let the boy do this for it would ruin the appearance of the forest. So he didn't let him try.

Poor Cenco had to think of another trick with which to fool the old magician. He thought and thought, and then popped out with this strange question to Sabino, "Are you very strong, Magician Sabino?"

"Of course I am," replied the man. "Why do you ask?"

"Oh, I was just wondering if you could squeeze a stone so hard that it would break into a powder," said the boy.

"I have never tried it," said the magician, "but that doesn't mean that I can't do it. Give me a large stone and I'll show you how strong I am."

Cenco quickly gave him a large flat stone and watched the magician try and try to break it. Finally, Sabino succeeded in breaking the stone in two. But while Sabino had been busy trying to break the stone, Cenco had quickly taken out his soft, fresh piece of cheese from his pocket, and then turning to Sabino he said, "Well you didn't succeed very easily did you? Now watch me break this stone."

Cenco proceeded to squeeze, apparently with all strength, the supposed stone in his hands. Of course the cheese easily crumbled to small pieces, and since it was fresh cheese, some few drops of water fell out of it too.

Sabino was not only greatly shocked but greatly impressed at the apparent strength of this mere boy.

"You see?" said the boy to Sabino, "I even got some water out of this stone. Do you not believe that I am stronger than you?"

But the old magician said that he did not. "You are tricking me in some way."

The boy did some quick thinking and answered, "Well, I'll give you another chance to show your strength. Let's see who can throw a stone the farthest." The magician agreed and picked up a heavy stone. While Sabino was warming up to throw the stone, Cenco put his hand in the pocket of his vest, where he had put the cuckoo. He got a good grip on him and then proceeded to watch Sabino throw the stone.

Sabino threw the stone with such might that it went very very far, so far that he was sure the boy could never equal the distance. He therefore turned smiling to Cenco and said, "Can you beat my throw?"

Cenco to Sabino's surprise nodded yes. He pretended to double up so he could throw the stone with more strength, and in this action he took the cuckoo out of his pocket and with all his might threw it a far enough distance so that it looked like a real stone. But the frightened cuckoo kept on flying straight ahead as Cenco had hoped he would, and instead of dropping down at the foot of the distant hill, as Sabino's stone had done, the cuckoo, a rock to Sabino, went over the hill and down the other side. The man was too shocked to say a word for a minute, and then turning to Cenco, he said, "My boy, with your strength and my wit, we will get along very well. Come, now, follow me to my house. We will have something to eat first, and then you will do the chores I give you." Cenco did not want to go but thought that he had better let Sabino believe in his supposed strength.

But Sabino was doing some ugly thinking. He was jealous of this mere boy, who had outdone him in strength, and was planning to kill him when he got home. They arrived at a great tree which had an opening in it and a staircase of stones going down through the earth. Before the magician began to descend the stairs, he ordered the boy to precede him. Frightened but determined to see this through, Cenco walked down the dark stairs and soon entered a spacious stone cave beneath the earth. There he saw large tree trunks near the fireplace that were yet to be cut into kindling wood.

The old man had come down too and now told Cenco to go and get some water from the well a little distance away which Sabino had dug himself. Sabino was determined, of course, not to let Cenco out of his sight and planned to follow him to see how much water he could carry back. But Cenco detected Sabino's thought and answered him quickly, saying that he would put his rope about the well and bring the whole thing to him.

Sabino was disturbed at this and told him he would go and get the water himself, but that Cenco should meanwhile cut two of the tree trunks in half so that he could have wood prepared for the winter. After Sabino had left, Cenco was struck with a bright idea. This time surely he would get the better of Sabino. He proceeded to split one of the trunks lengthwise. When he had placed stout wooden spikes between the two parts of the trunk, it seemed as though the trunk was only half split. Then he split the other trunk only half way through and put in even longer spikes of wood to keep the two parts separated.

When Sabino arrived, he indignantly asked how it came that he hadn't finished splitting the two trunks.

"Oh, I thought I would show you an easy way of doing it, which saves a lot of extra time."

"You did!" said the magician. "Well, show me then."

So Cenco put his hands through the first split trunk, which was really split all the way through, and with all his might separated the tree trunk in halves. It looked as if he had really split the trunk with his hands only.

Sabino was impressed and told the boy to show him how to do it on the other half-split trunk. Cenco told the magician to put his hands well into the already split part of the tree, holding them closely together so he could go in up to his elbows with more ease. Sabino stooped down and did as he was told. But he had not anticipated what would happen. Since Cenco had not split this tree all the way through, when he knocked out the spikes holding the trunk apart, the halves of the trunk tightly snapped together again, and Sabino was trapped. He could not separate his hands, for the closed tree trunk firmly held them, and he could get no strength to break the tree apart because he was caught right up to his elbows. He cried out in pain and demanded of the boy to be freed at once.

"Oh no," answered Cenco. "Don't you think I know what you will do to me if I let you out?"

"I won't punish you, I promise," said the wicked old magician.

But Cenco knew otherwise and told him so.

"And by the way," Cenco continued, "a magician like you ought to have some hidden money that you have robbed from honest people. I will search and see. I know you are trapped there for good, and since you are old and will soon die anyway, you might as well resign yourself to die now.'' With these final words to the old magician, he made a thorough search of the cave and found a bag of money in the floor. Taking this with him, he quickly began to ascend the stairs, saying over his shoulder, "This time I have outwitted you, eh, Sabino?''

So instead of seeing her son bring home a large bundle of wood from the forest, the mother saw him come home carrying a white bag in one hand. She ran to see what could have happened and was greeted with the boy's fantastic tale and the bag of money as proof.

They were poor no longer from that time on, and they both lived long and merry and were happy for the rest of their lives.

10. The Stone of Gold

There was once upon a time a king who had a very handsome son, but he would not let this son marry, even though he would not give any reasons why. However, it was thought that because the father would be jealous of any woman who came to live in the palace with his son, the boy had to accept his father's verdict. "You shall marry whom I wish and when I wish it,'' the father told his son when the latter brought up the subject, but the prince felt that his father was not fair. Since he loved beauty, kindness, and goodness, he often roamed the countryside to see nature in all its lovely colors and talk to the poor peasants and people whom he would meet on these saunters. He had come to believe so firmly in the equality of all men, whether kings or peasants, that he was glad his father was not talking about marriage for him because he knew that his father would choose a princess of another country, and whether he loved her or she loved him, they would have to become married anyway. He hated the thought that he couldn't choose the girl he wished. He dwelt on this so much that he finally decided that if he ever met a girl with whom he should fall in love, he would not care what his father might say, but would marry her.

In the same country in which the prince's father reigned lived a family of peasants who were very hard-working and diligent. They had orchards and farmland which they had to care for throughout the year. The family consisted of the father, the mother, and a daughter only, so that these three had to work very hard indeed to keep their land cultivated. As a result, some of it they had let go to grass and planted and sowed only as much as they could reap. One day the father decided that they would plow a little more land than they had plowed the year before, and he thought that, if they worked this hard, they would be sure to put away some money for the future. They were very poor and could not hire extra help, so the girl had to work very hard with her father to plow the extra land. The father told his daughter that he would plow deeper than he ever had before; then they could get the good earth below the surface of the ground near the top, and the crop would grow better.

One day they had been working all the afternoon in this new field when suddenly the girl's spade hit a rock. As she thought that it was only a little rock, she worked around it as best she could. But when she saw that the more she worked around the stone the bigger it became, she called her father to help her. Together they dug around and around until finally they had dug a little trench about the huge, solid stone, which would not break even when they used picks in trying to make it smaller. They were determined to get it out, though, and after some very hard labor, they succeeded in pulling it out. Then they concentrated on filling with dirt the large hole which was left and did not stop to inspect the stone very closely.

By now the sun was going down, so the two decided that they had better go home. Then the girl happened to look at the stone and exclaimed to her father, "Look, look, how the stone shines in the sunlight where it had been struck with the picks." Bending down to inspect it closer, the girl gasped out, "Father, I think this must be gold. It shines like gold, and it is heavier than an ordinary stone of this size. Let's take it home in the wheelbarrow and make sure."

The father hardly believed the girl, but thought he would give in to her whim and take the stone home. When he was able to inspect it more closely, he had to admit that there was a possibility that it was gold. His peasant mind could not grasp the fact that if it were, he would be a very rich man indeed. His daughter called in their friends from all around to inspect the stone and get their opinion about it. The men agreed unanimously that it actually was gold and congratulated the bewildered peasant on his good fortune.

The rumor spread throughout the kingdom that the peasant found a stone of gold on his land, and the word finally reached the palace. The prince became very curious and wanted to see for himself. But his father had other plans. He decided that since the man had found this gold in his kingdom, he would claim it in the name of the kingdom and thus enrich himself that much more. The prince did not know of his father's intentions. When he arrived at the peasant's home and saw his father's soldiers telling the peasant that he must give the stone up to the kingdom, he joined in with the protesting neighbors of the peasant, and the guards could not take the gold from the poor man. When the king heard this he was angered, but when he was given the petition signed by all the peasants of that region, begging him to let the peasant keep what was his own, he had to do it to avoid the consequences which they had threatened in their petition. The prince was very happy that this had happened to his father, for he saw that there were some ways of making the king give in to the will of others.

When he had gone to see the stone, he had noticed that in the peasant's house there was also a very beautiful girl, who shyly remained by her mother's side all during the examination of the stone. He had liked the girl immediately and decided that he wished to see her again. So one day soon after his first visit, he returned to the girl's house under the pretense that he wanted to see the stone once more. This time the father happened to be out on business about the stone, and the prince was able to talk to the girl. He liked her even more when he heard her speak, and before his visit was over, knew that he had found the girl he loved. He asked permission to visit her again, and it was granted. He visited the girl many times, until finally he was sure that she loved him too. Then one day he told her his feeling for her and asked her to marry him. The girl was very much surprised, for even though she loved the prince dearly, she had never imagined that he might love her, a peasant girl. Thus she told him that, since he was a prince and would become king when his father died, she, a mere peasant girl, couldn't possibly marry him. He assured her that he thought differently, that he was going to marry the girl he loved and not a princess whom he had never seen. The poor girl was overjoyed, and when her family heard the news, it was a happy group indeed that the prince saw in the doorway when he left them to return on the morrow.

The next day he arrived with many packages and had the peasant girl dressed very simply, but beautifully, to make her appearance before the king. The prince had not told his father that he had found the girl he loved and that he had decided to marry her, come what might. He felt that, if his father saw the lovely girl, he would have to admit that she was good enough to be a queen. So he drove his beloved to the palace and took her to his father. The old king was shocked at the news and would have nothing to do with the girl. He was very violent, for his temper got the better of him, and he had a bad one indeed. When the old king had finally calmed down enough to be spoken to, his only son coolly said, "I am not at all afraid of what you think. I want to get married, and I want to marry this girl. If you will not give your consent, I will leave the palace and become a peasant myself." This so horrified the father that he relented, under one condition. "Send this girl back to her home," he told his son. "Then I will send her a proper invitation to the palace; if she can come as that invitation directs, and successfully arrives here, I will give my permission for you to marry her."

The couple had no other choice but to accept this reasonable offer, and the prince told the girl to be brave, for he was sure it would not be hard. The girl was taken home, where she anxiously awaited the invitation. It came the following day, and when she read it, she was dismayed beyond belief. The invitation said that she should go to the palace and arrive there neither by day nor by night, neither by foot nor by carriage, neither clothed nor yet nude, neither having eaten nor yet hungry. She took the invitation to her mother, crying softly that she would now have to give up her beloved prince. But the mother studied the invitation carefully and soon a bright expression illuminated her face. "Do not worry, my poor girl, you can do all this easily." The girl sprang up with a happy cry and asked to be shown how.

"The invitation says you cannot go by foot nor by carriage, so you can go on our old donkey, who will carry you very well. Next it says you cannot be clothed nor nude. Well I'll give you my wedding veil, which I have always kept, thank goodness, and this you can put around you in folds. Leave your long hair free around your shoulders and that will cover the upper part of you. It will take you six hours to get there on the donkey, so you will not eat during all that time, but you can keep a dry chestnut in your mouth so that you will not feel hungry when you get there. And as for getting there neither during the day nor the night we will plan it this way. You can start out early in the morning, about one o'clock when it is still dark, and no one will see you. You can time yourself so that you will knock at the palace door just as dawn is creeping through the sky. It will be neither day nor night at this time, and the old king will have to accept you. Now let us get you ready." And the mother began preparing the happy girl for her journey.

The plans worked out wonderfully, for the girl on the donkey was not clothed with clothes, yet her beautiful long hair was like a mantle around her and covered her almost completely. She timed herself so that just as dawn was breaking, when the sun had not yet come up but the shadows of the night were quickly disappearing, she knocked at the palace door, which was opened immediately by her prince. He had been waiting diligently, yet anxiously, for her because he had read what his father had ordered. Now he was overjoyed to see how well she had succeeded. He called his father at once, who was indeed surprised to see the girl and to learn how cleverly she had accomplished the tasks he had set for her.

When the son asked him if he was satisfied, the king had to admit that he was, and he freely gave his consent for the marriage. Clothes were brought for the girl and a good warm breakfast prepared. Plans were put in motion at once for the preparation of the wedding, which was to take place without delay. The king came to like his son's wife so much that he was happy that he had accepted her as his daughter-in-law. He ruled the people with a wiser hand than before and closed his life a contented man. The young couple lived happily in the palace the rest of their lives, beloved by all in the kingdom; and the peasant and his wife, who had now become rich from the stone of gold, ended their lives happily on their farm, where they insisted on remaining.

11. The Story of Little Peter

Little Peter was the oldest and also the laziest and least obedient of a family of seven children. His poor mother was beset on all sides for aid and comfort by the younger children and badly needed a helping hand from Little Peter. But did Peter even offer to help his mother and the children? No! Right after breakfast he would sneak away from the house and start his daily rovings about the village, the fields, and the bypaths he came across. He would return home only when hunger prompted him to do so or when his conscience smote him for his cruel treatment of the children and his mother. The latter rarely happened indeed.

One day Peter's mother thought she would punish him justly for having made her worry all day about his whereabouts when he had been much needed at home. She locked the house and barred the windows; she put the children to bed and then prepared herself for bed. About eleven o'clock, when all were sleeping except the waiting mother, a loud knock, very characteristic of Peter, was heard. All was quiet! The knock was repeated, this time with kicking and loud calls. Little Peter was very indignant that no one was answering the door, but it only took him a short time longer to realize that no one would open the door. And then he heard his mother's voice which uttered some startling words to Peter's ears.

"Stop kicking at the door, Peter," she said brokenly, for she loved all her children, even Peter, her despair. But gaining control as she spoke, she continued, "I am determined to punish you for your very bad behavior, therefore do not try to come in tonight. You are a bad boy, and mean and selfish with your brothers and sisters and with me. I cannot love you any more if you continue to do all the things which you wish to do and none that you should do. So go away now, Peter. Go anywhere you please until you have decided that you will obey and help me and that you will love all the children too.'' With that she closed the bedroom window, and Peter was left to ponder over his mother's words. It never occurred to him to apologize and tell his mother that he was willing to help her in the future. He sullenly stuck his hands deep in his pockets and shuffled away in the dark.

Peter was deeply perplexed. Where was he to go at this time of night? Everyone was asleep, and all the doors were closed. He did not wish his boyfriends to see him vagabonding about without a home, even if it was temporary. He then bethought himself of the little park at the end of the village, where he knew many thick trees were situated, among which were some fruit-bearing ones. He was ravenously hungry, and, thinking of the pear tree he knew about in the park, he began to run. Reaching the desired destination, he quickly climbed the tree—thus hiding himself from observers—and picked off a large pear. He had only swallowed his first bite when he saw a dark shadow below on the grass. He stood quiet, still, hearing his heart beat very loudly, for now he was frightened. The shadow was that of an ugly old woman, as Peter recognized when she turned her face up to him. She was saying that, since she could not climb the tree to get herself some pears, she would cut the tree down. Upon hearing this, Peter called out loudly to wait until he got down. She answered him saying, ''Hurry down, then, and bring me down some pears.''

He filled his cap and slid down the tree. But Peter had not noticed that the old woman had a sack under her arm and that while he had been coming down, she had opened it. Now when he turned to give her the pears, she grabbed at him and pushed him into her sack. She tightly closed the opening so that the struggling Peter could not get out. As no one was about at that late hour, no one heard his faint cries.

You see, the old woman was really a wicked witch, and she had been out scouting for bad boys so that she could bring one of them home to her witch husband. She was very much pleased, therefore, that she had caught such a young and tender one as Little Peter.

She picked up the heavy sack with the struggling little boy in it and slowly made her way towards her hut on the hill near the town. Finally Peter became quite tired, desperately kicking and punching the sack as he did. He stopped, out of pure exhaustion, and began to think of his sad plight.

"Now if I had only obeyed my mother," he thought to himself, "perhaps this would not have happened to me." And he felt sorry for himself. Then he began to think of ways to get out of the sack. After all, he wasn't dead yet. So he searched through his pockets the best he could, and sure enough, in one he found his indispensable little jackknife. "Now I'll have a chance to get out," he thought. "I'll wait until she puts me down to take a little rest." And so he lay there quietly and waited, hoping that his weight would soon tire the old woman.

At last the old woman became very tired, for she had stood up under Peter's vicious kicking and beating and was indeed worn out with her heavy load. As she was passing by a little stream, which she thought an ideal place to rest and get a drink to make her stronger, she laid down the sack and went to the stream to drink. Little Peter quickly took the opportunity and cut the string that kept the sack closed. He picked up a large rock that was near him, which, together with a few sticks, he put into the sack and tied it again.

It was so dark that the old woman did not notice anything amiss. After she had taken her time about drinking and returned to pick up the sack, she was surprised to find how heavy it had become. She thought that the boy had fallen asleep, because he was so quiet, and was thankful that he was not kicking her anymore. So she trudged on up the steep hill towards her hut. Peter was curious by now, for he realized that she was a wicked witch and wanted to see where she lived. He followed her, therefore, but kept well hidden behind the bushes that ran parallel to the road.

When the witch had almost arrived at her hut, she called out to her husband that she had a tasty morsel for their dinner tonight. "I've had great luck hunting," she cried, "so put on the kettle full of water to boil. We shall have good broth tonight. My catch is very tender, my dear."

When the witch husband heard this, he ran to her and helped her carry the sack to the hut. They placed it in a corner while they prepared the kettle in which they would cook the game. Little Peter had meanwhile climbed to the roof of the house and was observing what was going on by looking through the chimney. He could hear what they were saying and shuddered to think what would have happened to him had he not escaped. "Oh how good I will be when I get home to mother," he thought to himself. The voices of the wicked witches were coming to him up the chimney and he could hear the man say, "You have taken a long time tonight, and I am very hungry. It is better for you that you have found a good dinner, for I would have been angry with you if you hadn't."

"Quick, then; the water is boiling! Let us put him in it, now while he is asleep."

Both went over to the corner and, lifting up the heavy sack, tossed it with all their might into the high, large kettle that was filled with bubbling, boiling water. The heavy stone that was actually in the sack sank to the bottom of the kettle with a great big splash, and its weight broke through the kettle. The scalding water was poured all over the two mean witches, and the scattered flames of the open fire began burning the floor and the wooden chairs and table.

Flames caught at the two witches' clothes too, and soon they were bright torches of fire. Their screams came to Peter's ears, but he felt no pity for them. He cried loudly down through the chimney, "So you thought you had gotten Little Peter, eh? Well, this time, my poor wicked witches, I have fooled you, and God has punished you; you deserve all that you are getting. Die wicked, as you lived wicked, and I will go home and be a good boy from now on."

When he saw that they were almost dead, he entered the hut quickly before it all burned and looked around to see what a witch's house looked like. In one corner he saw a wooden case, and hurrying to it, he opened it. In it was a small sack, and, picking it up, he heard that the contents jingled together. At this point, he rushed out of the hut with the sack, and, looking back, saw the building fall in on the two cruel witches who had done so much wickedness in their mean lives.

It was getting light now, for the morning was soon coming. He hurried towards the little town, feeling very repentant and sorry that he had caused his mother so much trouble in the past. He resolved that he would now be very good and obedient all the time, for he had learned his lesson.

When he had taken a glimpse into the sack he carried, he had seen that there was nothing but gold in it. "This will help my mother very much," he thought, "and now all of my brothers and sisters will be able to eat all they want and won't be cold anymore in the wintertime."

With those thoughts he hurried even faster and soon reached home. His mother had only gotten up, and when she heard a gentle knock at the door, she went to open it immediately. She never thought it would be Little Peter, for he always kicked at the door. She had been anxious about where he had gone that night, but she had resolved to carry through the punishment she had given him. So she was very much surprised when she saw a blushing Peter at the door. His eyes were downcast, and he was mumbling a sincere apology for all his meanness and selfishness of the past. He then asked his mother if he could come in again, and he promised her that he would always obey her and be good from then on. He said he had something to tell and something to give her.

She opened her arms wide, and with brimming eyes hugged him to her. "Yes, I forgive you, Peter, and I will let you come in. I am very happy, dear, to hear that you will be good from now on, for you would have come to a very unhappy end if you had continued as you were doing. But what is this you are carrying?" she asked him.

He sat down, but, before doing so, he had gotten his mother a chair too, much to that woman's hidden surprise. He then told his mother everything that had befallen him during that night. And then he showed her the bag of gold. He assured her that they could keep it, for the witches were dead now and didn't have any relatives to leave it to. The poor woman was overcome with joy, and kissing Peter again, she thanked God that he had been spared in this way.

When the children awoke and were told of the good news, they too were excited and danced around Peter very happily. All that Peter had promised himself on the way home came true. The children and their mother were clothed in decent attire and never again did they go hungry as they had done earlier.

Peter grew into a fine, honest man, and his mother reared her other children into worthy men and women.

12. The Three Brothers and the Fig Tree

There once lived three brothers with their parents in a small village far away. Their only means of income was the beautiful, tall fig tree in their backyard which grew larger and lovelier every year. The figs were known far and wide for their goodness and freshness, and the boys tended the tree day and night when it was in fruit so that no one would take even one fig.

But the brothers were very different from one another. The two oldest ones were a bit alike in that they both disliked to talk to people, and they positively hated to be asked their business. They had sharp cutting tongues and were not liked by the other villagers because of this. The youngest boy, though, was quite different. He was handsome, vivacious, smart, kind, and considerate. Everyone like him, and there were more than a few maiden hearts which fluttered when he went by. This eighteen-year-old boy was so gracious to all that he was to have some very thrilling adventures in his young life.

The fig season was at hand! The brothers and the old father were tending their figs as though they were nuggets of gold, for the money they would receive from selling the figs would buy the provisions for the winter and the wood for the fire to keep the family warm. Now a fig tree fruits gradually, so that there are a number of gatherings of figs, which diminish in size and goodness as the season progresses and nears the end. The brothers always made more money on their first few gatherings, for it was then that the figs were at their best.

It was always the oldest brother who would go out to sell the best figs, for he was trusted the most as to common sense and shrewdness in selling. Filling a large basket with the most luscious, juicy fruits every day, he would start out towards the city and the market. One morning, he had been walking for some time when he perceived in front of him down the road three lovely girls coming towards him. He lowered his eyes quickly and began walking even faster so he would pass the girls as soon as he could. But the girls had different ideas. They came upon him, merrily calling to him and asking him what he had in that basket he was carrying so carefully. He did not answer. One of the girls said, "A strange sort of a creature you are, not even saying good day to three maidens like us. Is it that we are ugly hags?"

"No," volunteered the boy gruffly, "I suppose I ought to say it. You are very beautiful."

"Well, then," said the second sister, "why not let us see what you have in your basket."

"That is my affair and none of your business!" snapped the boy.

"Are you going to market to sell whatever you have?" asked the third sister.

"What if I am?" he said. "I must get on my way and not waste time talking silliness to girls I've never seen before."

"But we only want to help you. We have heard that the king is looking for all kinds of good fruits and vegetables so he can stock up, and it would be more to your advantage if you went straight to the king's palace to sell your wares instead of to the market. We guarantee that you'll have more success," said the first sister.

"But we want to know what you have in your basket," clamored the two.

"Well, if you want to know," said the boy angrily, "I have some horse manure. Are you all satisfied now? Good day, I think I know how and where to sell my wares." And he departed in an angry temper. But he could not help overhearing the ominous reply of the three sisters.

"Manure you will have, then, young man!"

When the oldest boy arrived at the market, for he had not thought of taking the girls' advice, he found that most of the merchants had gone to the king's palace because he was asking to have the first choice of all the wares that came into the market to be sold. He hurried to the palace as fast as he could, and when he was beneath the king's windows, he started to call out his figs for sale. He thought to himself that here was the place to make a good bargain, for the king would not be too particular about the price since he was so rich, and therefore the boy would ask double the amount he originally would have asked per pound.

The king dearly loved fresh figs, and when he heard them called, he sent his valet down immediately to get some. The valet, though, knew the market price for figs and was prepared to offer the boy one franc more than that for the service. But when the boy heard the offer that the valet made to him, he laughed in his face.

"My dear sir," he said, "my two brothers and I have wasted many an hour just watching our fig tree fruit, and we have labored hard to get such delicious and large figs. We have to live all winter on the money we make from their sale, and six francs per pound is a miser's offer for the perfect figs I have to sell."

The valet was taken aback at the ungraciousness of the boy. "You are very stupid, my fine friend, to talk that way to the king's valet. But let me see these perfect figs for which you ask such a stupendous price."

"I'll show them to the king myself, for I'm sure he won't mind paying ten francs for my perfect fruit."

The valet was further stunned, but, being helpless, he decided to go and call the king. When he told the king the attitude of the boy towards himself the king was angered, but his love of figs overcame his bad humor, and he decided to go and see the figs himself. The boy made a sweeping, low bow when he saw the king come toward him, for now he was certain he could get what he asked for the figs.

"Come, come," cried the king, "what is this I hear about you and your figs? Let us see your fine figs that you brag so much about and ask such a high price for."

The boy very ceremoniously lifted the white towel that had hitherto covered the figs, expecting that the good odor of fresh figs would come forth and that the sight of the figs among their green leaves would induce the king to say that he would buy them. But what a stinging surprise he received, and what a horrified face he turned to the insulted king. For there within the neat basket was horse manure instead of figs.

The king was angered beyond description, and, screaming in rage, he called his guards to take this blundering fool to the lowest dungeon in the prison. "But sire," cried the poor boy, "I assure you that I never knew there was anything in my basket except my fine figs which I picked myself. Please listen to me and believe me, sire. I did not know."

"Quiet, you fool," cried the king. "You have insulted me, and anyone doing that deserves worse than just the dungeon for life. Take him away."

And the bewildered, frightened boy was thrown into a dark cell to starve and suffer for life. He thought and thought of how it could have happened, if perhaps his brothers had played a trick on him, but he knew that they would never have done that. And then he remembered the three girls. Could it be, he wondered, that what they had said had actually come true. And he repented that he had not treated them more kindly.

Now to return to his home. His parents and brothers were worried at the end of the week because the oldest boy was not yet home, and they hoped he had not run away. When a few more days went by and no sign of the boy, the second brother made up his mind that he would go and sell another basket of figs. He faithfully promised his parents that he would return as soon as he had sold them all. His parents gave him their blessing and Godspeed and settled back to wait and pray that this son, at least, would come home with some money so they would not starve. The youngest brother, meanwhile, tenderly took care of the last batch of figs on the tree, for they were the ones that he would sell. He tried to cheer his parents up and assure them that their two oldest boys would come back all right.

The second son was halfway along the road when he too saw three beautiful girls come singing towards him. He lowered his eyes in bashfulness and hurried his pace. The sisters stopped the second brother and asked him the same questions which they had asked the first. And he answered likewise and was told by the three young sister, "Manure it shall be, then, young man." He went on a short distance and soon met a little old woman coming towards him. She asked in her high-pitched voice what he had in the basket. And he rudely answered that it was none of her business and went on. The old woman was deeply hurt and walked silently on her way, marveling at the attitude of the young people of his generation.

The second brother did not act on the three girls' advice about going to the king's palace before he went to the market, so that he lost time going to the market first and then to the palace, when he found out he had to if he wished to sell his figs at a high figure. Very expectant and happy because he would be able to ask a higher price from the king, he began to call out his wares in the yard of the palace. The king, thinking that finally he would get his desired fresh figs and never thinking that the first scene might repeat itself, sent his valet down to get them. The frustrated valet returned to report that this boy wanted to see his highness and that he too wanted a much higher price than they asked at the market. But the king did not yet suspect the truth. He hurried down and asked the boy to let him see the wonder figs. The second brother took off the white towel that had covered them and was stunned at the sight that greeted him. The king could scarce be held, he was so angry. "Once it's forgivable," he cried, "but twice . . . ," and he remained speechless from anger.

The poor boy was quivering from fear and tried to explain that he did not know how this had happened for he had packed the basket himself. "Enough," cried the king. "Let this fool join the other fool in another of the deep dungeons." When the boy heard the king mention another fool, he wondered if perhaps the same thing had happened to his brother, and he was enlightened on the subject when the guard laughingly said, "Circumstance has given you a brother. He tried to sell the king horse manure for figs, too. Ha, ha, ha!"

Meanwhile, the parents and the youngest son were anxiously waiting for the second son's return, but the days sped by without sight of either one. Finally, the mother began to cry and lament the loss of her sons, for she would not believe that they had deserted their family. After waiting a few more days and seeing neither of his brothers, the youngest boy, who was eighteen years old, told his parents that he was going to market too and that he really would return. They gave him their blessing and wished him all the luck. "Come back to us, Bepi, don't forget," pleaded the loving mother. The last son was named Joseph but was called Bepi for short.

Bepi went along on his way, whistling merrily and greeting everyone with a nod and a bright smile. Soon he too was on the same part of the road that his brothers had been on when they met the three girls. Now he saw them too. They called out to him when he came close, "Hello, Bepi, where are you headed for?"

"Well, how do you know my name? I've never met you girls before," said Bepi perplexed.

"Oh, is it really Bepi?" asked the oldest. "We only guessed. How nice. But where are you headed for, Bepi?"

"Why, I'm on my way to market to sell the figs I am carrying in this basket. I can't offer you many, because I have to sell them to make money to take home to my parents, but I can give you one each so that you can say you've tasted fresh figs from this season. Would you like some?" he asked them pleasantly.

"Yes, thank you, thank you," they clamored and picked one fig each from the basket. Then the oldest girl told Bepi that he had better go right to the king's palace, for they knew that he was looking for fresh figs and would pay him even more than the market price.

"Thank you very much. I am obliged to you," said Bepi, "but now I must be on my way if I wish to get there before the palace is closed."

"Oh, wait a minute," they cried, "we have something to give you for having treated us so kindly." And the eldest presented Bepi with a little whistle that played a pretty tune. The second girl gave him a pocket knife that was new and shiny. And the youngest girl gave him a little wooden rod—a wand. He thanked them again but voiced his doubt as to the usefulness of the presents.

"You must remember, Bepi, that these little gifts have great power. The whistle will make anyone dance, whether he wants to or not. The pocket knife will be useful when you are in danger. The magic wand will give you protection, a fence, a moat, anything that will prevent evil from following you or overcoming you, provided you draw a circle about yourself. Good-bye for now, and use your gifts carefully." He expressed his appreciation to them and went on his way. Soon Bepi too met the little old woman who asked to see what he had in his basket.

"Why, of course you can, old mother, and I'll give you a fig too, so that you can say you had a fresh fig from this season." She was very grateful and went away smiling and happy.

Bepi went straight to the king's palace and began to sing out his wares loudly. The valet rushed down and told the boy to get off the premises, if he didn't want to be killed. He said the king was sick and tired of having boys come to sell him fresh figs and then to find it was only horse manure. "You'll get you head cut off at once, if you don't leave." On hearing the sentence about the boys coming to sell the king figs when it was only manure that they had, the boy thought at once that they had been his brothers and anxiously asked if those other boys had been killed. He was told that they were in the lowest dungeons for life and that he would end there too, if he didn't leave. Instead, to the valet's shocked amazement, the boy rushed into the palace and went from room to room until he came to the library where he saw the king reading. Leaving his basket outside the door he rushed in and confronted the king.

"What is the meaning of this, young man?" said the king. "Since when can anyone come in and interrupt the king without being announced?"

But the boy did not let the king continue. "It is you who ought to be ashamed of yourself, for you are the one who places innocent boys in dungeons. I am the brother of the two boys who came here to sell you fresh figs, as I have done, and I find that you have placed them in prison. Is that justice and mercy, your highness?"

"Don't mention those boys to me again. Of course it is justice. They insulted their king. What else did they deserve?"

"But I'm sure that if you had let them explain, they would have had an adequate explanation. I know that they had fresh figs when they left the house, and I know that they came straight to the city. You are not a good king when you condemn the innocent without even letting them tell their story."

But the king had heard enough. He cried for his guard to take the impudent boy away, but before they could lay a hand on him, he whipped out his little whistle and began to play it. The king, the guards in their encumbering uniforms, the servant and the valet, the house pets, the queen and the princess, everyone in the palace began to dance madly. The boy kept on playing and playing until the king cried out in pure exhaustion that he must stop. The boy heard screams from the floor above and rushed to see what was the matter. In one room he found the queen lying on the floor in a dead faint, and in another he found the beautiful princess begging him to stop because she could not go on any longer. He stopped, but no one came after him, for they were all too exhausted to move. He asked the girl how old she was, and she told him sixteen. He told her who he was, where he came from, and why he was punishing her father. She liked the boy at once and told him so. He was very much embarrassed and bashfully left the room.

By this time the king and some of his men had recovered and were in pursuit of the boy. He started playing again, and again they all began to dance. The girl called out, "Father, father, let the brothers out; do as he tells you, for I cannot go on. Please, father." And between breaths, the boy told the king that his wife was in a dead faint on the floor. "You had better agree to let my brothers out or your charming daughter will be in the same plight," warned Bepi. Finally, the king agreed, but the boy made him sign a paper to that effect so that the king would not be able to break his promise.

Bepi let his brothers free and gave them the money that the king had given him when he had shown him the good figs in his basket. The older brothers thanked him and went home to their waiting parents with the story of what had happened to them. The youngest boy decided that he would stay and ask for work from the king. He had fallen in love with the princess and wanted to get a glimpse of her sometimes, even if he could never actually ask her to be his.

Now a very tragic thing was going on in the hills surrounding the city. Here was where the king had his immense herd of sheep grazing, but every night seven of them would be missing. One day a shepherd had gotten a glimpse of a terrible dragon with seven heads. But no one had tried to kill him, for all believed that they would be eaten alive before they got close enough to cut off even one of the heads.

The embittered king told Bepi that he did have a job for him, that of taking care of his sheep in the hills. In this way, thought the king, "He will be away from the palace and out of my sight. And perhaps he will be eaten by the dragon with the seven heads."

The boy said he was honored to be in the service of the king and the following morning departed for the hills. When he arrived, he was told the tragic news that seven more sheep had disappeared and that the king's herd was diminishing rapidly. The boy, assuring the old shepherd that he would take care of the dragon, went to bed early. The following morning, he opened the sheep pens and watched the animals, like white clouds, run out and scatter about the hills. He realized that the sheep would wander while they were pasturing, and he was puzzled as to how he could get all of them back in the fold without having to go out himself when the time came for them to return. After a time, he decided to follow the sheep; he had a great curiosity to see if it was really true that there was a dragon with seven heads.

He went to one of the largest pastures where he could see for a long way around him. As twilight was falling, he knew that the sheep would soon return. Presently from afar off he saw a bunch of them running towards him with a hideous creature in pursuit. He saw seven heads protruding from seven long necks and realized that the dragon with the seven heads was coming towards him. Quickly he drew a large circle about himself and ordered a fence to be constructed so high and so thick that the dragon would not be able to reach him. But then he wondered how he could ever get all the sheep into the fenced-in place. And then he thought of the wand. Tapping it with irritation against his foot because he did not know how to use it, he was surprised to hear a voice cry, "At your command."

"I command that all my sheep in the pastures come within this pen so they will be safe from the dragon." And to his utter surprise there he was surrounded by all the sheep which had been in the pastures. The dragon, angered to see the sheep he had been chasing disappear before his very nose because of the magic wand, became infuriated, and bellowing horribly, he charged at the iron fence he saw. He rushed with such force that all seven of his ugly heads were caught in the fencing and he could not pull them back. One by one, Bepi cut them off with his magic knife, and soon all seven heads were strewn about the ground and the terrible dragon dead. With a motion of his magic wand he removed the fence and then led the sheep to their regular pens. When he told the aged shepherd in charge of the sheep what he had done, the old man would not believe him.

"Well, then," said Bepi, "go and see for yourself." And he told him where the dragon would be. The old man together with a number of other shepherds hurried to the place to see if it was true that now they would no longer have to fear the dragon. Sure enough there was the dead body of the horrible monster with all seven heads strewn about him in his own blood. They hurried back to the house to congratulate the boy. "However did you manage to kill such a monster?" they asked him, and he told them, "With my little pocket knife." They laughed at him, but that is all the explanation he gave them. Then one burst out excitedly, "Now the king will have to give you his daughter in marriage."

"What are you talking about?" quickly asked the boy.

"Why, don't you know? The king has promised that the man who slew the dragon so that it wouldn't kill any more of his sheep should have as a reward the princess for his wife," explained the shepherd.

"And a king can't break his promise, can he?" anxiously asked the boy. The men assured the lad that a king couldn't do that, and he happily went to the palace to demand his reward. He knew that the princess liked him, and therefore he had the courage to go through with it.

When he arrived at the palace, he demanded that the guard announce him. The guard looked at the poor boy dressed in shepherd's clothes and scornfully said, "And you think you can see the king? And who wants to announce you to his majesty?"

"You announce me to the king immediately and further announce me as the shepherd who has killed the dragon with the seven heads."

When the guard heard this, he laughed heartily and only called the boy a fool. But on seeing that the lad was going to go in even if no one announced him, he pulled back and ceremoniously, though sarcastically, announced him to the king. When the king heard the announcement, he jumped up and went to see the man who demanded an audience with him. Imagine his anger when he saw that it was the same boy who had almost made his wife die dancing. "You again," he bellowed, "I thought I had gotten rid of you for good. How dare you come here with the pretense of having killed a dragon that none of my best soldiers could get? If you think you will win my daughter by bluffing, you are very much mistaken. Take him away, guards."

"Just one moment, your highness, before I begin playing my whistle again." With an agonized look on his face, the king held up his hand to stop the guard. "I am telling you the truth when I say that I have really killed the dragon. Send your men to the north pasture, and you will see for yourself. You as a king have given a promise, and as a king you cannot break it. If your daughter does not approve me and does not wish to accept me as a husband, I won't be so cruel as to compel her to marry me. But if she is willing, neither you nor all your soldiers can prevent my taking her."

The stubborn king only laughed at him and told him angrily that he would see him dead before giving his daughter to a stupid, dirty shepherd. The boy was very much angered when he heard this and began to play his whistle. It took the king by surprise, for his rage had made him forget how terrible it was to be obliged to dance so hard. In a minute shouts and screams could be heard from upstairs, and Bepi said to the king that, if he didn't want his wife actually to die this time, he had better consent to let him see the princess. "I only want to know her answer to my question," he told the king.

"Then go to her," said the tired king, "as long as you stop your infernal music." And he sank down gratefully in a chair as soon as Bepi stopped playing. Bepi rushed upstairs two steps at a time and ran into the girl's room. She was seated on a chair breathing hard from having danced. He smiled at her and when she returned it, Bepi blushed. He began to stutter and stammer as he tried to tell her what he had done. Finally he told her that her father's promise had been that any man killing the dragon would receive his daughter for his wife. "Now, I'm not asking you to be my wife unless you love me, for I'm a very poor man and not educated. But if you feel towards me as I feel towards you, will you be my wife?"

"Oh, yes, Bepi," she cried, for she had truly fallen in love with him when she had first seen him. "Gladly would I be your wife, no matter how poor you were. You are kind, and good, and gracious. That is why I love you. I will go wherever you ask." The boy felt very deeply touched, and at that moment he realized that he could not take the girl away from the luxuries that she had known all her life to make her a poor man's wife. So he looked at her and said, "I fear that I shouldn't take you with me. You don't know how hard a peasant's life is, and you, who have been used to the very best all your life, could never adapt yourself to my way of living. I appreciate your love very deeply, but I must disappear from your life forever."

And with that he was gone. The princess understood why he had said that she could not be his wife, but she loved him too much to let that stand in her way. She knew that he was a shepherd for her father and she decided that she would run away that night and go to the huts in the pastures.

The king had smiled with satisfaction when he had seen the boy run down the stairs and straight out through the door with a pitiable look on his face. He was sure his daughter had scornfully refused him and was glad.

But that night the princess held to her resolve. She ran away and escaped to the shepherds' huts. She asked for Bepi at one of the huts, and she was so dressed that the shepherds did not recognized her. They told her where Bepi's hut was, and she hurried to it and knocked. Bepi opened the door and was much surprised to see a girl on his doorstep. She quickly entered and threw her hood and veil from her face. Bepi recognized the princess and gasped. "What are you doing here?" he asked.

"I love you, Bepi," she said.

"But you cannot remain here tonight. It would give you a bad name no matter how innocent we both are. You must return at once to the palace before they discover that you are missing."

But the stubborn girl looked at him and said, "I cannot do that. I will follow you wherever you go, so please take me." So Bepi planned how they would escape back to his parents during the night. He went out and killed two sheep. He skinned them, being careful not to cut the skin in any place. Then he blew and blew into them until they were like large balloons, so that they would float. Tying them securely and then putting some food into a bag, they were prepared to leave. To avoid passing the city, they had to go over a river. For the passage over it, Bepi had prepared the blown-up balloons.

Silently they slipped down the hill toward the river, and after Bepi had securely tied one balloon to the princess and one to himself, they were all ready to go. He paddled across, steering both himself and the princess. Once over the river, she turned to him and smiled. They thought that they were safe. They began to climb the step hill in front of them, and when they were halfway up, they stopped a while to rest. Far below, crossing the river on horses, Bepi saw the king's guards following them. The men had seen them because the two dark forms stood out clearly in the moonlight. Bepi's heart sank and he held the princess close. "There's a sort of cave over there," she whispered. "Couldn't we hide in it?"

"We can try, anyway," said the desperate boy.

If they had known that the cave was the home of a mother tiger and her little cubs, perhaps they would not have entered. But not knowing this, in they went and hid silently in the shadows. The men stopped outside and called to them to come out, for the king demanded them. They told the lovers that they had seen them enter the cave and knew that they had cornered them. The men said that the boy was going to be killed at once and that the princess was also to be punished. They had picked up their trail from the shepherds' huts, and the punctured empty skins lying by the riverside had assured them that they were on the right track. And then they had seen them in the moonlight.

"Come out, I say," roared the head guard, "before I come in after you." No sign of them. The guard got angry and rushed into the cave. His noise disturbed the mother tiger lying in a corner, and when she saw that it was a human being in the cave, she sprang at the guard and killed him. The men outside heard the cries, and they saw the tiger come charging towards them. They sprang on their horses and hurried away. "If the boy and the princess aren't dead now, they never will be," they thought.

But the boy and the princess had taken the opportunity, when the tiger was attacking the guard, to run out of the cave and up the road to the top of the hill. Then they went down into the valley where lay the home village of the boy. When he arrived at his parents' home and related his adventures, his parents called the priest of the parish to marry the two lovers. After the marriage, they lived in the pleasant house with the fig tree behind it for the rest of their lives. The king was heartbroken that—as he thought—his daughter had been killed by the tiger, but he was happy that in that way she did not disgrace him and that he did not have to punish her. Thinking her dead, he never looked for her again, and so Bepi and his happy princess-wife lived happily ever after.

13. The Twelve Doves on the Mountain of the Sun

Once upon a time in a little village in the mountains, there lived a poor widow with her only son. When the boy was grown, he began to think of earning a living. He saw how hard his mother tried to make ends meet and how poor they were. He also saw that his mother was getting old and weary and that it was his duty to go out into the world and make his fortune to help her. One day he suggested this to his mother, and though she hated to have him leave her, she was so in need of help that she let him go with her blessings and her wishes for his success. She packed him some food, and with tearful eyes she watched him set forth.

After walking many weary miles for days and days, the boy finally arrived at the large city. But it was late, and the gates were locked. Disappointed because he had to wait until morning to enter, he walked into an adjoining park to sleep through the night. It was early morning as the boy was about to leave his sleeping place when he heard hoof beats approaching and stopped to see who was coming his way. A rich-looking, well-dressed man stopped his horse in front of the youth and asked him why he was trespassing on his land. The boy explained that he had thought it was only a park and that he was on his way to find work in the city so he could support his poor mother. The man looked the boy over carefully and then said, "Young man, I am in need of a stable boy and am on my way to the city to find one. But since I've seen you, I think that if you are willing you can fill my requirements well." The boy was speechless with delight at having found a job so quickly and easily. He thanked the man and agreed wholeheartedly to do his best. The man guided him to his beautiful home and showed him where the stable and the horses were. He explained to the boy that all he had to do was to feed and groom the horses, cook the meals, and keep him company. The boy did his best, and apparently the rich man was well satisfied.

One day when the boy asked the man for an advance on his pay so that he could send it to his mother, the man agreed and gave the boy much more than he had anticipated. Joyfully he sent the much-needed money home and told the man that he would work even harder for such a good wage. The man assured the boy that he was doing all the work which he was required to do for the present and that soon he would be able to give him another, much more important job. And so days passed and then months, with the boy glad to have such an easy job and such good pay. He sent all the money paid him to his mother, who was indeed happy at her son's success and who no longer felt the pangs of hunger as she had done in the lean days.

One day the master told the boy that the next day they would go on a journey which would take about a week. "Pack up two mules with all the food they can carry, and saddle two of our fastest and strongest horses." The boy obeyed and asked no questions, believing that they were going to go on a hunting trip through the adjoining forest. Off they went. The horses and mules had a hard time breaking though the thickets. After a weary journey of two days, the master finally stopped at the foot of a very steep mountain. This mountain was strange in that trees, grass, and brush grew only halfway to the top, while above the timber line there was nothing but bare, smooth stone. As the boy turned to his master with a perplexed expression, the man said, "I now wish you to go to the top of that mountain." Curious, the boy asked why, and the master began to relate a most incredible story. He told the boy that on top of this mountain, the

Mountain of the Sun, there lived in a magnificent palace a very rich old magician who held captive twelve beautiful maids. "But they have no means of escape, and so must remain there always. What I wish you to get is a bag full of the precious stones which you will see on the ground when you reach the top. They will be strewn all along the edge of the mountain crag, and you must quickly and quietly pick up as many as you can carry in the bag, then throw them down to me, and hurry down yourself."

"But how will I ever get up there," asked the boy, "when the last half of the mountain is all sheer stone?"

"I have a plan which has worked before. You must kill and skin one of the donkeys very carefully so that you will not tear the hide and then sew yourself inside of it. The eagle, which has a nest at the top of the mountain, will think you are a real donkey and will come down and clutch the skin in which you are hidden and carry you to the top of the mountain. When he gets there, make a very loud noise, and he will drop you in fright. Using you pocket knife, cut your way out of the skin and start collecting precious stones as fast as you can. As soon as you have filled the bag and your pockets, throw the bag down to me. Then sew yourself into the hide, and the eagle will pick it up and carry you down again."

The master did not explain to the boy that all the other boys whom he had sent up had never come down because after they had thrown a bag of precious stones down the almost perpendicular mountain, the eagle would either carry them away, or claw them to death before they had time to prepare for escape.

The innocent, unknowing boy did as he had been told and killed and skinned the donkey. After sewing himself up inside the skin, the master warned him that the eagle was coming. It picked up the heavy donkey hide and soared skyward towards the mountaintop. When the boy felt the eagle lower him upon solid ground, he gave a loud cry which scared the great bird away. Then, cutting the stitches in the hide, he emerged from his case to see glittering in front of him many many beautiful shining precious stones. But he began to wonder before picking them up at once whether perhaps his master was doing some evil thing in stealing from the magician. Having been brought up so religiously and with strict ideas about obeying the law, the boy hesitated and decided he would first look around the mountaintop before going about the business of gathering jewels, which he didn't feel was right.

He wandered along, admiring the beauty of trees, flowers, and plants unlike any which he had seen before. Soon he emerged into an opening in which stood the most beautiful palace he had ever beheld. As the sun shone bright, it looked very glittering and magnificent. Hearing a window open, the boy quickly dropped behind some screening bushes. Soon he saw twelve doves fly down from a window high up in the palace and stop in front of the round pool of sparkling water on the ground. To his utter amazement he saw the doves remove their wings, which became small white shirts when they touched the ground, and suddenly change into twelve beautiful maidens. Each, as he gazed at them in turn, seemed more beautiful than the others, for they were all lovely to behold. They began bathing in the clear water, laughing and joking among themselves as they sported about. With one the boy fell deeply in love, and determining to make her his own, he decided to steal her shirt so that she could not become a dove again. While the maidens were playing with one another, he stole softly from his hiding place and succeeded in taking the shirt of the maiden he most admired and hiding it in his vest. Then he concealed himself again and waited to see what would happen.

After the girls had played for some time, one suggested that they had better hurry before the magician caught them out too late and punished them. With little squeals of laughter and much merriment they all began to put on their individual shirts and once more became doves. Eleven were soon ready to fly, but the twelfth was frantically searching in vain all around the pool for her shirt. At last the doves could wait no longer. They could not speak to the maiden, for now they were birds and did not possess the power of human speech. They flew back to their room in the palace, and the window closed behind them. The poor girl, abandoned by her friends, was very much frightened and wept bitterly. At that the boy thought he dared come out of hiding and ask her if he could help her. He knew that she wanted her shirt, but he thought that he could persuade her to go with him. Of course when she saw the boy, she was terribly startled and cried out, "Oh, now I know how my little shirt disappeared. You took it, and you must give it back to me at once."

The boy pretended not to understand what she was saying and very kindly asked her why she was crying and what she meant by the "little shirt" she was looking for. Trusting him, she told a sorrowful tale about an evil magician who lived on the mountain-top and who had stolen twelve girls from their homes and would not let them return to their parents. Then the boy explained that he was lost and did not know how to get off the mountain and begged her to tell him any way to do so that she might know. "If you will tell me how I may leave the mountain, I will help you escape from the magician."

But with fright in her eyes she told him that the magician was very powerful and that she knew of no way to escape from the mountain nor from her master. "He even flies when he wants to," she said, "and as soon as he finds out that I have escaped, he will go after me. No, I'm afraid I am not able to help you." The boy, though, caught at the phrase "he can fly when he wants to" and wondered whether perhaps the magician did not have some magic ointments or salve that enabled him to fly. He asked the girl where the magician was, and she said that he had gone on a trip and had flown from the top of the mountain. The boy then told the girl what he had thought, and she agreed that perhaps the magician had some such ointment as the boy suggested and that perhaps in applying it to himself he had spilled some. She also agreed to take him to the magician's room when the boy asked her to do so, and sure enough, there they discovered some drops of ointment on the floor. They stooped quickly and moistened their wrists, their foreheads, and their ankles with it. Thereupon, feeling very light and airy, they realized that if they wished they could fly. Then the girl began to think of her dove friends and thought that she did not want to desert them. The boy began to tell her how much she meant to him and how he would take her home to his mother and make her very happy. He told her about the precious stones and explained that, if the magician was as evil as she had said, he would feel no hesitation about taking some, for the magician was so rich he would never miss them. "With

196

the precious stones in our possession we would be rich and you could lead a happy, luxurious life with me.''

Now the girl had really been moved by the boy and knew that she liked him very much, so she agreed to go with him to his home. He gave her his long jacket to put on but was very careful that she did not see the shirt hidden beneath his buttoned vest. Outside in the air they felt themselves lifted from the ground and smoothly gliding through space. When they got to the edge of the mountain, the boy descended and filled the bag his master had given him and all his pockets with precious stones. Then he flew away with the girl to his home. His master had long since given him up as eaten by the eagle and had gone home angry because the boy had not been quick enough to throw down the stones.

When the two arrived at the boy's poor home, he explained to his mother that the girl was going to be his wife and that they would never have to worry about going hungry or having to work, for with the precious stones he was rich. He clothed his mother and his wife in expensive garments, remade his house, and lived very luxuriously. He sold his precious stones a few at a time when he visited the city, and in this way time went on. The girl was happy, for she had nothing to complain about, and she loved her husband very much; but many times she yearned to see her eleven companions who were captives of the terrible magician. Formerly they had agreed that they would always help one another until the time came when they were able to escape. And she felt guilty that she had not kept her part of the agreement. So some days she would pine but would not explain the cause of her sadness to her husband and her mother-in-law.

One day when the boy was planning to go hunting, he called his mother aside and explained to her his secret. ''I am telling it to you only because I want you to keep the little shirt locked up and out of my wife's sight. I love her too dearly to lose her now, and you must help me keep her.'' His mother, who loved him very much and who would do anything for his happiness, agreed to do as he directed and told him he need not worry. Reassured, he kissed his wife and left. The old mother took the little shirt that her son had given her and put it in a dresser drawer that had a key. She thought that she had locked it, but really she had forgotten to do so, and since it was time for her daily visit to the church, she set forth.

The girl was very restless that day because her beloved husband was not at home, and she began to wander aimlessly through the house. As she chanced to pass her mother-in-law's room, she noticed the dresser drawer a little open. Going over to close it, she was filled with curiosity to look inside. She was greatly astonished at what she saw, for there, on top of all the linen, was the clean white shirt that she had lost when she had been on top of the mountain of the sun bathing with her sister doves. Her longing to see them again overcame her love for her home and her husband, and she removed her clothes, opened the window, and put on the little shirt. At once she became a dove and flew swiftly out of the open window toward the Mountain of the Sun.

After a long flight she arrived, and pecking at the window within which she could see the other eleven captives of the magician, she drew their attention and was greeted by them with joy and excitement. They wished to know all that had happened to her, and she told them about the adventures and the life she had experienced. She told them how much she loved her husband, but how great the urge was to return to them and keep her part of the agreement about sharing their troubles. As soon as the doves entered the window and came within the room, they became girls again; in that capacity they prepared the food and the table for their dinner. They looked upon the young wife as their leader and treated her as such. They celebrated her return to them by offering her dainty tidbits of food and told her that, as the old magician had returned to the palace, they would never be able to escape.

And now to return to the old lady. Having finished her prayers, she walked home happily, for she loved her son's wife very much and looked forward to her company. But when she arrived at her house, she received no answer to her calls. Alarmed, she began to search the house and soon came to her own room where she saw the clothes on the bed, the open window, and the open drawer. Realizing that her son's beloved wife had flown away and that now he would be very lonely and unhappy, she sat down and sobbed because she had made him a promise which she had not kept. Thus her son found her when he returned. Very much surprised, he asked her what caused her to cry so bitterly. When he was told that his bride had gone, he was plunged into dark despair. But he determined to go out and search for her. "I shall go back to the Mountain of the Sun and rescue her again. I shall try to trick the magician into freeing all of the dove-girls." And with these words he made preparations for his long journey. His mother, eager to atone for her carelessness, helped him, so soon he was ready to go.

Once again he walked towards the city to which he had gone before in search of a job to support his mother. When he came to his former master's property, he began to cross it in the direction which the master and he had taken when they had gone on horseback to the foot of the Mountain of the Sun. Now he was careful not to be seen by anyone and walked quickly until he was a long way into the thick forest. Since he was making the journey on foot, he had to carry his food, so he could take but little. He was determined, though, and walked all day through the forest until he had to rest from exhaustion. Then, because he was hungry, he ate most of his food and impatiently prepared himself for a night's rest. The next day when he had gone on for a few hours, he began to hear the voices of men quarreling. Fearful lest one of them was his master, he approached the place softly and peered through some bushes to see who the owners of the voices were.

He beheld two ragged men whom he had never seen before, quarreling over who should keep the high boots, the beautiful tablecloth, and the magic cloak, which they held in their hands. "I was the one who had courage enough to go and steal them," cried one of the men, "and I think they should belong to me. You did not risk your life for them as I did; but now you want to share them."

"Oh, is that so!" furiously cried the other, at the same time pulling at the boots. "Was it not I who planned the robbery for you? Did I not tell you where the things were and how to steal them? It is only right that I should have a share in them. By right I deserve all that you claim."

When the boy saw that he did not know the men, he boldly stepped into the clearing and was soon noticed by the robbers, who stopped their quarreling. "Ah, here we have someone who will decide for us who should have the booty," said the first robber.

"Young sir," said the second robber, "we have here some very precious loot. I was bold and courageous enough to risk my life in getting it. This man here claims that because he first got the idea of how to go about stealing these things, he should have them. Now I think I deserve them more than he does. What is your decision?"

"Well, let me see what they are," said the boy. And he was shown the three articles in dispute.

"This tablecloth, sir," said the second robber, "is very valuable, because when you spread it and think of the meal you would like to have, it will appear on the tablecloth all prepared to eat." With that he handed the cloth over to the boy for inspection. The boy tucked it in one of his pockets so that he could more easily handle the boots which the robber next displayed to him, saying as he did so, "These boots help a man to travel faster than the wind. All he need do is to put them on his feet and command them to convey him as fast as they can to his destination." The boy took the boots and put them on his feet, telling the man that he must test them and see if all that was claimed for them was true. Sure enough, he had to agree that he felt as light as air in them. Then the men took the black cloak from the ground and told the boy that, when he put it on, he would become invisible to the world. When the boy asked if he could test it by putting it on, the men gave their consent, and, sure enough, he was invisible. "Am I truly invisible to you both?" asked the boy.

"Verily, you are," said the robbers, "but now remove it so we can see you, and tell us which of us you think should keep these things."

"To tell you the truth, good sirs," cried the boy, "I think I should keep them, for I have greater need of them than you ever will have. So good-bye gentlemen; thank you very much."

When the outraged and indignant robbers yelled after him that he return their property and that he take off the cloak so that they could see him to fight him, he was right in front of them still, and startled them half out of their wits by yelling into their ears, "Here I am. I'm not deaf. But since I know for sure now that you can't see me, I am departing with all my thanks to you

200

both." The bewildered robbers, realizing that they could do nothing to regain their possessions, made the best of their loss by vowing vengeance on the boy if they ever found him.

Now that he was so equipped with magic power, the lad thought that he would soon reach the foot of the mountain. But not remembering clearly the course which he and his former master had taken through the forest, he soon realized that he was hopelessly lost. Neither his boots, nor his tablecloth, nor his cloak could tell him in which direction he should go, and so he continued in the hope that he would find some good hermit or hunter who could direct him to the right road. If he had but known it, he had started in the wrong direction when he left the robbers and, because of his swiftness, had gone a great distance out of his way. When he realized that night was approaching, in desperation he ran even faster. To add to his troubles thunder began to rumble and rain to fall in fearful torrents. But at last, with a sigh of relief, he saw, a little distance ahead, a light in a large window in a huge house. He went up to the enormous door of the house and knocked with all his might. To his amazement the plaintive voice of an old woman inquired, "Who is it?"

"O good mother, would you be so kind as to give me shelter for the night? I want a refuge from the pouring rain; I am lost and need help. Won't you aid me?"

"O my poor fellow," cried the old woman without opening the door. "You must not come in here, for this is the home of the seven winds, and any human flesh which they smell, they will devour. You are in grave danger and must run away from here quickly. One of my sons will soon be home and will eat you up if he sees you."

"But I assure you that he will not see me," said the boy quickly. "Please open the door and let me in." He begged so hard that the tenderhearted old woman yielded to his request.

"Where are you, boy?" she cried when she saw no one outside. "Here I am, good mother," said the boy, who had not yet removed his cloak and therefore was still invisible. He had entered when she opened the door and spoke from behind her back. Startled, she turned and still could see no one.

"This is very strange," she said. "Do not play pranks on me, young sir, for I am serious about the cruelty of my sons. Where are you?'' The boy, not yet removing his cloak, assured her that if she could not see him neither would the seven sons, and in that way he could be safe in her house until the morning. The old woman was indeed mystified and said that, if he could remain invisible, she saw no reason for not letting him stay. ''But remove your cloak for a moment until I can see you and get you something to eat.''

Thereupon the boy took off his cloak and showed what a handsome lad he was. ''You look very hungry,'' said the good mother. ''I will get you a good meal.''

''Oh, you do not have to trouble yourself,'' said the boy. ''If you will eat with me I will provide the food for both of us.''

To the old woman's amazement she saw the boy take a cloth from his pocket and, calling out all sorts of good foods to eat, spread it over the table; and all the food appeared on the cloth, ready to be eaten. Thankfully she sat down to eat with the hungry boy, and when they were through and he returned the cloth to his pocket, everything disappeared. Then it was that the old woman reminded the boy that her sons would soon be coming home very hungry and that he had better hide while she was preparing their food. She took him to the cellar and put him under a barrel. Of course he had his cloak on and could not be seen, but just in case the sons should be able to see him, she made him hide.

Soon he felt the earth trembling a little, and he heard dishes and loose articles rattling in their places. Next he heard loud footsteps approaching and a slamming of the door above him. One of the sons had come home.

''Mother, I smell a strange odor like that of a human being.''

''Oh, I'm sure you are wrong,'' said the poor mother as she busied herself about the fire. ''There is no human here; but you may look.''

''If there is, I shall eat him at once. I hate the human smell.'' But he did not bother to look for anyone because his mother had filled his large plate with good food, and he was more interested in that for the moment than in a human. Soon another son came, and he asked the same question and received the same answer from his mother. Finally, the last son, the fiercest and the strongest of them all, arrived.

"I smell human flesh!" he roared. "Where is it that I may eat it at once?" His mother assured him, too, that there were no humans in their home. But this son was not easily satisfied and began noisily searching through the house. He looked from the attic to the cellar, and the boy could feel the hot breath of the wind when he lifted the barrel and threw it to one side. But the giant wind could find no human being in the house. Now his mother felt better, for she knew that her son, if he had not found the boy, could not have seen him. But the giant wind would not be satisfied. When he had finished eating, he insisted that there was a human being in the house and threatened his mother unless she told him where the person was. The poor woman denied and denied her son's charge until he was very angry. Meanwhile the boy, having heard all that was going on, ran upstairs so that the mother of the giants would not be punished on his account.

"I am here," said the boy; and the wind turned in the direction from which the voice came. He was astounded to see no one and called out, "Where are you?"

"Your mother was right when she insisted that no human was in your home because a human could not make himself invisible. But if you promise me that you will not harm me or your mother, I will let you see me. But remember that I have power too and that you must not harm me. Do you promise?"

"I do," said the curious giant, and his mother drew a sigh of relief, for once her son made a promise, she knew that he always kept it. The boy, seeing the thankful expression on the mother's face, was not afraid and without hesitation threw off his cloak and stood revealed to the giant. The wind showed admiration for so courageous a youth, and they became very sociable and began to talk of their different lives. The boy began to steer the talk toward the places where the wind had gone and asked him if he had ever passed by the Mountain of the Sun.

"Oh yes," said the giant laughing. "I have often passed by there, for that is the place where twelve beautiful maidens are held as captives by an old magician. I like to go there because the place is very beautiful, and I blow the apples down from the trees so the maidens will be able to eat them, and sometimes I blow a little colder and have fun watching them scurry back to their room. But the place is very far from here and it takes a long time to reach it.''

''Where will you be going tomorrow?'' asked the boy.

''Why, now that you mention it,'' said the giant, ''I plan to go to the Mountain of the Sun tomorrow. But even though it is far, I rest only once,'' bragged the wind. The boy, seeming very much interested in that place, asked the giant where he rested. He told the lad that once he had blown down a giant oak tree and that he had enjoyed laughing at the owner of the tree when he had found his mighty oak grounded. ''The oak is exactly half of the journey to the Mountain of the Sun from here, and I always like to stop there and sit on the fallen trunk of the oak to rest.''

''But how do you get there?'' asked the boy very innocently. And the giant, well pleased at having so attentive an audience, told the boy how to get there and from there to the Mountain of the Sun. Now to humor the giant, the boy said, ''I wonder which of us would get to the oak first if we started out at the same time.'' The giant laughed and assured him that no one could go faster than himself. Then the boy suggested that they have a race in the morning and see who would reach the Mountain of the Sun first. ''Remember I have magic powers at my command,'' he told the giant good-humoredly. Since the giant liked the boy very much, he heartily agreed to his proposal that they have a race. ''It will take me four hours to arrive at the oak,'' the wind told the boy, ''and four more to reach the Mountain of the Sun. However could you hope to get there before me?''

''We shall see,'' said the boy, and the mother received instructions to call them at four o'clock the next morning.

When the mother called them, the boy spread his tablecloth, and much good food instantly appeared on it. The giant was dumbfounded and complimented the boy on his fine powers. They ate heartily and were then ready to depart. When the boy put on his cloak, he was no longer visible, and so he bade the giant good-bye until they should meet at the oak. The wind was very sure that he would get there first, no matter what powers the boy possessed, and so he blew along at his usual rate. If he had only known that the boy had magic boots that could go faster than the wind himself, perhaps he would have tried to go even faster. But as it was, the boy kept ahead of the giant all the way and reached the oak tree two hours before him. He was thus able to catch up on his sleep, but when he felt the wind coming closer, he awoke. However, he pretended still to be asleep, and when the wind arrived, he received a great surprise to see the boy, as he thought, asleep. Then the boy woke up, yawned sleepily, and cried, "Oh, there you are, Sir Wind. It is already two hours that I have slept. I thought you were faster than that."

"I would never have believed it. But you won only because I did not really go fast so that I would not have to wait too long for you. Now let us see who will get to the Mountain of the Sun first. I assure you that I shall go very fast this time and reach there before you do." The boy asked in which direction he would go, and the wind explained. "Agreed," said the boy. I shall meet you there, but I assure you that I shall get there before you do." The giant laughed and hastened on his way, certain this time that the smart boy could not outdo him. The boy started out and of course with his swift boots was on the Mountain of the Sun two hours before the wind arrived.

In his magic cloak the boy could not be seen, and with palpitating heart he waited by the familiar pool for the doves to come. It was not yet time, he noticed, so he wandered over the mountain, saw the beautiful palace from all sides, and noticed that there was no door at all in the section of the palace in which the doves were kept. He went back to wait again, but no one came. He began to worry for fear that the maidens were no longer there. He did not know that when the magician discovered that one of his maidens had escaped, he would not let them out anymore but went himself to give them food. And now it was time for him to do so. The boy heard the wind coming then, saw the pears and apples fall, and then saw an enormous, ugly man come out of the palace and begin to fill a huge basket with all different kinds of fruit. He tied the basket to a rope, which hung down from the window of the doves' room, and gave it a pull. A little bell sounded inside the window, and the boy knew then that the maidens were still there and would soon come out to pull the basket up. Quickly he went to the basket, and taking some of the fruit out, he hid himself under the rest and waited to be hauled up by the maidens.

But they had heard the wind coming and were waiting until he had passed so that they would not be blown out of the window.

The giant soon arrived and of course did not see the boy. He laughed to himself and thought that this time he had won. He had enjoyed the boy's company, but he had important work to do, and so, wishing the lad good luck, he departed chuckling. When he had gone, the maidens opened the window and began to pull up the basket.

"My, but the basket is heavy today," he heard one of them remark. "Come and help me, girls."

They all came to help her, and with much labor, they finally hauled the basket into their room. The boy quickly escaped from it while they were busy getting the dishes in which to put the fruit so that they could let the basket down again. When they came back to the basket, they marveled at the little bit of fruit that was in it now.

"But it was so heavy before and was full right up to the brim, and now it is only half-full. Has one of you already taken fruit out?" asked his own little wife, for she was considered the leader and so took charge of any emergency that arose. They all denied very hard that they had taken or eaten any of the fruit, and the boy had to hold his mouth tightly shut so his laugh would not escape. He was very happy that he had seen his wife safe and commenced to observe the life which the girls led in their room. He had to admit that it was a very beautiful room and that the girls lacked nothing in the way of food. Only they could never return to their own people, and he was angered at the ugly magician whom he had seen filling the basket. His eyes had been enormous and very red and evil looking. Great big bushy eyebrows protruded from his forehead, and his teeth were yellow and big. The boy wondered how he would ever be able to overcome him so that he could rescue the beautiful captives.

When all of the maidens were prepared to sit down to their dinner, the invisible boy stationed himself by his wife's side. Suddenly, one of them cried out, "Oh, the soup is hot. Let us go on the roof and see what the wind has done this time, while the soup cools." And they all trooped up to the roof. He laughed softly to himself, and being hungry and not wanting to spread his cloth, he sat down and ate his wife's soup. Soon the maidens returned, and he hurried to one corner of the room to see what would happen. They all sat around the table and were just preparing to commence eating when his wife cried out, "Oh, you tricky girls! Someone has eaten my soup. This is not a funny joke, and I am surprised at you!" The maidens all looked at one another and stoutly denied that they had eaten it. But because there was some soup left, she forgave them and ate the extra bit in the pot. But when the meat and potatoes came, while she was serving the others, the boy ate some pieces of the meat and potatoes on her dish. And while she was eating, he took pieces of meat and potatoes from her plate, until she had nothing left. This made her very angry, for she had only eaten a few mouthfuls, and this time she was sure that one of the girls was tricking her. "I did not mind too much with the soup, because there was some more left. But I am hungry too, and now all of my meat and potatoes are gone." And when she reached out to drink her wine, her glass had been emptied. At this sight she burst out crying and told the bewildered maidens that she would never forgive them. They denied over and over that they had taken the food, and when she was about to leave the table very angry with them, she felt her shoulders grasped by two hands which she could not see. She gasped out to the maidens what she felt, and they told her that it must have been a spirit who had eaten all her food.

"No, I'm not a spirit, my dear," came the boy's voice, and all the maidens looked at the wife in amazement. The boy kept on. "I am only invisible because I have on a magic cloak." And removing it, he stepped in front of his happy wife while she ran to him and clasped him to her. The other girls were very happy to see the young man that their beloved leader had talked so much about. He looked at his wife and asked her why she had run away from him that day. She explained to him that she had promised her sister prisoners that she would always remain with them, and she assured him that she could never leave them even though she loved him so much. The young man was very much grieved, but suddenly a bright idea came to him. If he were to find a means of escape from the mountain for them all, would the girls be willing to go? They assured him that they would, and with this he began to descend the doorless house. He had hidden his cloak, and the boots, and left the tablecloth with the girls. When he reached the ground, he stuck his hands in his pockets and began walking toward the palace of the magician whistling loudly and merrily.

The magician heard this strange sound on his mountain and rushed out to see who was making it. He knew that his doves did not whistle, and when he beheld the young man coming toward him, he hailed him lustily. "You, there! Where are you going? How did you get on this mountain?"

The young man spoke up quickly, for the bellowing tones of the magician made everyone fearful of him. "The wind blew me on this mountain and I do not know how to get down again. I am only a poor, wandering young man looking for a job. Could you hire me to do anything for you, sir?"

The magician looked the young man over and exclaimed incredulously, "The wind must have been a very strong one. But, yes, I have a job for you. If you are faithful and do as I tell you, you will be rewarded; but if you disobey me in any way, I will punish you severely." After telling the young man to follow him, the magician took the lad to a third section of the palace. When the magician opened the large doors, the young man saw a sorry sight in front of him. There were eleven horses in a row in the stable, as the third section of the palace turned out to be, but the poor horses were the hungriest, weakest, sickest-looking steeds that he had ever seen. He felt great pity for them, and turning to the magician, he asked what his job was to be. The magician looked threateningly at the boy and told him that he was to beat each one of the horses twelve times with a hard stick after he had given them a very small amount of oats for their daily food. The cruel magician told the incredulous boy that, if he didn't beat the horses, he would change him into one too. He showed him where the heavy sticks were kept and told him to go ahead and begin to beat the poor horses, which were in such a weak state that their legs were giving under their weight. The magician left them with the pretended sincere assurance from the young man that he would really beat the horses with all his might, as he was feeling in just such a mood. The sly magician sneaked to the attic of the stable where he could hear whether the boy beat the horses or not. He put his ear to the floor and heard loud heavy beats accompanied with cries of pain. He listened for a while until satisfied that his new groom was doing his job properly.

But the young man was not actually beating the horses. When he had hit the first one lightly he was greatly shocked to hear the horse cry out in pain, "Oh, my back. Please don't beat me. I will soon die anyway." The young man then realized that the horses must be human young men like himself whom the evil magician had turned into horses. He whispered to the horses that he would not beat them but that they should pretend they were being hit. He then proceeded to hit the ground as hard as he could with loud convincing whacks. This was why the magician thought the horses were being beaten. The young man was sad with pity for the poor, starved horses and gave them all another ration of oats while he watched them ravenously gulp it down. Then he left for the house of the magician and there was told that as soon as they had eaten they would go to bed. But the young man sneaked out after he heard the magician snoring in the room above him and went to the girls' window, where they pulled him up in the basket again. He took his cloak, which he had hidden there, and told the girls that he planned during the night to find out how they could escape from the mountain. He told them to prepare themselves; they should be ready to escape at any time that he called them.

They wished him good luck and watched him as he descended the palace wall. He put on his cloak and ceased to be afraid, for now he knew that he could not be seen. So he hurried to the magician's room, and opening the door of it, softly he slipped inside. Upon looking about him, he was astounded to see the ugly, red eyes of the magician wide open, while their owner snored loudly. But as he had on his cloak of invisibility, he went to the magician's dresser and found, upon opening the first drawer, that many bottles of ointment were in it. He did not know which was the one that had permitted himself and his wife to fly away when they had escaped, so he went into the closet in search of some directions for the use of the different ointments.

After looking through almost all of the pockets of the magician's clothes, he finally found in one of them a folded sheet of heavy paper. As he read by the light of the moon, he was astonished what it contained. It not only told him which bottle contained ointment that would enable him to fly, but it also told him how the magician could be killed. It said that the only way to do this was by cutting off his head with the knife that he always kept underneath the pillow on which he slept, and unless the severed head was thrown far from the body, the magician's powers would not be broken. The directions said that the head would bounce until the magician's tough heart stopped beating and that the spells which the magician had cast would be broken only if certain procedures were followed during the time that the magician's head continued to bounce. As the boy read further, he came to the spell which lay on the eleven horses in the stable and with much interest learned that a tooth had to be pulled from the mouth of each horse before the spell would be broken. The spell on the doves would be broken at once when the magician died.

With this information the boy stealthily crept up to the bed of the magician and cautiously began to pull at the long knife that was projecting from underneath the pillow. At first the magician stirred, then snored a little louder as the young man succeeded in securing the sharp, long knife. After making sure that the window was open, with all his might he cut off the magician's head, grabbed it by the stringy hair, and slung it out the window to the ground.

Then returning to the drawer, he took out the correct ointment which he identified by the color and hurried to the stables. As he went, he could see the head bouncing about to counteract the spell on the horses. When the animals smelled him they shied and kicked, but he went up to all of them and, opening their mouths one by one, pulled from each a tooth, broke their imprisoning chain, gave them a sound slap, and pushed them through the wide doors of the stable to freedom.

As soon as he had finished liberating the horses, the roof of the stable fell in, the magician's head stopped bouncing, for its owner was dead, and the gaunt horses became eleven young men like himself. He told them to follow him quickly, for they had yet to rescue the twelve maidens from the other section of the palace before it too caved in. By this time he had taken off his cloak. He could be seen by the eleven men and therefore was seen by the girls when he called to them from below their window to lower themselves to the ground. They let themselves down in the basket none too soon, for when they were all safely on the ground, their part of the palace crumbled to dust.

By now morning was about to dawn, and soon the rays of the rising sun fell upon the main part of the palace where the magician had lived. With a fearful, thundering crash this part of the building toppled down into ruins. The young man quickly ordered the girls to put some of the ointment he was about to give them on their wrists, for that would enable them to fly. While they were doing this, the boy said that he would take his wife with him to his home, but he asked the other girls what they were planning to do. They told him that they wished to return to their homes and see their parents again. The boys briefly explained how they had been stolen from their homes to become the magician's horse slaves, and they wanted to see their parents again. But one of them suggested that they should meet all together in some place so that they would be able to celebrate their liberation from the magician's tyranny and get better acquainted with one another. With these plans in mind they all departed, flying in various directions to reach their homes. As they started, they looked back once more to see the place where they had been kept captives so long and were greatly surprised to behold that the mountain had disappeared.

A few months later, true to their promise made on the Mountain of the Sun, they all met to celebrate their liberation. The eleven young girls and eleven young men fell in love with one another, and the eleven couples planned to get married at once. So at the same party at which they celebrated their victory over the magician, they were also married. The young man and the girl, who had been married a long time before, smiled at the new couples and were very happy that all their troubles and fears had come to an end and that now they would all live merry and content.

Legends and Religious Tales

14. The Bloodred Evil Elf

It is heartily believed by all the small children of Faller (and by some of the grown-ups too) that an evil elf dressed in bloodred garments lives in the surrounding hills and mountains. This elf, it is believed, is out purposely to lure children from their proper ways and to persuade them to follow him to his little hut on the top of one of the mountains.

Whenever a mother wishes to instill fear of wandering in her child, she will warn him about the small, evil *sanguenell* in the hills. If the child still insists on having his own way, she will then tell him the story of a little boy who disobeyed his mother and was lured away by the elf.

Once upon a time, in a pleasant village in a fertile, green valley, there lived a little boy with his widowed mother. He was a good and obedient boy in everything except in his great wish to follow his mother to the next town, to which she often went to find sewing to do so she could support herself and her small son. But because she had forbidden him to follow her, he wished to go all the more and would get sulkier and sulkier the more times she explained to him that she could not take him.

Now, one reason the mother did not let her son go with her was that it was very much too far for a little boy to walk; but more important still, a wicked witch lived by the road they must pass to reach the town, and if she ever caught someone passing by who had disturbed her, she would make that one perform some evil, cruel, dangerous deed to atone for it. Many ugly tales had been told about the wicked things the witch had made some victims do, and everyone in the town was afraid to go by way of this road.

So the mother really had some good reasons for not taking her young son with her. This day, though, he was determined to follow her at any cost. Thinking that he was secure and safe at home, the mother hurried on her way, never glancing back. The boy had waited for a little while before starting out after her, for he did not wish her to see him. A few friends of his mother stopped him as he was leaving the town to ask where he was going. He told them that he was on his way to meet his mother, so they all let him go.

On and on he walked, dodging behind bushes and trees when he thought she would look back, and she was so far ahead of him that she never heard him. As they went along they began drawing nearer and nearer to the witch's haunts, and the boy began to get nervous and a little bit frightened when he realized that he would have to pass by the terrible place all by himself. The road curved sharply at a certain point, and when he came around the curve, instead of seeing the familiar back of his mother, he saw no one at all. The road continued on very straight until it made another curve, but he saw no mother on that long stretch. Really frightened by now, he resolved not to follow the road but to take a shortcut through the woods as he believed his mother had done. "In this way," he thought, "I won't have to pass by the witch's place." Thinking that he could get through the woods easily, he kept on walking buoyantly until he noticed that he was not getting out of the forest at all. Now he was really scared and began to call his mother in a loud, frightened voice. He kept on calling and calling, but no answer came except the hollow echo of his own little voice. Finally he began to sob and cry miserably, but he would not give up. He continued walking on and on, going farther into the forest and getting more hopelessly lost every moment.

The mother had gone off the road, but only far enough so as not to pass the witch's house. She later came out on the same road and continued her journey. So the little boy was really lost and no one, not even his mother, had the slightest clue as to where he was.

When the forlorn boy was at the lowest ebb of despair, thinking that he had better sit down and die and believing that he would never see his dear mother again, he was surprised to see a small boy like himself standing in front of him. The poor boy was so happy to see someone who looked like a human being and who perhaps could tell him how to get home that he did not notice that the other boy was really a little elf who was dressed in bloodred clothes, a peaked hat, and pointed shoes. He jumped up joyously and asked the elf if he would show him how to get home. The elf smiled at him and said, "You're not lost, little boy. Come with me and I will take you to my home on the top of that hill where your mother will soon come to take you home." The boy was reluctant to go at first, but when the elf told him that he would give him chocolates, sweet candies, and a lot of toys to play with, the boy agreed to go at once. Taking the elf's extended hand, he went with him up the steep hill. It was strange and unbelievable how quickly they reached the top of the hill and were out of the dense forest. The house which the elf said was his home was just a little hut which the boy's uncle owned, but the boy did not know this. Of course there were no chocolates or candies or toys in the hut, but by magic the wicked elf made the boy see all these things and truly believe that he was eating candy and playing with pretty toys. In reality the wicked elf was waiting for the moment when the boy would die; then he could take his body away to the witch and the other evil elves.

In the meanwhile, the mother had gone to and also returned from the adjoining town, and when she reached home and did not find her son, she asked her neighbors about him. None had seen him except the two women who had talked to him, and they told her what she had been afraid to hear all along. "Yes, we saw your little son. He told us he was on the way to meet you, and naturally we thought you were returning from the other town, where he said you had gone." Soon the whole town knew that the little boy was missing, and the men of the town told the frantic mother that they would go out and search for him. They followed the road and looked for some distance on each side of it, but they could not find him. When they reached home late that night, they assured the mother that they would search again in the morning and that she would not need to worry. But what else could the loving mother do?

The following day, the men started out early and made a more thorough search, dividing into groups and going up the mountains and into the woods around them. Again they had to return home at night with the sorrowful news that they could find no clue as to the boy's whereabouts. The mother cried harder still and soon was reduced to such weakness that she took to her bed. The people thought surely she was going to die.

The men started out again the next day, and this time the boy's uncle went with the searching party. Though he was old and rather feeble, he was determined and entered the forest at about the same place his nephew had entered it. Naturally he did not know this, but he did know that he was on his way to his hut to see if perhaps his nephew had wandered there. He did not have much hope of finding the boy, but he was not going to let one stone go unturned. On and on he went, and soon he was at the foot of the steep hill. But the wicked elf from the top of the hill had caught sight of the old man and had hurriedly entered the hut to warn the weak boy that he had better hide because a terrible old giant was on his way up the hill. The elf succeeded in hiding the boy under some hay, leaves, and sticks that lay in a corner.

When the old uncle gained the top of the hill, he hurried towards the hut. Opening the door quickly, he was much disappointed and very sorry to see the room empty. But he noticed at once that the hay, leaves, and sticks that he had left in one corner were now in the opposite one. The little boy, meanwhile, was sneezing and wheezing beneath the hay, and the uncle, hearing these sounds, thought that there must be some wild pigs or an animal underneath the rubbish. Then all sounds stopped, and he thought that perhaps he had only imagined that he heard things. He was about to leave without searching when a sudden idea struck him. Suppose some robber or someone else had hidden something underneath the pile, perhaps a chest of money or good clothes. His mind ran on excitedly about what good things could be under the stack, until he decided to pull it apart. As he did so he came upon the little boy—thin, hungry-looking, and very weak.

The uncle was exceedingly happy that he had found him yet alive, and the boy was very much surprised to see his uncle. "Why, uncle," he cried, "What are you doing here? When is mother going to come and get me? The little boy dressed in red said that mother would soon come and get me. Is she with you?'' The uncle thought that the boy had gone insane, and, seeing his condition, he told him that his mother was waiting at home for him and that he must hurry to her. The boy replied that he did not want to go because here the little red boy was giving him chocolates, and candies, and toys everyday, and his mother only gave him candies on special occasions. The bewildered uncle asked him where the boy in red was, and his nephew, looking around to call to him, was surprised not to see him.

"But he was here just a minute ago," the nephew said, "and told me that I must hide, for a great big giant was coming up the hill to get me." The uncle really believed the boy crazy by now, but, thankful that he had at last found him, he picked him up, and old as he was, he carried the boy all the way back to the village. The mother was very ill in bed, but when she saw her boy still alive and well, she began to cry and cry for joy. The woman helping her took care of the poor starving boy at once, and after bathing and feeding him, they put him to bed for a restful sleep.

With good care by his mother the boy soon recovered, and when he had been told what had really happened to him before he had been found, he became very good indeed. From then until he became old enough to take care of himself properly, he always minded his mother and never begged her to let him go with her to the neighboring town again.

Many stories about the *sanguenell* have been passed down through the generations, and the children all believe that, if the wicked elf catches them, he will show them beautiful bridges and roads over deep precipices, and if they follow his deceptive illusions, they will get killed.

15. The Dark Men

In an obscure little village in the Alps of Italy, there once lived a small family consisting of a father, a mother, and their nine-year-old son. But this family was never happy, for the husband was a drunkard and a lazy, good-for-nothing bum. Any bit of money that he might earn he squandered on drinking and gambling, while his wife and son had to starve and suffer at home. But this was not all; every night when he came home from the drinking house of the town, he would mercilessly beat his wife and curse her with vile words. The poor woman was very patient though, and all through the day she would pray fervently that her husband's ways be forgiven and changed for the better by the help of God.

She often told her little son, who was her joy and life, that he must never never do any of the evil things that his father did because she was sure that the "dark men" would come and get him if he did. She told him that his evil father would surely be punished by God for his behavior and that the boy must never imitate him. The boy believed his mother and prayed with her for the redemption of his father's soul.

One night not long after she had told him about the dark men, who, she explained, were devils taking the form of dark men, the father came home very angry. He had lost all his hard-earned money gambling and thought that surely someone had cheated him. He was mean and impatient and ordered his wife about with curses. Every time she got near him, he hit her for her slowness. He pulled her hair, pricked her with his fork, pinched her cruelly, and punched her with his fist. He took delight in doing this, to the poor woman's sorrow and anguish. Tonight he was worse than ever. After she had served him with the food that they had left from the meal before this one, she went into a corner to pray to God to forgive him. When the husband saw this, he suddenly became infuriated and began to curse all the saints, angels, and God in heaven. She begged him to stop, but he only dragged her from her corner and began to beat her until the poor woman was almost in a dead faint. The boy kept crying out to him to stop, lest the dark men get him and punish him. But the father only flung the poor boy into the corner, where he cowered from fright and from the kicks that his cruel father occasionally gave him as a diversion from the task of beating his poor religious wife. The woman prayed more fervently, and this spurred his anger on. Finally the half-crazy man took his wife by the neck and cruelly strangled her to death. When he saw that she was dead, he laughed uproariously and told his son, "Now I need never be bothered with her stupid prayers!"

And then the boy cried out, for he saw, emerging from another corner of the room, two dark figures, which he realized were the dark men that his mother had so often warned him about. They did not come towards him, though, but went towards his evil, laughing father. To his horror he saw that they caught the man in a grip from which he could not escape and then wrenched off one of his arms. He cried out in pain, but no one came to his rescue. Then the dark men tore off another arm and thrust this, together with the first, into a sack which they carried for that purpose. Next they tore off his legs one after the other, then pulled off his head, and finally cut the rest of the body into pieces, which they put into the sack with all the other mutilated parts.

The boy was so horrified by this terrible murder that, when he saw the dark men leaving, he rushed to his room, locked the door, and hid himself beneath the covers of the bed. Here, after much sobbing for his dear mother, he finally fell into an uneasy sleep. Then he began to dream. He dreamt that there was a trapdoor beneath his bed, which he was supposed to open. In a daze he left his bed and crawled underneath it to feel the floor. To his great surprise he found that what he had dreamt was really so. There was a trapdoor under his bed, and something made him open it and look into the hole that it revealed. There appeared at the opening a basket, in which he sat and which he felt begin to go down. It kept going down, down, down, never seeming to come to an end, but finally it landed on the bottom of the dark hole, and he climbed out of the basket and looked about him.

He found that he was in a sort of cave and that a little farther on there was a hole through which dim light came. He went towards it and, looking out, saw a vast pasture of dark grass as far as his eye could see. There was no sun shining—only the dim, dead light. But he summoned all his courage and decided to walk through the pasture. He soon came upon two fierce-looking lions, which were chained a little distance from each other, who looked so cruel that the boy was afraid to go on. Being a brave lad, though, and seeing that the lions were chained, he finally rushed between them and was able to go on again.

Then he unexpectedly came to a hill in whose side a great iron door had been built. He was curious, and, deciding to investigate, he knocked. No one answered, so he tried the door himself and found that it was open. Entering, he was met with a very strange sight indeed. He saw a dim and dreary-looking dark tunnel, on each side of which were dim figures of people sitting on chairs or making them. He walked on down the dark corridorlike tunnel, fascinated by the mysterious-looking figures of people all about him. Soon he became accustomed to the darkness and so could see better. He then realized that those people looked very sad and pained indeed, and he felt sorry for them. Then to his great surprise, he saw his uncle, who had died some years ago, sitting on a chair and working feverishly on another. The boy called out to him, and the shocked uncle looked up to see his little nephew before him. "What are you doing here?" asked the uncle in horror. "Leave immediately if you don't want to remain here to suffer like the rest of these condemned people." But the boy insisted on telling his uncle how he had come to be there, how he had dreamt of the trapdoor, and how he had entered the hole and the basket had brought him down here. He told him how his father had killed his mother and how the dark men had killed his father. "Do you know where my parents are now?" asked the orphaned boy.

"Yes, I know," said the uncle. "Your father was very cruel to your mother and God is punishing him, as he is punishing all of us in this place for having been so evil during our lives. Your sweet, good mother is in heaven now, receiving her rightful reward for having been so pious and enduring. But you must not stay here any longer. Do you not know what this place is?"

"No, uncle, I do not. Those lions out there in the pasture frightened me. What kind of a place is this in a hill, and so dark?"

"You are in hell, my boy, and you must leave as fast as you can, unless you wish to be kept here all eternity, to suffer as we are suffering."

The little boy was awed, but he wished to know all about it. He asked his uncle why he was sitting on a chair and making another chair. The uncle explained that he had suffered enough to earn the chair on which he was sitting. Then he said to the boy, "Your father is undergoing many punishments before he can get a chair, and it is my duty to make him one. That is why I am so busy working.'' But as soon as he had explained all this, he warned the boy again, and this time the boy thought he had better leave. He wanted to kiss his uncle good-bye, but the man warned him not to touch him and had to push the boy back with his hand so he would not embrace him. The boy cried out in pain, for the uncle had pushed his hand away, and where he had touched the boy, he had left a bad burn. ''You see, my poor boy,'' said the uncle, ''I am as hot as fire, and that is another form of suffering that I shall have to endure for eternity. Now hurry and escape while you still have time.'' So the boy bade his uncle farewell and went out though the door in the hillside into the open air.

Outside, he was arrested by what was occurring. He saw two dark men on top of the hill putting a man into the hole of a miller's grindstone and then pushing it down the hill. The boy saw it roll with all its heavy force and then hit the iron door leading into hell. But the door did not break. The boy had hidden behind some shrubs that grow near the hill and could observe what was going on without being seen himself. To his great surprise he saw that the man who had been forced into the hole of the grindstone was no other than his own father. When the stone had rolled to the bottom of the hill, the boy saw his father pull himself out of the hole in the stone with great pain and with much labor begin pushing the heavy grindstone up the hill. His father was then put into the hole with his head only and was rolled down the hill in great pain because his body was twisted and turned as the grindstone went around and around as it rolled down the hill. Again the stone hit the door, but without opening it, so his sweating, bloody, pain-racked father had to push the heavy stone up the hill again. But even the third time the grindstone did not break the door down. The two dark men then came down from the hill, thinking that the man had received enough of this kind of punishment and must go on to the next.

Two other dark men came out of the door, and to the boy's surprise he saw that one of them was a noted drunkard of his village, who had died some years before. One could see that he had suffered a great deal of pain and seemed to be suffering yet, as was the case with the other dark men too. These two had a great caldron of molten lead and a funnel. To his horror the boy saw them lay his terrified father on the ground and, opening his mouth, place the funnel in it and then begin pouring the molten lead through it. The man writhed in anguish, but the dark men emptied the caldron even though the body of their victim became so swollen that it seemed it would burst. Then the other two men took a great rolling pin and began rolling it over the stomach of the boy's cruel father. The hot lead came pouring out of the man's eyes, nose, ears, and mouth, but when they stopped the rolling, his father was still alive. The boy then realized that his father would never die in hell because he had died on earth, and now he would have to suffer forever for his former wicked ways.

The poor boy saw his father led inside the door from which he would never be able to come out. By now the boy was resolved that he would hurry back to earth and lead a good, pious life so that he would never have to be sent to hell and punished so cruelly and painfully for all of eternity. He ran past the lions, who again did not harm him, and finding his basket and the ropes which guided it up and down, he pulled himself up to earth again.

It was morning by this time, as he noticed when he came out from under his bed, and he went at once to the priest of the village. He told him what had happened to his mother and his father and where he had been. The priest would not believe him, but the boy told him to come to the house and see his dead mother, and he also showed him the burn which he had received when his uncle had touched him. The priest came and had to believe that the cruel father must have been punished by the dark men as he well deserved.

The townspeople were glad to hear that the evil man was dead and that the pious woman was now in heaven and out of her misery. They collected a fund to bury her, and the priest sent the boy to a monastery in the next town, where he later became a faithful brother of this order. Many believed his story when he showed them the proof of his burned hand, and they changed their ways of life so as to be spared from eternal pain in hell.

16. The Good Priest and the Rich Stranger

There lived in the small village of Lamon in northern Italy a kind, good priest who did all in his power to help the poor and the farmers of his parish. He went about in threadbare clothes because he would give everything he himself didn't absolutely need to the poor and the unfortunate. He was a very faithful, pious priest, and his great faith in the mercy and power of God had endowed him with the supernatural power to order harmful things away to places where he willed them. Thus he would command that a frost fall where it could do no harm instead of on the wheat fields or on other parts of his parish where crops were being grown. Many times his praying would save the poor farmers from a ruined crop, and the people loved and honored their kind priest very much indeed.

This priest would take his pail of holy water and his prayer book with him every day and tour the countryside. He would bless one field and then another and would command a storm to wait until the crops were ready for it. On a certain day the priest went out to the fields of the farmers who lived some distance from the village. It was very solitary there, but the priest did not mind this because it was as it should be and as it always was. But today the priest suddenly came upon a rich-looking gentleman, resting his foot on a stone while he gazed far off into the sky. The priest, who knew everybody in the village and all the farmers who lived outside it, did not recognize this man and thus spoke and asked him who he was. "I am only visiting your beautiful countryside," he answered.

"Oh, I see. A very beautiful day, is it not?" murmured the priest.

"Well, it won't stay so beautiful for very long," said the rich-looking man threateningly.

"But I know that it will," answered the priest, who had decreed only the day before the postponement of a heavy rainstorm so that the tender stalks of corn would not be broken down.

"We shall see!" cried the man. And with this he strode off and was soon out of sight. The priest could not understand the meaning of such conduct, but something told him that his man was evil and wished to do evil to others. The words he had said implied that the weather might turn bad, so the priest hurried back to his house to pray even harder that the bad weather would hold off until the tender crops could better stand the lashing of a hard rainstorm.

But when the tired priest got home he felt very queer. He became exceedingly sleepy and tired and couldn't keep his eyes open any longer. He called his sister, who was the housekeeper for her brother, and told her that he felt so sleepy and tired that he would be forced to go to bed. "But remember this," he said to his sister, "if you see even a speck of a cloud in the distance call me at once. You are to sit by the window until I get up and watch for any sign of a cloud." The bewildered sister promised and sat down at the window to watch for clouds. Soon she saw something black in the sky near the horizon, but thinking that it was very far off and could not possibly mean anything and being sorry for her tired brother, she decided that it would not be necessary to call him. But before she realized it, there was a loud peal of thunder, and lightning began to break through the dense, black cloud that was coming nearer, faster and faster. She started to run up to her brother's room to call him, but he met her on the stair and scolded her fiercely for not having called him. "I can hear the storm myself now, and it is too late."

Taking his holy water and his blessed book and rosary, he ran out towards the dark, menacing cloud, commanding over and over that rain should fall only on the cemetery, where it would harm no crops. But the dark cloud kept on approaching, and the priest was almost desperate. Then, when it was right over the cemetery, he cried out fervently, "O my good God, my power is not enough. I have tried, but only your power can help us now. I have faith in you. Help me!" And to his great joy he saw the black cloud begin to shrink. But his faith had taken so much of his energy that he sat limply on the ground and covered his eyes in sorrow, for he thought that he had been too late to save many of the crops that the cloud had passed over.

The black cloud had by now become the size of the cemetery, and after another peal of thunder, it began to hail so fiercely that it seemed as though an ice sheet was falling. The hailstones were almost as large as hens' eggs and came down into the cemetery with hard, loud thuds. It hailed and it hailed until the cemetery was filled with hailstones. The village people, who had run after the priest when they had seen him so frantic, were overjoyed to see that the terrible hailstorm had been kept from ruining their crops, and they thanked the good priest over and over again. They told him that he could look up, for his prayers had really availed and the hail had fallen only into the cemetery. So he raised his head and realized that he had been in time. He thanked God for the deliverance of his people from a season of want, as it would have been if the hail had ruined the crops.

But then the good priest suddenly thought of something, and turning to the villagers, he told them that he knew there must be someone who had ordered the terrible hailstorm and that he suspected the rich-looking man he had seen that day. They could not understand him because they had not seen this man, but they were told that, if they would get shovels and dig through the hailstones, they would find a human being under them. So they did as the priest told them to do, and to their amazement they found the figure of a well-dressed man. But he was dead and ugly to look at. He was black all over and looked like a devil. The priest told his people that this man must have been a witch who had ordered the storm so as to ruin the crops of the people.

They buried the evil man and helped the priest back to the village, for he was still so weak that he could not stand on his legs very well. He became weaker and weaker, and the sorrowful people had to realize that the days of the kind priest were numbered. Soon after, he died peacefully in his sleep. The whole town mourned for the loss of this good man. Upon lifting the coffin in which his body had been placed, they found it felt as though nothing was in it; they believed that he had gone to heaven in soul and body and that by God's grace he had become the saint of the poor.

17. The Monk and His Cloak

A kind monk was planning to leave the village in which he had been preaching and journey to another one to teach the law of God to other people in that country. He had become so loved by the residents of this little village that they hated to see him leave. It was in wintertime, and they were sorry that the monk should travel in such cold and snowy weather. When they noticed that he was going to start out without even a cloak, one of the women ran into her house and came out with a beautiful one with gold buttons on it that had belonged to her father, who was then dead. The people happily presented it to the kind monk, and he was told not to give it away because he needed it more than anyone else. Finally he was ready to start out on his journey through the hills and valleys to go to his next destination.

It so happened that on the same road upon which the kind monk would travel there were resting a man and his wife, who had been married only a short time. They were high up the road on a hill; since the road wound around the hill, they could see, far down beneath them on the curving road, the kind monk with the beautiful cloak of the golden buttons. "Oh, look at that monk with a good cloak," cried the wife. "You'd think he'd be ashamed of himself and give it to some poor beggar who is too poor to buy clothes to keep himself warm. I think I deserve it more than he does." And with this she told her husband to think of some way in which they could get the monk to give up his cloak.

These two people were really petty thieves and did not care from whom they stole; rich or poor, it made no difference as long as they got something for nothing. So the husband eagerly thought of a plan and soon was ready with it. He told his wife that she would pose as a dead girl in the snow and he as a stranger who had come upon her and found her. She was to take off her clothes, lie down on the snow, and pretend to be half frozen. He would come from the direction opposite the monk's, and they would arrive almost at the same time at the place where the girl was lying, though he would be the first to cry out at the sight of her. Then we would ask the monk for the cloak to cover her up with, and the monk, out of pity and duty, would naturally give it to him. So the wife took off all her clothes, and her husband hid them in some bushes beside the road. Then she lay down on the cold snow and presently was really blue from the cold, though of course she was not dead but only pretending to be so.

The two men were getting nearer to each other when the monk saw the young man hesitate, look at something on the ground, and then give a cry of pity. He looked up at the monk and said, "Brother, brother, have pity on this creature that I have just

226

found on the snow. Look at her. She is blue from the cold and looks dead, but perhaps there is still hope. Could you give me your cloak so that I may cover her? She must have been maltreated by some vicious man, the swine!'' And the husband put out his hand for the cloak that the kind monk only too gladly removed. He stood at the side of the road nevertheless, for being a modest monk he did not dare look at a naked woman. Before giving the young man the cloak, he looked him in the eyes and said, ''Does she really need it, son?''

''Of course she does. It might save her life,'' impatiently answered the husband, who was now worried lest the monk change his mind about giving it up. The monk gave the cloak to the young man, but the husband felt uneasy when he took it, for there had been a queer look in the monk's eyes. ''Will you take care of her, then?'' asked the kind monk. The other answered that he would wrap her up in the warm cloak, which perhaps would save her from her death, and take her into the next village, from which she might have been stolen by whoever had maltreated her. ''I hope you succeed, my son, and may God reward you as you well deserve for this act of mercy,'' were the last words of the kind monk. Then he went on toward that other village, shivering a bit from the cold, but praying as always for the sick, the prisoners, the robbers, and all the other people on this earth who needed help for their souls.

Soon he arrived at the end of his journey and was happily looking forward to the warm fire that would greet him in the home in which he would stay while he preached Christ's gospel. But before he had fully entered the village, he heard calls behind him from a frantic man. He turned and recognized the young man whom he had met on the road and who had used his cloak to cover the nude woman. But this time the young man was frantic in another way. He was sincerely desperate and greatly worried, and he gasped out to the kind monk, ''Brother, brother, please forgive me. I lied to you about the frozen woman so that I could get your cloak. She is my wife, and we planned that she should pretend to be dead in the snow so that you would give up your cloak to us. But the cloak over her did not help to bring her back, for my wife was really dead. I repent sincerely and thoroughly.

Won't you come back and bring her back to life? I am sorry to have robbed you. Here is the cloak. Please won't you come and bring my young wife back to life?''

The husband pleaded with all his heart, and the kind monk, looking at him and smiling, said, ''I think you have learned your lesson, now, so I will accept your sincere plea and return your wife to life. But you must go back before I reach the body and put some clothes on it, or I shall be unable to look upon it.'' The overjoyed young man ran all the way back to the body of his wife and had it dressed by the time the monk arrived. He touched the young woman and told her that their sin had been forgiven and so she would be forgiven from the punishment. They gratefully thanked him and promised him that they would never again rob anyone and would from then on lead good, lawful lives. And so they did. The kind monk had helped two lost souls gain a chance for heaven once more.

18. The Monk and the Mason

A very pious, kind monk was walking along the city streets one day, going towards the monastery in which he lived. He had been to visit the prisoners and the sick to comfort and pray for them. Soon he was approaching a place where a house was being built. He saw the mortar-makers carry the buckets full of mortar up to the masons who were laying the bricks. Everything about the construction signified business and activity, and the monk stopped a while to see the men working so diligently. They were already working on the fifth floor of the house, and bricklayers were on the scaffolds high above the street.

Suddenly, to everyone's horror, one of the bricklayers slipped and fell off the high scaffold. He was falling fast and soon would be killed. But the kind monk raised his arm and cried out, ''Stop, stop where you are, in the name of God!'' To everybody's amazement and joy, the falling man stopped as he was halfway between the scaffold and the hard pavement. The men all ran to the monk and thanked him as they cried, ''A miracle, a miracle!'' while they rejoiced to have witnessed this sight. Then one of the men, seeing that the monk looked perplexed and did not do anything about getting the man down on the ground, asked him,

"Kind brother, won't you let him come down now?"

"That is what is troubling me," answered the kind monk. "I do not know whether I should do it or whether I should not."

"But why, brother, why?" asked the men when they heard this. "If you have performed the miracle so far, surely you can finish it and let him come down."

Then the kind monk told the men a perplexing story. He told them that his brother superior in the monastery had forbidden his ever making miracles again. It did not seem suitable that a mere monk, a plain brother, should perform miracles while the superior himself, who had so much more honor and age, could not. It did not appear seemly in the eyes of the world, and so he had forbidden the kind monk to perform another one. Thus he found himself debating whether he should disobey his superior, whose demand was a command, or should allow the man to come down safely. When he explained all this to the men, they began cheering him and telling him that they would have that settled in a few minutes.

Forming a large group, the men quickly ran to the superior's office in the monastery, which was not very far away. The poor monk panted along behind the men, but they got there before he did. By the time he arrived, they had duly convinced the superior that the kind monk should be permitted to perform as many miracles as he could because that is what God wished, not what the superior wished. They had shamed the superior, but they told him that they would forgive him and never mention it again if he would give his full consent to the kind monk.

When the superior agreed, they took him and the kind monk to the scene of the miracle, and the monk was told to go ahead and finish his miracle, for the poor man was still sprawled in midair with his head downward, frightened half to death at the thought that he might have to stay in midair for the rest of his life or until he fell and was killed. So the kind monk, only too glad at having received permission to perform miracles, raised his hand once more and told the man to come down to the ground gently. The man slowly continued downward, head foremost, as he had started. "Come down with your feet first, good man!" ordered the monk, and sure enough the man made a turn and landed safe, though very pale, on the pavement.

The monk was cheered over and over again, and the superior had to recognize the powers that the kind monk possessed, which he was not destined also to have. Therefore he congratulated the monk and praised him very eloquently. The kind monk was overwhelmed with happiness and vowed that he would perform miracles to the best of his ability in the cause of mankind.

19. The Old Man Who Couldn't Die

There are customs in some villages in Italy which have been observed for many generations. One of them in the northern villages of Italy is to visit friends from other villages in the evenings, to discuss the weather, the crops, and interesting occurrences that may have happened to different people in the village. In other words, they go to gossip and enjoy an evening with cronies and friends. The people who are visited also enjoy these meetings, and if they know ahead of time that visitors are coming, they will perhaps plan an entertainment for the evening like a game of cards for the men with roasted chestnuts and wine for refreshments.

There once was a certain little old man who particularly loved to visit in the meeting places of other villages. But the people to be visited, who almost never knew when he would go to them, dreaded every minute that he was to be with them. This little man had a mind of his own, and everything that he said, did, or believed he thought was so, and everyone who disagreed with him was wrong. He had a fiery temper and a more fiery vocabulary, and the poor mothers who had virgin daughters would pale and gasp at hearing the curses that were cried out aloud by the vigorous little man. He loved to debate because he believed that he had to convince his listeners—mostly involuntary listeners— that his point was the right one. They sometimes could not get rid of the little man for hours, but there was one remedy that always worked.

It was the custom in some villages for the people to say the rosary at the end of their social meetings because they were very pious people. Now the little man thought this act such a waste of time and so futile that he would get up with disgust, began to swear to high heaven, and indignantly tramp out of the place in which he had been visiting. But since this custom meant that the meeting had come to an end, the people were reluctant to turn to the cure for this sacrilege too soon. So the little man really succeeded many times in boring or annoying the people he visited.

One day there came the news that the little old man was very ill in bed. The story ran that once, while he was returning late at night to his own village after having visited his neighbors, he had been confronted by a dark shadow who had swung a rosary at him, the thing he seemed to hate most of all in the world. Instead of becoming frightened as he properly should have done, he laughed at it and cursed and swore at it and walked on home, not giving it another thought. But the next morning he had not felt well, and the following day he was unable to get up at all. He became worse and worse, and the people who visited him could not understand how the poor man could bear such suffering and continue to live. It seemed that he could not die, try and wish as hard as he could to do so. Of course he had forbidden anyone to carry a rosary inside his house, or to pray, or do anything else that the people thought would help him, so no one had done so. But one day when the suffering old man had drifted into an uneasy sleep, one of his old cronies, who was very religious and pious, thought that he would say the rosary for the old man's sake, and perhaps God would take pity on him and let him get better. He devotedly began his rosary, and as he watched the old man, he saw the pain-drawn, withered face slowly turn peaceful and happy. The man noticed how relaxed and rested the little old man was getting, and then he saw him open his eyes. The old man saw his crony praying for him and realized that the rosary was what was giving him the peace he felt and the power to die. He gave a deep sigh of content, turned his head, and died. The saying of the rosary was the only thing that had let him die in peace; otherwise he could not have died.

20. Saint Peter Gets His Way

When the Master and his apostles were walking to a certain town one day, they became weary and hungry from their long, hard walk. Evening was drawing near, and they were still many miles from the town. They decided, therefore, that they would rest underneath a great walnut tree they saw nearby until the next morning; then they would resume their journey to the town. Though the ground was hard, the tired apostles slept soundly all through the night. Toward dawn a hard walnut fell from the tree and hit Saint Peter soundly on his head. He sat up with a cry and woke the others. He indignantly gazed up into the great tree and had to bear the laughter and jests of his friends. Looking about him, he noticed a pumpkin vine heavily laden with large pumpkins. Then he looked at the great tree which bore such a small fruit as the walnut. Turning to the Master he observed, "Good Master, I do not think the Lord was very fair when he made the pumpkin vine and the walnut tree."

"Why do you say that?" inquired the Master.

"Only look at that poor pumpkin vine over there," and he pointed to the heavily laden vine. "It is a frail, small plant and yet bears such enormous fruits as pumpkins. They are so heavy, it can hardly carry them, and it is dragged down mercilessly. Now look at his great, tall tree. Its fruit is this small, light walnut. Is it fair that so large and strong a tree should have such light and tiny fruit while a frail small vine bears such enormous and heavy fruit?"

The Good Master told Peter that his logic was very good, and since it was so good, he would let him have his will about the pumpkin vine and the walnut tree. "You make them grow as you wish, Peter, and show us that your plan is a better working one." Saint Peter was very flattered at receiving this power and immediately turned the pumpkin vine into a walnut-bearing plant and the giant walnut tree into a pumpkin-bearing tree. Indeed, the vine looked better capable of carrying the lighter fruit, as was the case with the walnut tree. It carried the pumpkins without effort at all, it seemed. Saint Peter was very happy that his logic had worked and was respected even more by his fellow apostles.

It was now time to continue on their journey to the next town, and they set out refreshed. When they reached the town, they preached Christ's Way to the people, and when they were through here, they had to go on again to another town and carry the gospel to those people too.

The next town was also very far away, and that night they had to rest once more beneath a tree. It so happened that they slept underneath another walnut tree, or, now that Saint Peter had changed the walnut tree and the pumpkin vine around, underneath a pumpkin tree. Toward morning the same thing happened as on that other time they had slept underneath a tree. But this time it was not a small walnut that fell on Saint Peter's head but a large, heavy, solid pumpkin.

With a cry of great pain, Saint Peter woke the apostles, and when they saw what had happened, they had to roar with laughter. They teased Saint Peter about his better logic, and the Good Master said to Peter, "It is your good fortune that you have so hard a head, for the pumpkin is a mighty fruit. Especially when it falls from so high a tree is it harder and harder." So Saint Peter assured him at once that he saw how well the Good Lord knew his job when he had created the world and why he had put a little fruit in a high tree rather than a heavy fruit, which might kill a person when it fell if he didn't have a hard head like himself.

21. The Story of the Black Sheep

It is the custom in the small, tucked-away villages of northern Italy to pass pleasant, warm evenings during the cold winter months in the stable that they fix up appropriately for meeting places. Here the boys may come to see the girls they like while the ever-present, watchful mother hovers over them. While the mothers are busy weaving, knitting, or rolling flax into yarn, the younger people play games, tell stories, or listen to the older men tell of their adventures during their youth. Until time for the rosary—a custom which is yet generally prevalent among the very religious northern Italians—the people enjoy themselves as they please. But at that time all frivolous acts, thoughts, and deeds, must be forgotten and the mind and heart turned to God. This is a very solemn occasion and means the end of the evening's entertainment.

On a certain night a young man from a neighboring town came to visit in the stable of the village family. The daughter was very charming, and the boys of her village were jealous that this outsider should come and perhaps endanger their chance with her. But they had to accept him for that night to please her, and so they played and sang songs and had a jolly time. Soon it was time for the rosary, and the people stopped their work and play to pray. But the boy from the next village surprised and shocked the people by beginning to blaspheme and curse God and heaven, laughing at them for wasting their time. The indignant mother sent him out of her stable, a thing that was done only in extreme cases. He only laughed and said it was a pleasure to get out of the hearing of their silly chantings.

When the boy got outside, he was surprised to see a beautiful black sheep. It was right in his path and looked at him with eyes that held an almost human expression. She looked at him in a mocking way and began to trot off towards his town. Very happy at this occurrence and thinking that if he could catch the sheep and tie her with his handkerchief he would be able to take her home with him, he ran after her. He got very near to her and had almost succeeded in catching her when he found himself grabbing thin air and saw the sheep a few steps ahead of him. He tried this a number of times with the same result. Satisfied, though, that she was still going in the direction of his town, he kept on following her. She would run ahead and hide behind some bushes and then stick her head out and play a sort of "peek-a-boo" game with him, always with that mocking look in her eyes. Either he was ignorant or just didn't notice how strange the sheep's behavior was. Nevertheless, he kept on. Now she would be in front of him, and again she would be following him.

Soon they came to a church, and because the sheep was then following him, he did not look around while he passed the church. But having passed it, he turned around to make sure the animal was still coming with him. To his surprise he did not see her, and he was worried lest she had hid in the bushes and would no longer follow him. He went back and looked all around but could not see or hear her. Finally he gave up, thinking that it would have been too great a piece of luck to have the fine black sheep actually follow him all the way home. So he continued on his way. But a few yards on, he again beheld the black sheep playing peek-a-boo with him and giving him that strange look. The boy was overjoyed and tried again without success to catch her so he would make sure to get her home. She trotted on ahead again, and the boy quickened his steps, for he did not want to lose her again.

234

They were passing by a small saint's niche—a common sight on the roads and mountain paths—when something perplexing happened. The sheep was in front of him one second and the next she had vanished in thin air. He passed the saint's niche quickly to see if she had hidden again and was relieved to see her a few yards along the road. By this time he was beginning to feel panicky, for it was late and he was the only one on the narrow path. Soon they got to the crossroads, and the sheep stopped and looked at the young man. "Fortunately," he thought, "there is a fence which surrounds someone's property, and I will corner her against the fence and surely catch her this time."

But as he advanced toward the sheep, she kept retreating. He was pushing her into the little nook made by the fence and the crossroad and was sure that he had her. But when he quickly put out his hand to seize her, he again felt just thin air and saw her on the opposite side of the nook. He rushed to that side to get her and then saw her on the other side again. He kept this up until he was wet from perspiration and completely tired out. The sheep, on the other hand, seemed to be just as cool and fresh as when he had first seen her. She just stood there and stared at him with her peculiar meaningful expression.

It suddenly dawned on him that this was an extraordinary sort of sheep. She had black wool instead of white like all the rest, and he had never seen any animal look at a person in that mocking manner. And then the way she escaped from him every time he thought he had her was simply uncanny. Suddenly he was struck with fear. He remembered how the sheep had always seemed to disappear when he passed a holy place, and so he realized to his horror that this must be either the devil in the form of a black sheep or some other evil thing that God had created to show his power.

The boy believed in a God from that second on, but not knowing any prayers or how to pray, he felt lost. He did know how to make the sign of the cross though, and doing this quickly, he was able to take his eyes from the hypnotizing sheep and escape. When he made the sign of the cross, the sheep vanished, and the fearful boy rushed home.

On his arrival he found his mother waiting for him. Seeing him in such a lather of sweat and with such a frightened look on his face, she asked what had happened. The boy was too ashamed to tell the dreadful story, so he went to bed. He shivered all that night, thinking of the sheep with its almost human expression of mockery, which seemed to say, "You fool, you fool!" He could not sleep, for when he slipped off into unconsciousness, he was immediately aroused by a terrifying vision of the sheep in different shapes.

Finally morning arrived. The boy was suffering from a burning fever, and the mother, seeing the red face and glassy eyes, called the doctor. When he arrived and was taken to the boy's room, he asked him if he knew why he was feverish. "Have you eaten anything that has disagreed with you?" asked the doctor while he was taking out his instruments to examine the patient.

The poor boy burst out in unashamed tears and cried heartily for a few minutes. Then he decided that he would tell the doctor and his mother what had befallen him, and smoothing back his hair in preparation for talking, he was greatly shocked to feel that it all came off and left his head as a greased ball. The mother gasped, and the doctor was so surprised that he couldn't speak. The boy cried afresh at this additional catastrophe and punishment for his unbelief, and in tears he told the two perplexed and stunned people of his night's experience. The doctor said that he could only help him physically and that the boy would have to do the rest. The boy promised his mother that he would always pray and be good from then on and that he hoped God would forgive him for having cursed and blasphemed against him.

But the shock had been so great that the boy never fully recovered from his fever. A few months later he died, a bald old man before his time. He looked old and worn out because he had never been able to forget the sheep's eyes and would often dream of them and awake in a cold sweat. He was completely bald because his hair had all come off on that eventful morning after his experience with the sheep!

22. The Old Man and the Rosary

The following story has been told may times by the older people of Faller, and it is claimed that the events related actually happened.

It is the custom in Faller to send sheep and cattle to the mountain grazing land during the months of July, August, and September. The people do this because of the better grass in the mountains and because they wish to make the cows produce more and finer milk. But to get on with the story. An old man of the town was taking his herd of cows and sheep to his mountain hut during the three months. He had about four other men with him to help him watch the herds, milk the cows, and do other chores about the land. One of the men was a young lad of about eighteen, the nephew of the old man. This young fellow did not care for God, never said his prayers or his rosary, and was more or less an evil-minded boy. The old man—his uncle—was taking the lad with him because he wanted to try to convert him, being himself a very pious, believing, Christian soul.

The climb was long and wearisome, but finally they all arrived at the tumbledown hut. Since each year they remained in the shack only during the warm summer months, they had merely the barest necessities in it, and they had taken with them enough foodstuffs to last a week. Every week one of the men took his turn in returning to the town and bringing back fresh supplies. After some work, they had the hut in living order, and it was time for their supper. Before beginning to eat, the old man said prayers in thanks for the food. The young boy paid no attention and was very disturbing and noisy. But the old man said nothing that first day.

Before going to bed it was the custom to say the rosary through. That custom has passed down from generation to generation and is still practiced in almost every home in Faller. That night the boy went to bed early because he was tired, he said. But the three men and the old uncle said their rosaries through, and the men whispered to themselves in horror because the uncle had allowed the boy to go to bed without saying his rosary too.

On the following evening though, the uncle besought the boy to stay up with them to say the rosary. The boy refused and called his uncle and the other men a pack of fools for wasting their time like that. They irritated him, he claimed, and he demanded more than once that they stop their irritating chanting. The uncle said that, if he didn't want to hear them, he could go outside. And so the boy did, very angry indeed.

The following night, the men were once more very devoutly praying when the boy cursed loudly and called his uncle evil names for not keeping quiet and playing some games instead of praying. The uncle talked to him kindly and sagely, but the boy would have none of his advice. He became so angry at his uncle that he threatened to go home, and the uncle, knowing that it would be a sacrilege not to say the rosary, told the boy he could do as he liked but that the men would pray.

The boy went out and slammed the door after him. It was raining and lightning, but the stubborn boy was determined to keep his threat. Of course he realized how much he was needed at the hut, but he was determined to show his uncle that he meant what he said. After he had walked some way, he arrived at the little bridge that stretched between two mountaintops and permitted a traveler to cross over the deep abyss between the mountains without having to go all the way down one steep mountainside and up the other. A stone wall was built on one side of the little bridge, and when the cursing boy was halfway across, to his horror he saw an arm extend out from the wall and reach for his throat. It held him in a strong grip and slowly tightened and tightened until the boy was gradually choking to death.

Meanwhile, the men had finished praying, and the old uncle, feeling repentant that he had scolded the boy and sent him out, thought he would go after him. He never thought that the boy would actually think of deserting when he did not find him around the hut. Feeling a strange anxiety overtake him and as if he was guided, the uncle started walking swiftly towards the little bridge. When he reached it, he was shocked to see the young boy, almost black in the face with his eyes popping out of his head and gasping for breath. As the old man did not see the arm, he could see nothing that accounted for this. Quickly saying a prayer and calling upon God to have mercy upon the boy, he threw his rosary about his nephew's head. When the boy felt the hand release him and saw it return into the stone wall, he gasped and fainted.

The frightened uncle took the boy on his back and carried him to the hut. The men helped to warm him and restore him to consciousness. When the boy opened his eyes and saw that he was safe, he began to cry. The uncle asked what had happened, and the half-dead boy told what had happened to him. He swore he would always say his prayers and rosary from then on and thanked his uncle for having saved him.

For two years from that time, he was the most pious, saintly boy in the village. But by the time two years had passed, he had forgotten the frightful episode and had begun to return to his evil ways. Again when it was time for the cattle to go to the mountain pastures, the uncle took the boy with him. The boy was twenty years old now and was looking for a girl friend. A little way below them in the pasture land was the grazing land of another family, and this summer the boy noticed that a young and pretty girl accompanied her brothers and father.

He began to visit her and to boast to the other men that he had a sweetheart. He also began to stop saying his prayers and to hate the rosary once more. The poor uncle was frantic and one night reminded the boy of what had happened to him two years before. The boy scoffed and laughed at him and said that he had probably had something bad to eat and that that was why he had been dying. He blamed his uncle for his sickness and became hateful again. For a few days he acted this way, relishing his newfound freedom in not saying the rosary. Nothing was happening and he was having a good time with his girl friend, so he forgot all about God and his respect for him.

One night he left the hut earlier than usual to go to see his girl. Halfway down the mountain he saw her coming smiling towards him. She was laughing gaily and gave him sly, canny looks. She told him that she had come to meet him that night, and he suggested that they go to his uncle's hut and have some refreshments. She agreed, and they soon arrived just before the men started their rosary. When the boy entered with the girl, he told them all to get something to eat and to have some refreshments.

The uncle looked askance at the girl, for he thought that all good girls should be home with their parents at that time of night. But they all assembled around the table and ate, until after a while the old man was through. The girl was very gay and witty and carried on with all the men. They, not accustomed to girls and their ways, were flattered and taken in with her free manners. The old man didn't like it, and lowering his head in an unapproving manner, he chanced to see the girl's feet under the table. He stared in horrified stupefaction. What he saw were the hoofs of a goat and its hairy legs. He began to talk rapidly, lisping and stuttering in bewilderment. He told the men that they must start their rosary at once, for it was late, and the young girl had better go now. When the girl heard the mention of prayers, she sprang to her feet and said that she must really be leaving.

The uncle agreed and was insisting that she go when the boy broke in furiously and asked his uncle what he meant by practically sending his girl out of the house. He further told him, cursing terribly, that the prayers could be damned and that he was going to stay in the house with his girl as long as he wished. But the girl said she would go and asked him to accompany her home. He agreed, angrily answering his uncle's pleading that he remain because the girl was the devil.

While they were walking along, the boy sniffed something burning, and when he kept smelling this, as they walked further, he remarked upon it to the quiet girl beside him. A strange laughter greeted him, and turning toward her, he was paralyzed to see, not the pretty girl of the farm below, but the devil himself. He had a long, ugly face with red eyes and sharp horns. It was the devil who had been burning the grass as he walked along beside the boy, and that had caused the burning odor the boy had smelled.

The lad was so struck with fear that he could not move. The devil began to dig a deep hole and soon had it large enough to force the boy into it. He took him bodily and pushed him down into the hole up to his chin. He then piled the loose dirt all around him in a granitelike hardness. He laughed and said that the boy would surely like it in his hole and wished him a merry time. He promised him that he would soon see him again, for he was his. The pressure of the dirt around the boy was growing greater and greater, and he was experiencing the greatest pain and dizziness. Surely he would die, he thought, as the devil kept dancing around him, laughing and stamping his feet, which burned a print in every place he put them.

The poor old uncle had explained what he had seen to the men, but they did not believe him and went to bed. After saying his rosary, the old man went out to look for the boy. He too smelled burning and began to run quickly towards the place where it seemed to be coming from. He was praying in a loud voice, calling upon God and all his saints to help him in time to save the boy, for he imagined what must have happened.

When the poor old man arrived on the scene of the boy's punishment, the devil ran back to hell, for he could not exist in front of so holy a man. When the uncle saw his nephew fainting and dying, buried to his chin in the dirt, he again threw his holy rosary about the boy's head. The lad began to breathe again, and the pains left him. He cried and besought God to give him one more chance to be good and worthy. The old man rushed back to the hut and told the men to bring picks and shovels to dig the boy out. They worked until morning to loosen enough earth to get him out, for the dirt about him was as hard as granite.

The whole village heard of this terrible happening, and when the boy came home, they could hardly believe he was still alive. In time he left the village and went to the adjoining town, where he became a brother in a monastery. He would tell all unbelievers his tale, and the village people and priest testified as to the truth of what he said. Many evil men he converted with his tale, and many boys obeyed their elders when they were told his story.

Narratives of Personal Experience

Work in Italy

Clementina's Childhood

I had five brothers and sisters. My younger sister was able to do the chores around the house; she could milk the cows and make the polenta. There was always enough to eat compared to our neighbors, who were always in misery. I often went to visit the Zampieris who were always cooking polenta. Oh my, what an aroma! I was always so hungry, I could have eaten all the time. But I saw that they never had cheese, nothing, just a little polenta. I used to ask, "Where's the cheese?" Zia Beta would say, "Oh well, we finished it. We don't have any more."

Then I would wait until my stepmother would go into the stable to tend to the cows or pigs or horses or until she would go to a friend's house, like the teacher or the lady who owned the little restaurant where my stepmother would drink a little wine or whiskey and beer. Anyway, then I would run to my grandmother's and say, "Hurry, hurry, grandma. Go inside and cut a nice piece of cheese so I can take it to Zia Beta!" She said "Yes, yes." But she was afraid of my stepmother, you know. Zia Beta was so poor that they didn't even have ricotta or beans or meat.

We had plenty to eat when I was a girl, before I was married. And when I married John, they didn't have a blessed thing there. I wasn't used to it like that. So I said "How about having a pig?" I mean, Grandma Todesco came from a poor family herself. She used to say her family counted potatoes before they cooked them—two for each person and the larger ones for the men. They were very pitiful times long ago. But anyway, I was working hard, but I had plenty to eat—every kind of stuff, you know. And then Grandpa Todesco had a vineyard. He made wine, but that didn't even last three months, because he drank it all before it was all fermented—even before it was wine. And then nothing. So anyway, I told my two aunts, Patrizio's wife and Giuseppi's wife, "Let's see who makes the pig grow the biggest." I took the small one because they were there first and picked what they wanted; ours was the smallest one. So the pig was our pet, since we didn't have any dogs or cats. And we let him go down and run in race contests. You know you can make a pet out of pigs, believe it or not. And I took a big basin of water and soap and brushed and washed his back; he just loved that. And I made him grow bigger and bigger. They used to say, "You're down on your hands and knees with that pig." My pig grew bigger than theirs. So we always had bacon and salami in the house.

But Grandma Todesco was too stingy, poor old lady. She even accounted for the little bit of oil for the salad. I mean I shouldn't speak like that because it seems I'm criticizing, but it's the truth. Our house was always like this when I was a child: there was always plenty of work, but also there was plenty to eat. There—in Grandma Todesco's house—it was always pinching a little here and a little there.

Hardships of Children
Well, my grandfather had a stroke in 1927 when I was a young girl. I remember he died one day while Zia Beta was combing my hair. Nobody wanted to comb my hair—it was very curly and took a lot of patience to comb it. And my grandmother called Zia Beta to come because my grandfather Giacomo was dying. He took so long to die while he was in a coma. His heart wouldn't break. Let's see. He was alive when my father remarried and lived a few years beyond that. I don't know exactly. He was twenty-five or twenty-seven when he married my grandma, who was fifteen.

My grandmother lost her mother when she was very young, and her stepmother from Premiero wanted my grandmother to go, go, to leave the house. So her stepmother talked to my grandfather's mother and said, "She's old enough to get married. She's cute, so." That's the way they did things. Her name was Trento, Coronna [Coronna Trento]. And she had only one brother, who had lots of land, lots of sheep. She didn't go to school. She used to go out into the field to help her brother, when she was very young. Most of the time, she said, she used to fall asleep hungry. And one time, the brother went home with the sheep but without Coronna. It was already dark. So the stepmother said, "Where is your sister? There are dishes to be washed here." He said, "I haven't seen my sister. I thought she came home." Then they took the lantern and looked all over, and they found her asleep in the middle of the field. One other time, she fell down the outside stairs and dislocated her shoulder. The stepmother didn't take care of her, so she was a little hump-backed. And she never complained.

One time I remember they gave me a two-liter bottle of wine to take to the men in the field. I tripped and fell and broke the bottle. I had a cut over my mouth, and nobody took care of it. So one side of my face is crooked. See, right here, it's just like a half-moon.

Clementina Lives with John's Family

Mother was not a big woman, not a strong person, like I said. And John doesn't like to say anything, and nobody likes to say anything. But the truth is truth no matter what. John's mother was an epileptic . . . how do you say it? And I tell you I picked up that old lady so many times when she fell down you know. [Tears.] And when I used to go to take care of the corn or potatoes—you have to work on them twice—I had to leave the house and was worried about Bruna all the time. Grandma Todesco was in charge of taking care of her, but when they start feeling that sickness, they fall no matter where they are. One time I was coming outside, and I saw the priest run up, and he started yelling, "Filomena, Filomena, hold tight, hold tight" because she was on the outside stairs of the house having an attack. And I ran and took my baby Bruna from her because she was beginning to fall down the steps. If she had fallen down the stairs, both she and

Bruna would have been killed. And when I saw that, I felt bad. The priest then told us that he kept an eye on Grandma Todesco.

Anyway, Grandma Todesco wasn't a strong person. Yet I was young and strong and trained to work very hard, and I took care of things. John, instead of sending me money from America, sent it to his father, the old-fashioned way. He would write to me twice a week; but with money, he thought he had a family there that had to be supported, so he sent money to his father. And you couldn't say anything, because over there, father and mother are everything. So I just swallowed and swallowed all my pride and never could say anything. And Grandma Todesco was crying and everything, and she said, "Dear God, God really answered my prayers. I never had a daughter and here you are, Clementina, you are better than a daughter." I used to take care of her and take care of all the things. And I said, "Well, I hope some day I can go to America, because I really feel lonely and tired of this miserable life."

If I went to see my sister, John's father would come right over. It looked like he was jealous. And she was so old-fashioned, John's mother. I used to make Bruna little dresses; I kept her like a doll. And Grandma Todesco would say, "Bruna has her skirts too short, too short. I don't like them that way." I said, "She's a little girl. She has panties on, long socks. What's wrong with Bruna?"

In fact, one day she took apart one of her own skirts and made a little skirt for Bruna. I was working in the field not far away from the house there, and I saw this little girl falling all the time as she came toward me. Grandma Todesco had told her to come to me to show me Bruna had a new skirt. The skirt was so long that Bruna was stepping on it all the time and falling over. Bruna was only two years old. Finally, Bruna was so tired from falling down that she fell asleep. So in a little while when she didn't show up, I went and found Bruna there, exhausted and sleepy in this long skirt. So I said to Grandma Todesco, "Well look, mother, that is your style, but this is a new era. I'm me, and this is my little girl, and I want to dress her in the style of the day." I talked in a nice and kind way, but she was like that. She just thought ladies should have long sleeves below the elbow.

246

Patrizio

Patrizio's Father and Mother

Patrizio's father was also a smart man. He did not have much schooling, but he was the mayor of the village. That man was thirty-five years old, and he went to Servo to do his duty as a mayor. And when he started back home, he never reached home, and they never found his body, and they never knew what happened to him or what. It was during the winter with quite high snow, and she [Patrizio's mother] used to say maybe it was the hungry wolf that devoured him. Or somebody hit him and killed and buried him. She never, never, never knew what happened to her husband.

The widow told me she never found out what caused the death, and she was left with two children—a boy and a girl. She began to have toothaches. She went to the drugstore and he [the druggist] gave her a liquid—a few drops in the water and rinse your mouth twice a day. She was so worried, this poor widow. She forgot how much to take, and she took a full mouth of this water and rinsed her mouth. [Laughter.] All her teeth came out the day after. Healthy, she was twenty-two. So I used to say, "Why you lose your teeth, every tooth so even." You know when you're a child you don't stop, and you just say it like that. She told me a story. She said, "I did that." Well, instead of complaining, she did nothing about it. I remember she used to take the chicory and put it inside the mouth behind the tongue and used to swallow it like that. And then she used to say, "I wasn't able to sleep well all night." And then she had this [trouble] . . . their son Patrizio who didn't want to immigrate and didn't want to help in no way.

Patrizio as Trickster and Educator

I have to tell a story. I just remembered it now. We used to have a nice place, but on one side it was very steep and they cut down big trees. So my father came down the street, and these three men stopped working and came to help my father with the tree he had cut down. He was sneaky and sharp, so Patrizio said, "Let's just pretend to help him." They wanted to know how strong my father was, and he was a strong man. Well, anyway, they started

yelling, "Ah-up, ah-up." They made believe they were pulling
hard—the two of them—and then Patrizio said, "He's like a
horse." When he reached the end, they helped a little bit, but not
much, and then he sat up and said, "Bonaventura, you know
you're strong. You can make it without our help." "How?" he
said. "We don't pull," Patrizio said. [Laughter.] He just loved to
do tricks like that and tell stories and so on.

He used to wait until the afternoon when the priest finished the
paper and gave it to him. He read all the paper, every single
word. When we came back from working, we had a nice space
outside . . . you know and then . . . what do you call it? . . .
That bench there; anyway a bench like that . . . we used to sit
outside. So he came out from his house and came to the top of the
stairs and said, *"Compare,* you know *compare* Ventura, you know
what happened." He used to tell everything. My father didn't
have time to read the paper, and he used to tell us everything . . .
like reading *The Gazette* every evening. That time anyway, he was
hungry for news, and he said, "I'll tell you what happened in
Russia. Lenin went to power." That was 1917 or 1915 or something like that. I was a little girl. I just wanted to hear what they
had to say, and he used to tell us everything that was in the paper
every evening. In the meantime he had eaten supper. All the
bad things that happened in Italian cities, you know, robberies,
people dead, whatever, smash-up train, all the news we heard
from that mouth, every evening he had to tell. Report everything
. . . so anxious to. He should have been a reporter.

I remember the priest didn't allow the people to talk about the
Bible because they didn't have the capability to interpret it, to
really know what it said. There were two brothers; Patrizio and
they used to go hide in the woods and read the Bible, and then he
used to come to our stable and tell us all about it. He used to
say, "You know what we read today? There's got to be a car
going without horses. Instead of horses driving the car, the car
will drive the horses. And we will be in the air, the ocean, the
ground." He even mentioned the moon. "Someday we will be
able to reach it. It's not far." The people they was a little bit . . .
not poets . . . but really hungry for news . . . hungry to know.
And they used to learn from the Bible . . . like Leonardo [da

Vinci]. He had the brain of a giant, and they used to explain his things one hundred years later. And so we used to stay there and look and listen . . . so carefully.

Where you go to school . . . they had only fourth grade at the time . . . The time of my father, they have the priest to teach an hour a day in the room. All together . . . the alphabet, just enough to write their own name and add up 1 + 1 = 2. That was our grandparents. Then our parents, they made it mandatory for them to have school. And then it was the priest who taught school. You know priests used to teach catechism most of all. The priests are interested in teaching you the Catholic faith. And in the meantime, you learn to write and read and that was not to have the diploma or anything else. Just one classroom for everyone . . . so they weren't very smart at all. That was very much the way it was in that little town up in the mountains. In the city they had schools and the high schools and whatever. I can't remember all the different grades of schools anyway.

Patrizio just had the knowledge of a teacher. He talked about the Bible, the lives of the saints, and many other things . . . international news . . . how many soldiers each nation drafted . . . Lenin in 1917. I remember that time when he told my father, "O Ventura, in Russia Lenin went communist. And they grabbed bishops, nuns, and priests, and put them in prison. And they put the horses in the churches and stole everything." We were terrified hearing these things. I was fourteen years old then in 1917. Like I said, he used to tell us everything that happened every day. During the war, Patrizio kept score—how many were dead, how many were taken prisoner. Zio Patrizio was anxious to let people know what was going on. He was proud of his knowledge and the fact that he could read. And he wanted to transmit this news to the people. He was so smart. He was even able to detect hidden meanings in what was being printed. In other words, it was fun to be with that man because he was an instructor, in his own way. Well, like I said, I was happy when I could bring something to Patrizio and his wife because they used to love us like their own children.

Zio Patrizio told me all the legends, which he read in a book. He read all the lives of the saints. He used to go into the archive of the rectory. He had nothing to do, so he used to read for hours and hours. He was so intelligent. He remembered everything that he had read.

Most of the stories, you know, they are told in one evening or two, and then most of the guys fell asleep. And me . . . I was there . . . open eyes and open ears, and then Patrizio said to me, "Clementina, I bet you can tell me back this story." I said, "You want me to try?" He said, "Yes." So the next day was Sunday, and he said, "You sit here," and I told him the whole story, which he took two evenings to tell me.

Patrizio in the Stable
Patrizio had something special. Not everybody was like him. In the summer we used to eat a big dish of soup at night. Then we went into the courtyard because it was so hot. And my father would sit there at the head, and we children would all sit around my father like a little army. So Zio Patrizio would come and say, "Compadre, Ventura, listen, I've got to tell you this." He always had something to say. He knew everything—how many inhabitants were here and there, what this or that country was doing, what they produced, all this. It was just like a school. To tell the truth, my father didn't have much time to read, but it was possible to get a complete education free from Zio Patrizio, who read everything in the newspapers.

Every night it was like that, as long as the weather was good. And we used to eat outside. Otherwise we ate in the kitchen. In the winter we ate earlier—at five or five-thirty—then washed the dishes and went into the stable. Even Zio Patrizio's only child, a girl who was one year older than I, would go into our stable.

Zio Patrizio didn't have a stable. They had only four chickens. And they ate very poorly. He had a little land, worked in the woods a little, had a small vineyard. He was not used to continually doing heavy work like the rest of us farmers. He did his work a little at a time, easy; when there was the chance to work in the woods, to cut down trees, he went; he did what he could. He wasn't the kind who liked to work hard, but he did what he could. It wasn't that he was really lazy, because he provided food for his family to eat. He really didn't have a fixed way of making a living. Sometimes, when the government made the state highway there, near Faller, and the road had to be repaired, it was Patrizio and another man who went to help repair the roads. He did that for years. And then he got old. His daughter moved away. He was left alone. There was no more work. He ate only when it was necessary. There wasn't any money. He began to sell his vineyard and the little bit of garden he had for fruits. Then he had only that little plot of land for beans and potatoes. It really wasn't enough.

But I was little, mind you. I really didn't know. And then, I remember, he used to make polenta, but it was just enough for two. And I didn't understand. I would always ask, "But where is the cheese?" "It's finished," he used to say. And I used to run to my grandmother and ask her to go into the pantry and cut a slice of cheese for Patrizio—ricotta.

There was always a conflict between my grandmother and stepmother, because they each wanted to be boss. "As long as I'm alive, I'm the head of this household," my grandmother used to say. Anyway, Patrizio was a good man. He used to go to church but he didn't believe everything the priests used to say. He was too intelligent. He couldn't believe everything. But some priests, you know, are ignorant. They have nothing to say.

Patrizio's Death
He died at home. The daughter went to France in 1925, two years after she got married and had two children—Patrizio and Angelina, who is my godchild. And then her husband sent for her a couple of years later. The daughter couldn't send any money from France to her father, so he suffered in silence. There was no charity for the poor or the sick. Everybody had to think for themselves. There were a few things, like the Daughters of Mary, and when they knew some people were sick, they used to report to the priest and ask that he pray for that person. And then they took turns visiting that person or staying up all night watching him before he died. And they brought something according to what was needed—food, clothing. But really, it was not organized for the people. In Italy there were really forgotten people. That's all.

Well, when I knew Zio Patrizio was sick in bed, I went over to visit him, and he said, "Clementina, I feel so bad I feel really sick." I said, "Well, don't worry. Just pray. You know, we are made out of breath. If it's your time, you'll be prepared. Just pray and just think you'll be going to see our creator, and you'll be much better off." To encourage him to feel better at his age, would have been a lie. He was over sixty for sure. With his starvation and having gone through the agony of the war and all the suffering, he just looked much older than he was.

It was 1924 or 25 . . . May 1926, because I had Bruna and she was already three years old. Zia Lizabetta had gone to mass that day. So I told him to accept death if it was his moment to go. And he said, "All right. Pray for me." And I knelt down on the foot of the bed. In a little while, he just turned yellow and then a little blue. So I called Zia Lizabetta, and she embraced him and kissed him good-bye, and she cried, because he was so alone—poor and hungry. There was just hurt.

Social Behavior

Courtship

When people went to the stables, they behaved as if they were in the house. They knew the rules and regulations. They had to behave. And they had to stay for the rosaries. When they reached fifteen or sixteen, they didn't want to stay for the rosary, because they thought they were men. But in our family my father used to insist that they stay there and wait for the rosary; then they could go. "Tell your friends not to come to our stable if they don't want to stay for the rosary."

The girls sat in front of their own parents. They were really embarrassed, somehow. I remember looking at my older sister when two or three young boys would come together and ask permission to sit next to her. But John was the smart one. He wanted to stay in the kitchen. We sat on each side of the open fireplace, while I made bread with pumpkin and raisins. In the meantime, my stepmother or grandmother or brothers would come in and out of the kitchen, getting the second wine or something like that. You know, in the stables it was warm, and when somebody was telling a story, he would get thirsty, and somebody else would come up and fetch some wine for him. They used to put the wine, which was in the basement, into a terra-cotta jar—

nice and cold. Anyway, you didn't stay alone a minute, that was the regulation for young boys and girls. Me and John were the first to start to say "tu" [you], and we were the first who went on a honeymoon in Venice. All the old ladies used to say, "They want to go to Venice for a honeymoon. If I had a young daughter who wants to do that, I'll put her up in the chimney where they put the ricotta." [Laughter.]

Anyway, in the stables everybody is sitting right there in the stable, and the boy is bashful, and the girl feels ashamed. The boy doesn't have enough courage to ask the girl anything; he just tells her what he did during the day. And the girls were always sewing and making socks. I remember, once my sister was so nervous that even after she made a mistake while she was making these socks, she kept on going. The next morning, she had to take everything apart to begin again. The shoemaker, who had a limp, proposed to my sister, then my younger sister. But nobody wanted him. I don't know why. Later he married a widow. He wasn't bad-looking, but I don't know, not so attractive. I remember there was another young man named Giacomo Slongo—much younger than the shoemaker—who proposed to me. It was very silly. I was fifteen years younger than he was. One morning, this Giacomo came to my father to borrow an instrument for pulling a log. He said to me, "Good morning, Clementina." You see, he had written me a letter of proposal, and I wrote back to him accepting. The busybody mailman had given my letter to the old shoemaker instead of Giacomo, and Giacomo never received my letter; I was so embarrassed and felt so terrible that I slunk into the house and tried to do my work. Later, I found out he proposed to my cousin Mary and to a lot of other women. So I said to Mary, "Let's get a really funny postcard and send it to him, inviting him to come to see us." We laughed and laughed till we had tears in our eyes.

Work Activities during Storytelling

We had our own big stable that was really big. And it was really big with plenty of room in the middle for everybody. Yes, well anyway, they don't have no way to get warm during the winter. So they used to come down there every day and part of the night until they go to bed. And so the ladies used to make socks, sweaters, *filavano* [spinning] wool and *canope* [hemp]. My sister was making socks and underwear around the oil lamp in the center, and all the men were laying down on the dry leaves in the back against the wall, and those who were interested listened to the story, and there were others who just slept. The children played or listened to stories or fought or whatever. And that was the life of the story in Italy.

In general in those mountains there, everyone went into the stables because in order to keep the kitchen warm it was necessary to burn a lot of wood. So we went into the stables and the problem of warmth was solved. Those who didn't have a stable went to the stables of others. It was very warm in the stables. In the evening the whole family would go to the stables.

The women always found something to do in the stables. They were always busy mending, sewing, spinning. And the men shared experiences of the day or played cards. They formed little groups according to age and occasion. Or the men spoke about business among themselves, and the women spoke about their domestic business among themselves—whose daughter was getting married, whose was expecting a baby, and so on. Or the men would say things like, we had a good crop of fruit this year, or the thing they plan to do in the springtime, where they planned to plant the wheat instead of potatoes. Like that they talked among themselves—familiar and business matters. Sometimes certain men would talk about their experiences during the day when they went into the forest to cut wood, or the hay, or whatever. They spoke about the real things that happened to them during the day. And the young boys played checkers. And the young girls learned how to darn socks and crochet or help with something. It all depended on their ages. Oh well, the old people could have stayed if they wanted to, otherwise not.

The stories were stories and weren't very interesting for adults. No, the stories were mostly for children. There was nothing else to do. There were no comic books, or movies, nothing at all. So, the stories were really the only thing. I was young, eight or seven years old, when I began to tell the stories—after my father remarried. Most of the time in the winter, when there was a lot of snow, everyone gathered in the stable—the young people—but old people had work to do. Zio Bepi and Patrizio told the stories that they learned from their own grandfathers. Certain stories of Zio Bepi and Patrizio are, who knows, three hundred years old, for that matter. Some of them—not all, but some of them. Zio Bepi didn't only go to John's father's stable. He went to his older brother's stable and to his own stable. So he went here and there. Patrizio, Giuseppe, and Bernardino were the three Todesco brothers. But Zio Patrizio Zampieri would be at our stable almost every night.

I heard all the stories I told to Bruna from Patrizio and Bepi. But also, I read some stories from old books before the war. Certain stories—I don't remember which ones—I read from my books. We always said to Zio Bepi, "Zio, tell us a story tonight." Then he would say, "Which one did I tell you the last time? Okay, I'll tell you another one," He told lots of stories, but I don't remember them all. Just the ones which made the strongest impression on me. These are all old stories. It was all over there—telling these stories because they didn't have records or books for children and that's the way they entertained children. It was always that way, I think. The old style was to say the rosary, and for the children that was a long, long prayer. They said the rosary in the early part of the evening. And then whoever wanted to sleep was free to go. But we ended the evening in the stable with a litany where everybody sang, so loud. It was a choral. A lot of fun, even if you didn't understand all the words.

Before I was married, I used to listen to stories in my father's stable all the time. That was the big one with all the people. I told stories to other boys and girls. You see, there were many young children in Faller—every age. And my brothers and sisters and I had lots of friends who would come into our stable on winter days, starting early in the morning. And one of us was there all the time. The older people would come in the evening. After supper the women would work in the stables. There used to be an old-fashioned oil lamp, and the ladies who were working would form a circle around it, while the men would sit or lie farther back against the walls on top of the leaves. So whenever a story was being told, everybody was silent. Most of the people fell asleep before a story ended. When I listened to a story, I was all ears, openmouthed. I just loved stories and was excited to tell other people stories. Sometimes my brother in Detroit would say to me, "Stop, stop, I've heard that story twice. Stop it now. You annoy me." But later he would say, "You know, I really admire you. You really tell the whole truth like Uncle Patrizio. You remember every word. How do you do it?" Yes, it was a simple life.

After I was married, I went to my father-in-law's stable. That was where Zio Bepi came. He used to come over and say hello and would talk about what happened during the day and what news there was from the emigrants and what they were doing and this and that. A little bit of everything in general. And then, finally, Maria Trento's mother would say, "Zio Bepi, please tell us a story." "Oh," he would say, "I'm not in the mood to-night." "We want to hear another story or want you to finish the one you didn't." And he was a good, jolly man, clever. He really had a way with words to keep you in suspense. And then he would say, "I don't remember anything else." And we would say, "Yes you do. We want to hear the end. You'd better finish." And so he used to tell a lot of good stories because he traveled a lot. He was like Zio Patrizio, men who had great memories and who would read a lot, like *1001 Nights*, many things about the Medicis, all these things, like the Milan revolution—all the things we knew nothing about, and so we just tried to remember so we could pass these things on to our children.

For children of seven, eight, nine years old, they would be fascinated by the stories, sitting there in the stables with their mouths open. We would be inside the stable, sitting in the area where the leaves were kept to make the beds for the cows. And we would sit there on top of the leaves where it was really warm. We would sit there, all ears, hanging on every word of Zio Bepi. . . .

He had a little of the clown in him, you know. He gave grand importance to all these little stories. He had a way of attracting our attention. Everyone watched him. There in Faller, there was nothing else to do. Bepi had traveled a little around the world, had read some books, and had heard and read lots of stories which he told, and Zio Patrizio did the same thing. Zio Bepi had learned lots of stories from the books in the rectory in Faller. He would go into the archive of the church and borrow books.

Illness, Death, and Miracles

Infant Mortality, Illness, and Folk Religion
Zio Patrizio and Zia Beta had nine children but only one lived—
Antonietta. She was the fifth or sixth child. Imagine—she said
one time that, after she had a baby, she heard the door open, and
she didn't have the strength to open her eyes; she was so drowsy.
Patrizio was sleeping, and she didn't hear any noise, but she
found the baby, who was next to her, dead with a big slice of
polenta on his chest. And she said, "That must be a *strega*
[witch]."

They still believe in witches in Faller. Before the Council
Trento, there were really evil spirits loose in the world. All the
bishops at the council had condemned these evil spirits to the sea
and the mountains, where they couldn't hurt people. Some
people believe all these kinds of stories. "Why," I asked, "do
all your babies die?" And she told me the story. You know, she
said the midwife would give castor oil to a newborn child, and
probably the little baby choked to death. With the polenta, Zia
Beta threw it out the door.

Anyway, all those little children suffered from malnutrition,
because they were poor. Zia Beta had a sewing machine and
would do a little work. She was a dressmaker. You know a pregnant woman shouldn't do this kind of work, hour after hour. It
just disturbs the child. Anyway, somehow the children were anemic, not strong at all, and in their house it was cold, no heat at
all. The poor suffer. They never have enough to take care of
themselves. Anyway, I remember the last little girl. She was like
a doll—all blond and blue eyes. Then she got pneumonia and
died . . . no doctor. And we took her to the cemetery and left
bouquets of flowers with a little flag with the baby's name on it.
There were more white flags for infants than for old people. The
infants died from pneumonia or from the milk of a cow with TB.
Before the war, there was no pasteurization. The milk was fresh.
Nobody boiled it. Lots of children had bellyaches from worms. So
after the war, they said that milk had to be sterilized. It had to be
brought to a boil, then cooled off, then reheated before giving it

to the baby. They didn't have diapers, couldn't sterilize anything. Only the strongest children survived.

Patrizio lost many, many children. When Antonietta asked the
doctor what she could do to save her children, the doctor told her
that she was anemic, and her children would be very, very weak.
They would die if there were a complication. He told her to drink
milk. Then Antonietta said they were too poor to buy milk, and
her husband wasn't working. Well you know, all the poor were
welcome in the cheese house in Faller. They made butter from
milk on the first round, then cheese on the second round, ricotta
on the third; then if you boil the liquid left over, honey. Can you
imagine how much a cow gives us? Anyway, they used to give the
poor the *scolo* [drainage] which was the liquid left after the ricotta
had been made. They were given a liter or two of this instead of
milk. So the third child of Antonietta survived on this honey from
the cheese house—a beautiful, blond child. Another of her children died of scarlet fever, and still another died of pneumonia.
They suffered so much. When you are really low in nourishment,
you're in a lot of trouble.

A Village Miracle
Zia Beta was a sweet lady—kind. I remember her curly hair. My
grandmother was so busy, and my older sister was busy too. And
besides that, over there when they combed your hair, they just
pulled it. And I was always crying. I didn't want them to touch
me. So Zia Beta, with the patience of a saint, used to comb my
hair once a week. Without a mother, nobody cared. Well, Zia
Beta was a kind person . . . very, very good. Patrizio's mother
had a sister who never got married. I remember, she went to the
cornfield to work and it started raining so hard, but she couldn't
stop. And since that time, she began to hemorrhage. She was
pale, yellow, sick. When she died in her sleep, after a few hours
she became completely white. Incredible!

And she was a young girl, eighteen years old on her death bed.
That was a miracle. I think it was a good twenty years after that
her grave was excavated, and she looked the same as she did on
the day she died. So the priest was called to the grave, and the
priest said, "Oh yes. She is a saint. But please don't say anything
to anybody because to make a saint costs a lot of money. We are

poor people, so there's no way . . . no way. Don't say anything!''

Well it happened that the cemetery was in the middle of my father's property. I used to go on top of the brick wall and sit there and watch the cows. And so I saw the guy digging her grave. You know, the burial grounds are forever here in America, but in Italy, every twenty-five or thirty years, they crack up the bones of the dead. You know, there was a lot of water in that cemetery and the water preserved the corpses much longer. I remember one time, they dug up a body . . . the father of somebody . . . I don't remember . . . and the body was in good shape, but they had to crack up the body anyway. So with his shovel, he used to crack up the body. I thought that was disrespectful to the dead.

Death of Clementina's Mother

We were a bunch of brothers and sisters—eight from my mother. She died of double pneumonia, seventeenth January 1909. I was five. And she was six months pregnant. She caught double pneumonia when she came to take care of us. We were all sick with measles. And over there the snow was so high, and they had the doctor for all five villages [Sorriva, Zorzoi, Servo, Aune, and Faller], and he was at Servo. The doctor used to come on horseback. But there was too much snow, so he didn't come for two days. And the doctor was a widower. He had a beautiful young wife, and I don't know how she died. He opened his office and did good work, but he drank too much. So he—the doctor—arrived after two days, drunk. He began to speak with a Florentine accent to make us believe he was a gentleman. But my mother fainted from his cigar smoke. She had a high fever. My father was the mayor, and he went to call the doctor three days in a row. But anyway, he had a meeting there and he had to stay. So the doctor came and my father came a couple of hours later. When my father visited her and saw her, he could tell she had fainted from the cigar smoke. And then my mother, who was an intelligent person, couldn't talk in this condition.

So Grandma was there, Zia Beta was there, and my mother finally became conscious and sighed, ''I thought I was dead. Call all my children.'' When my father realized that the doctor had placed bloodsuckers all over my mother's arm—my God, a pregnant woman and the doctor puts on bloodsuckers to take all the blood out—my father yells "What in the world did that doctor do? He killed my wife." So he took off all the leeches, and he bundled up my mother in blankets and put her on the carriage—he used to have two horses, and I don't know how much he beat those poor animals—but he brought her to Feltre to the best hospital there and called for the best specialist. It was too late. She was too weak. She lost too much blood. But she was conscious.

Before he took her away to the hospital, though, she told my grandma to bring her all her children. And she told Coronna, my oldest sister, who used to be very good at sewing, crocheting, and art work . . . she went to the nursery school at the monastery. She was cultured, so my mother said to her, "Listen, I have taught you how to sew. I don't know whether I'll live or die. But don't cry for me. I'll accept. You're the oldest. I taught you how to take a jacket, wash it and iron it, and then put it over your material and measure it and then sew it. You can be a dressmaker any time. Remember you have to take my place. If I die, you have to be able to do that." Coronna was twelve years old.

I was a twin. My sister twin was beautiful, fat, fresh. She seemed very healthy, but she lived only three days. Then she died and I instead—skinny and ugly—I'm still here. So then the doctor tried to save the baby . . . fetus. He was born alive, was baptized, and then he died and was buried in the arms of my mother. It was so sad.

"Bring me all my children," she said to Grandma and Zia Beta. "Please remember, find out every night whether my children have gone to bed with enough food. Promise me that." Every mother worried about that, is worried about her children. My mother said, "Mother, I'm giving you the job to watch over my children. Do what you can. They're good and obedient, but make sure they've eaten before they go to sleep, so they will grow normally." This is what Sant' Beta—Zia Beta—and my grandma used to tell me. I didn't remember. My mother's last words, "God bless you all." Then she left.

My mother had two sisters and brothers and they were all there in Feltre. My mother was born and raised in Feltre. She had fallen in love with my father and had come to Faller in the mountains, to marry a farmer, my father. She was not accustomed to the life, but *chi piace un giallo, piace punarro* [he who marries a farmer marries want].

Stepmothers

Stepmothers in Peasant Society
The first wife *e meschina, e la seconda e regina* [is a slave, and the second is a queen]. That's really the slogan of Faller. The first wife suffers, bears children, loves the husband and family. She suffers and then dies. The second one enters the house and finds a complete family. Just like in the story, the stepmother tells her husband to take the children into the woods and abandon them. The children talked to an old woman who gave them *rise* [rice]. No, she gave them rags—white rags—to be put here and there as they were taken into the woods. Then, I think, they were able to return because of the rags they had left as landmarks. But then the second time the husband took them into the woods, they were captured by a witch who took them to a house made out of chocolate. And . . . I don't remember anymore . . . Oh yes, the witch wanted to roast them in the oven. But then the children said, "Wait, wait, we're still too skinny." And then, when the old witch opened the oven to put in the little girl, the little boy, who had cut the wood and fetched the water—the old witch had planned to eat the little girl first—gave the old witch a good kick into the oven and then closed the oven door. And she was roasted. And the little boy remembered how to get home. So he led the sister home, and they arrived at night, and then instead of going home, they went next door. So these were all stories of children mistreated by their stepmother.

My stepmother was always fat. She never suffered from hunger. She would take the bread and store it in a chest—under lock and key. The bread box or cedar chest, there is where she kept the bread under lock and key. So at dinner at night, she cut the bread and passed it around with some soup made of foul-tasting weeds that even the horses wouldn't eat. I don't know how we didn't die . . . really. She had the keys, so she would eat as much as she wanted and so could her own children. They ate double what we ate.

The Family

My father wasn't rich. He was the only son and had five sisters— all with ten, eleven, twelve children. We were sixty-two cousins in all. In those times there was no birth control. And everything that happened, happened. That's why my mother said to my father, "I'd like even you to go to Germany to give me two or three years' rest."

When my mother died, my grandmother took charge and cooked for twelve or fourteen people. Her name was Coronna Trento.

Well, he married after eighteen months, and he married a widow from another town, Sorriva. She was nice looking but short, fat, and had a beard like a man. It wasn't too long, and it wasn't too full, but it was really a beard . . . just like a man . . . a tomboy. They married down in Sorriva, and when they came up with all the relatives, she was taken to see the church and then to the restaurant and then she was taken to see the neighborhood. She was proud to be escorted and taken around like that. She was already the boss, the underboss. She did exactly what she wanted to do, whether you liked it or not. For my father . . . perhaps the second marriage was not for love, maybe for necessity, he thought, because there were lots of children. Anyway he was forty-five years old. And she was almost the same. Or maybe she was under forty. She married young the first time. Anyway, my father was always busy between being mayor and veterinarian and also teaching the older brothers how to work. He always worked in Faller. And then my stepmother had a daughter from the first marriage, and she took her with her. She was a pretty young girl, but the mother brought her sweets and cookies and chocolates always and made her a pretty bed where she left her sweets. She was obsessed with raising her own daughter to grow up and be beautiful. And instead, with us, she treated us badly.

My mother was like a saint—humble, good, loving. Everybody knew this. The other one always said, "Me and my people." She was partial. Then she had three other children with my father.

Well, she was all for them. For us, big and little, all of us, she ordered us around and demanded three times as much work as we were able to do at our age. We came home from school, had a snack—bread—and the orders began. "Fetch the water. Go here. Go there." There was always something to do, since we had lots of animals. In fact, this woman was not exactly a saint.

No love from my stepmother, and not much from my father either. He was a good man but too busy to show love. So we decided to love one another and protect one another, and that's the way it was with our stepmother.

So my grandmother packed up her things and then left and walked to Fonzazo, poor old lady, where she had a married daughter. And after Fonzazo, she went to Feltre where she had three other children. My father had four sisters. My father's only brother died in the revolution of Milano. [About five hundred people were killed or seriously wounded in Milan in 1898 in demonstrations protesting desperate economic conditions.] There, they threw down boiling oil from the roof, thinking there were enemies below. Instead they killed Italians, including my father's brother. So when my father came home, I was in Zia Beta's home, crying and telling her how my stepmother had thrown out the cup of my grandmother's coffee and how grandmother had left in despair and how we were all in despair because we loved our grandmother as if she were our mother. So Zia Beta said, "Patrizio, go into the stable and look for Clementina's father, and get him alone so you can tell him how things have developed. You've got to tell him, because she doesn't tell the truth." So Patrizio told my father. And my father said to my stepmother, "You have everything you need here. You're the boss." From then on she closed the cabinet filled with wine, cheese, salami, and all the other stuff. Only once in awhile did she leave it open, and then I would go to see Grandma, begging her to cut me a slice of cheese for Zia Beta. The room where we kept the apples and pears and everything else we cultivated in the field— although we sold a lot, a lot remained—this room was always locked. Also it was locked for my poor old grandmother, who also lived there.

Before my grandfather died, he had made a will and had left half to my father and the other half was to be divided equally among his sisters. That was the custom in Italy. It was the custom, but I think the law has changed. So she—stepmother—was cunning. My grandfather always went out to the fields here and there to do his work. She would send him a double order of food, double ration, a whole sandwich, a bit of cheese and wine. And we went with the basket of food and took it to him. So he was very happy. She was cunning. She wanted to be liked by my grandfather. Yet she wanted to be the boss of the provisions, even of the food and the pots and pans. Anyway, once my grandfather came to the door, and my stepmother was inside with my grandmother. My grandfather knocked and said, "Hey, you are the boss here. You can do what you want, but not with my wife. She's older than you, and as long as I'm alive, respect her. Otherwise I won't leave anything to you in my will! And here in my house, I want peace. Don't mistreat anybody. There's enough for everybody!"

To get back to the account of my grandmother who went to live with her daughters for three months that winter. She finally had them take her back to my father's house. She returned on a wagon pulled by a beautiful, black horse. The husband of her oldest daughter, Uncle Fiorino, took her to my father's house. She said, "Before I enter this house, I want to talk to my son." So my father was there, you know, and he didn't know why his mother wanted to spend the winter with her daughter. My grandmother didn't write to him, so he thought everything was all right. She said, "Son, I've returned to your house, but you must permit me to say to your wife that she must respect me more and that I can make all the coffee I want; otherwise, I will turn around and return to my daughter."

Stepmother's Abuses

You know what she did one time? That time I called her *barbosa* [tiresome]. "Ugly old hairy witch. I hate you, I hate you." Why? My grandma, poor old lady, was almost eighty years old. She drank a cup of black coffee, without milk, just a little bit of sugar, you know. You buy coffee beans and roast them over the fire— one teaspoon of coffee and two teaspoons of barley, which didn't cost anything because we grew barley ourselves. So she wasn't eating or drinking everything in the house. But she hated my grandmother. Poor lady. She went to mass every day, every morning. She went to communion and then returned from church and drank some coffee. Instead of preparing the coffee, the stepmother got angry. She said, "I have to prepare the food for the pigs. What have you done here? What have you done?" She talked just like a man. Oh yes, she went crazy when she was nervous. She was always pregnant, and she didn't want any more children. So then in those times she acted bad. She was at least forty years old, so the last two times were natural abortions. She was very nervous, and she fought with everyone and everybody. So she took the coffeepot in which my grandmother was making coffee. The front door was open, and she threw out the coffeepot, and it rolled down the street as my brother arrived. And he saw the coffeepot and picked it up and took it inside. And my grandmother said, "Do you want me to die? I can't kill myself before God calls me. I'm still here. I've been here before you, and I worked very hard to provide my family with a living and for a little black coffee without bread or milk. You have been bad and cruel. And I want to tell my son what you're like." But my grandmother was too saintly, and she didn't want to start trouble between a husband and wife. She suffered and kept silent.

When I saw how my grandmother was treated, I began to cry. My grandmother said to her, "Now I'm going to my daughter's, and I'll never step inside this house again." And she went out the door. So I went there, and I grabbed my stepmother by the skirt. I was very tiny. "You ugly old hairy witch. I hate you. You drop dead, not Grandma who loves everybody." So my brother entered and said, "What happened?" Grandma couldn't say anything, so I told the whole story. I was about to burst into tears again. I was angry. So I said "Cruel old liar. You're a liar. You're everything evil and nothing good." Oh, there was a commotion. She would spit in your face when she was nervous and would speak. A little while later, I came to understand that she was a nervous personality. But I'll never forget that house where I had the courage to call my stepmother ugly names. So, then she hated me and called me a billy goat because I talked back to her.

Another time I was behind my sister in the field to gather the hay, and we two and my little brother were gathering. The stepmother always had us doing something more than we were capable of, but we were used to it. And we were obedient, obedient and respected here. Fine. So I called my younger brother to call the cows and also the five sheep. One of the sheep was black and the wool was used to make stockings for men and sweaters. So he took these sheep to another part of the field to graze, and when they had eaten enough, I said, "Go get them and take them home." He had a little cart like those we have here for little children with four wheels and a handle. Poor little baby, he was little over six years old. He tied the oldest sheep to the handle of the wagon, and inside the wagon he put a lot of squash.

The sheep was expecting, and perhaps my stepmother was afraid that the sheep would lose the fetus before it was born—I don't know—because she was worried a lot about the sheep. She took off a wooden shoe, a hard one, and began to hit my baby brother over the head, screaming all dirty words, "You want to kill the sheep! Don't do that." And she kept hitting him. I began to scream, and my older sister began to cry, and she didn't say anything, even though she was older than me. I said, "What are you doing, old hag? Leave him alone." And I was running against her. My brother fell to the ground, full of bruises. I took my brother and helped him up and unharnessed the sheep. I took my brother home as we both cried. And, that's the way she was, rough and tough.

Going Home Again
When I went to Faller in 1950, my stepmother was still alive and she had only one tooth. When I saw her, I tried not to laugh, but she looked so funny, just like the witch in the story. So it was just like nothing had happened when I saw her after all those years of trouble. I thanked her for having taken care of my father, and she started crying and said, "Nobody ever told me that before." And then, before I left, I knelt down and asked her blessing. And she said, "O dear, you're asking me that?" "Yes," I said. So she said, "If I did something wrong without knowing, will you forgive me?" I said, "Yes." And she was happy. She knew she did much wrong. When she first saw me, she said, "Don't come and condemn me for anything, because I'm innocent like the Blessed Mother." I said, "Mother, I'm not coming here to judge you. In

fact, I thank you for having taken care of my father.'' She was touched. I think she lived another five years.

World War I

War Comes to Faller
I remember the war well. . . . The General Cadorno went and said, ''You've got to retreat. Because if in the three years we can't penetrate the German lines, we pull back to Monte Grappa.'' My older brother was there, and he said he was under a rock for twenty-four hours when there was continuous bombing. We had, in my father's house, a house with three floors, where Flora lives today: first floor was kitchen, dining room, and storage room; above was the grandmother and mother and father's room; and above was for the children in the two large rooms—three or four beds per room. From this house it was possible to see the explosions of the bombs . . . day after day . . . the murder of mankind . . . steady and steady . . . three days and three nights.

The Italians couldn't take Panerote and the other mountains against the Germans. So the Italians waited for them in Monte Grappa, and it was that part that saved Italy. We were at Faller. The Pointe Sierra was blown up; we couldn't go into Premiero. The soldiers came into Faller on foot with a little bit of canvas wrapped around their feet and on horses, horses that were so thin that they could hardly walk. The Red Cross was there—this caravan of soldiers and Red Cross—about one hundred people. They were cruel, those Germans, ''The Barbarians of the North.'' It is ironic that the first Germans who marched into our village of Faller were the storm troopers, those who enlisted in the military for life. They were called companions of death. They were ferocious. The wife of one man—a beautiful woman—they tied him to a chair with rope, put her in a bed, and twelve of them raped her. They were savages. They had a license to kill and rape and murder. They were ex-convicts who had been freed from prison in Germany and had not seen women for years. The husband was there in the room, and as they raped his wife, they beat him. So she was almost destroyed by that experience, and her husband could no longer sleep with her after that horror. She would have nightmares at night. And he couldn't sleep unless it was absolutely quiet afterwards. He slept with a gun under his bed, and nobody could make a sound.

My other aunt, who lived in the apartment under theirs, heard my other aunt crying and screaming. She had five sons; the youngest was my age, and the others were about twenty years old. So, they had a closet between the kitchen and the dining room, and they went out and gathered a lot of wood and placed it in the closet. At night, they gave their other aunt and uncle a little wood and a little hot water and whatever they could give them to eat. They stayed in that apartment for one week without ever coming out—until all the German savages left and advanced to Monte Grappa.

War, Hunger, and Sharing

November 1917 through November 1918, when the Germans left Faller, that was the worst time. November 1917 through November 1918, many people died . . . husbands and wives dying in bed together. One would die and not even have the strength to say good-bye. One couple in particular, I remember, the wife went to boil some water and returned to the bedside and said, "Giovanni, I've brought you some hot water." There was nothing left to eat. "You don't hear me? Well, it's better that I leave you rest." Then she returned to the kitchen and went back to bed one hour later, and she spoke, and her husband didn't answer. So she touched him, and he was cold already.

There were only old people and small children in the village. The other men were either soldiers or like John and my brother, who were about to be drafted by the Italian army when the Germans came, and the Germans conscripted these men into the German army—all the men up to sixty years old. The Germans made them watchmen on the roads, had them cut wood, and be guards. But the Germans always watched them closely, as if they were prisoners. They gave them beets to eat, boiled with lots of water. That's all. There was hardly anything to eat, and the Germans used to add sawdust to flour to make bread. The poor Germans didn't have anything more to eat, not even in Austria.

They had lots of ammunitions, but nothing to eat. They were dying of starvation. My stepmother used to get some milk and mix it half with water and boil it together with a pinch of salt to make milk. Then she would bottle it: seven or eight bottles to make eight liters of milk. Then we made shoes out of rags, dresses out of blue canvas which the Germans had left behind . . . really bad. And we never knew what time it was because the bell in the tower had been taken down by the Germans, as had been all the alarm clocks. One night we went to Fonzazo, because school was no longer in session, and we arrived at the barracks, where the soldiers slept in the straw like the beasts. The worst sight was to see the wounded who were carried into Fonzazo from Monte Grappa. Poor things. It was too pitiful . . . such sadness . . . so much bleeding. We used to exchange a bottle of milk for a loaf of bread at the barracks. That's why they put sawdust in the flour—to give some roughage to soldiers in their weakened condition. And soap . . . it was half soap and half lime; it was revolting stuff. There was nothing. The soldiers were dying of hunger. In fact, in the stables there were the horses of the officers. I remember the wounded horses bleeding . . . awful.

And then there was the captain's headquarters, which was on the third floor of our house. We were altogether fourteen people, and we were all thrown out of our rooms. In the evening when we finished cooking, boiling water, or whatever, we had to make other beds for more soldiers. We used to go to neighbors' houses in order to sleep. We did what we could. The whole thing was a nightmare. I used to say to myself, "O God, what will we do during the winter of 1917-18?" That winter broke the record. There was not one speck of snow. It was warm, serene, and beautiful. We never saw any snow that whole winter. It was a miracle. No one died that winter from double pneumonia. We hardly had houses, beds, and had little to wear because the Germans had taken away everything. Anyway, it was a terrible year. Every company of men who came through Faller . . . some stayed and others went . . . as replacements to the front lines.

Finally, after the interval when the front line troops were being replaced by the new soldiers, we always dug up the food and supplies and divided them among ourselves. When the partisans came to Faller, crying that they were hungry, my father would say, "All right, tonight we'll dig up some food, some beans, and tomorrow the partisans will come in the morning, and there'll be a little for everyone. As long as there's a little to eat, we'll live, and then we'll die together." My father wanted to save the seeds for the spring, so he went out and planted seeds for beans, potatoes, lettuce, cabbage, and so on. And when we went to sell milk in Fonzazo, we returned to Faller with two or three loaves of bread.

War and the Enemy

Our house was the German headquarters, and at the house where my brother now lives was the officers' dining room. There were some soldiers in the German army from Trento, the cook and those who were valets of the officers. They spoke Italian. Lots of Trentini knew how to speak Italian, but they never warmed up to the villagers in Faller. Those Trentini just listened. If someone spoke too much or bad-mouthed any of them, that poor person was taken before the officers. "Keep your mouth shut or you'll be finished!"

Anyway, it was a terrible time. They took away all the chickens, all the food. And then each time a new company of troops would come, they wouldn't believe that we didn't have any food, that everything had been taken away. One soldier wanted eggs for his commanding officer. He made all kinds of motions and imitations, "Ko-Ko-Deck. Ko-Ko-Deck." I said, "Nothing. Nothing. There's no more food." He pulled a knife from his boot and was about to kill me. My brother happened to be returning from the stable at that time. He yelled, "Stop. Don't try to kill my sister. I'll kill you." Well, that soldier was from Trento and he understood my brother, so he stopped with the knife in his hand. Can you believe that? He wanted to kill me because I didn't give him any eggs. He was Italian from Trento, and Trento and Trieste were the parts that started the war. Trento and Trieste were under Austrian rule. The Italians wanted to reclaim these regions. You know, we only went to the third grade in Faller, but they taught us a little bit of everything—history, sewing, embroidery, and woodworking.

War and the Desire to Go to America

I remember in 1918 when the Italians marched into Faller. This man was cleaning up the mess the German soldiers had made, and he picked up a bomb which was made in the form of a clock by the Germans. He thought he had found a clock, but it exploded, and all of his intestines burst out into the plaza. I could see the flash of the bomb on the wall of my room, and that man blew into pieces. He had just finished digging the grave of a woman who had died just one hour before, and the priest said, "Just a minute. This has to go on record, because it's really strange." They put him in the grave he dug for the woman. Wasn't that something? And John's best friend also picked up one of these little clocks which exploded in his hands, and he lost a hand and damaged the other very badly. That was Monica's husband, Carolina's brother-in-law. After that everybody had to go to the church to be told not to touch anything, because it might be a bomb. We could look and report it but not touch it. Finally the Italian army came and collected all these things, and there were no more casualties.

We saw a little bit of everything. Really, when you are young, you really are impressed by this terrible war and you ask, "Why? Why?" The Alpini used to sing "In Trincerea" about the injustice of the war. War doesn't help anything. It just brings diseases, death, and misery. The poor people have to pay for all of this and fight and die for nothing. So that's why I thought I had to run away from that miserable place where there was a war every twenty years. I wanted to come to America. Maybe I would suffer as I had there in Italy, but I wanted to go. I waited a long time and arrived in America in 1930, when there was nothing so special there. But no matter where you go, life's troubles are everyday things for everybody. Only sometimes you see people who were lucky to be well-off, and they are loved, spoiled, healthy, and have what they desire. It doesn't seem fair. You know, you don't miss what you don't have. That's the way I feel, so we don't have anything to complain about.

Immigration to America

Dream of America

It was before World War I that my cousins came to America and would write to me that there was work in America and that you could live well. In Faller we ate meat very rarely, you know. It was really miserable in Italy. But in America, when you worked, you earned money and could eat and drink what you wanted. And there was freedom, no war, no soldiers. So as I said, I was sort of a rebel. I hated ugly and brutal things. I hate injustice and prejudice. So I said to myself, when I get old enough to marry, I'm going to marry the first man who promises to take me to America.

Marriage to John and the Voyage to America

In Faller we got married and stayed there five months. Then John left because in Italy it was impossible to get the chance to come into America. The quota was ten thousand people, and everybody wanted to run away after the war. A lawyer suggested to go to France because maybe the quota wasn't covered there. John stayed there a year, but there was no chance. So he and my brother, who is in Detroit now, went to Luxembourg and lived in a boarding house and were working there together. They required a lot of men in Verdun because everything was knocked down during the war. John could hardly understand French. Anyway, the couple who rented a room to my brother had a son who wanted to come to America. He went to the office of immigration and signed up and came home. He was so happy and was talking to his parents that he had the chance to go, to line up everything and be ready. My brother said, "You mean you have the chance to go to America?" "Yes, yes," he said. "You can come too." "Can you be good enough to take me to the office?" The Luxembourg man said, "All right, I'll be happy to." He rented a bike, rode to the office, and took him with him and signed him up. My brother said, "I have a brother-in-law. Can he come with me?" He said, "Yes." So he telephoned John, who was in Zarne.

After he worked all day, John rented a bike and went to Tony.

He said, "Stay here tonight and tomorrow. I'll take you to the office." You don't have any idea how happy John was to sign up. At the office they said there were three more openings to complete the quota, and then the boat could take off. There was Tony and Guido from Faller. My brother and John went to them and said, "Don't say anything to anyone else, because all the other men from Faller would like to go to America also. You were there and understand the language and were miners, both of you. We would like to be able to help you so we can all go to America—to Export, Pennsylvania, where they have the coal mines and other minerals." They were working very slowly—only one or two days a week. To make a long story short, John sent a telegram to me and his father and said "Send me the four thousand lire I sent you last week, because I got the key to go to America. Three days to get ready, so I don't even have the time to get ready and see you once again and meet my little daughter, Bruna." Like I said earlier, we had five months together; I was pregnant and then he had to leave.

John was living in France on the border of Luxembourg for fourteen months altogether. He left and took the boat from Avris. In the meantime, I had Bruna, our little baby. He never saw us for seven and one-half years, mind you. My dear, that's right. Bruna was six years old when he came. That was seven years—the best time of our life apart. Of course, he was a good man, and he wrote twice a week. I have a bushelful of letters—all love. [Laughter.]

Oh boy. I lived with his parents and his younger brother, Pietro. Of course, Pietro wasn't there much. First he was with John in France, and then, when he came back, he had to go into the army. Pietro wanted to come to America. Pietro knew that from Italy it was impossible, as John had struggled so long. After Pietro came back from the army, I was still there and he found a job up in Bolzano. Then his mother passed away. I sent him a telegram. Anyway, he finally came home and decided to get married. He said, "Clementina, you're a good woman. You were here helping my father and mother, working hard, and everything else. But now I would like you to give me your room"—there were only two bedrooms. I said, "Well, I have to write to your brother and see what I can do." So he said, "Well, you stay there." I was waiting for the papers from John to take off. I asked a lady who had three or four bedrooms in her home and who was alone with her daughter if she could rent me a couple of rooms. She said, "Yes. To you, anytime." So I moved out and gave the room to Pietro. He got married, and they were happy and loved one another and everything was fine there.

And me, I was expecting the papers. After fourteen months in France and five years to become a citizen in America, John received his citizenship, and he came back. He didn't have a chance to see his mother; she passed away two years before. He said, "I'm going to see my father once again." So he left Chicago and came back. Then his father passed away.

Between the two brothers, they decided to divide what was there, and Pietro said, "I don't care for the old house." It was so old that they didn't even pay one penny of taxes. It was falling down. So he gave the woods, vineyards, and grazing land to Pietro instead of the old house. John got the house and left the rest to Pietro. He took time to fix the house; he even put the post under the second floor. I said, "Why in the world do you want to spend money to fix an old house?" He said, "You never know. Maybe we can't stay in America, and we'll come back. Or we can rent it and have an income. And when we want to come back, we'll have a place to live."

In the meantime, I was pregnant with my son. So I said, "What do you plan to do? Hire some men and do it quick!" I said, "John, that's all! I'm six and one-half months pregnant. Do you want me to come to America with you? Stop right now and let others finish it." So he paid the men to finish the old, leftover job, but they never finished it, because when you pay ahead, that's the way it is.

On the eleventh of July we took off for Genoa. Anyway, I was feeling bad. I didn't even go to see our relatives to say good-bye. In the morning I fixed the trunk and all the things I was supposed to do. This man . . . he did things the American way—simple. The condition I was in, I didn't have breakfast, didn't have lunch, and we were supposed to. We called the taxi from Fonzazo or Feltre. People came up, and I said good-bye. I told the lady next door to take the last chicken and roast it. We could eat it the next day, before we left. But there was not even time to eat that. I bundled the chicken up and said maybe I can eat it on the way to the train at Feltre. On the way down to Feltre was a girl who made a motion that we should stop in the middle of the street. She said, "Stop, I'm going to Fonzazo. Give me a ride." You know, she was a sixteen- or seventeen-year-old girl named Maria, who married John's other cousin. I said, "Honey, it's not that I don't want to give you a ride, but we're on our way to go far away from here. You're not supposed to interfere." John said, "Oh, come on. There's room for her too." We reached Feltre, and John took Tony Moretto with him and went to the lawyer's office, giving Tony Moretto the power of attorney. Me and Bruna were in the car. It was a hot day, and I didn't have the nerve to take the chicken out and eat it. We finally took off for the train. The way I left Italy, I almost starved to death. We finally reached Genoa and went to the hotel and took a good bath and ordered dinner. We ate good and everything was fine until the next day when we took off.

We went to Naples. When I went up to the boat, I was scared and said, "Dear God, I don't know how to swim." But I was happy inside, because I said, "Finally, we're going to America." And I was happy. . . . The trip from Genoa to Naples was beautiful. I enjoyed it, looking out all of the time. When we reached Naples, we stayed there, and the ship was rocking, and I started to get dizzy and feeling sick. I said, "Oh dear, days to go across. How in the world can I make it?" I was upset all through the voyage, especially the last three days when even water didn't stay down. I was in bad shape. Anyway, we reached New York. There was a big boat; it was French. They had to finish loading. We were stuck for three hours on the boat. John wanted us to go upstairs on the deck to see the skyscrapers. I said, "John, I can hardly stand up." He was all excited.

Settling in New York City
The second night we were in New York staying with our friend Irena and her husband, John looked at the paper and saw an apartment for rent, two months' rent in advance required, and John went to see it and said it was really nice and asked me to go with him to see it. Even though I didn't feel like it, I went and

looked at the apartment. When I saw it was near Central Park, I said, "Well, my baby always wants to go to the park for fresh air." So we spent the first five or six months there in that apartment.

Thank God I knew how to sew, because I went downtown to get work. The first time I took the subway, I met Irena and her husband as I was coming up from the subway. She said, "Clementina, where are you coming from?" It was early in the morning. Before Bruna went to school in the morning, she had to watch her baby brother. John, meanwhile, was always looking for a job. Bruna was there with her brother, a beautiful baby—fat and heavy—and he was crying. Bruna was crying too because she had to go to school and it was late. So Irena asked, "Where are you coming from?" I said, "I've gone downtown to Canal Street to pick up my work orders . . . clothing." She said, "Alone?" I said, "Yes, alone!" She said, "I've been here for eight years and I don't have the courage to ride the subway alone because I'm afraid of getting lost. My God, you don't even know how to say bread in English and you go downtown alone?" [Laughter.] I said, "Yes." She was so surprised. Then I told her about all these little sewing jobs, and she started going downtown to get some work too.

That was a rough and tough time for Irena because her husband was a bricklayer, and he wasn't able to find a job at all. Like I said, between us girls we tried to help out, and we made it without any struggle at all. With a little bit of money, you went to the market, and for five dollars you came home with a full shopping bag of everything. That was really nice. From there came a time when we weren't able to pay for the rent . . . no money. I said to John, "You write to my brother to ask for a hundred dollars, and we'll pay the rent for three months." Gas and electric was ninety cents per month. Very cheap. Now, it's a hundred dollars a month. My brother wrote and said, "Only a hundred dollars?" My brother sent two hundred. We paid the rent and stayed a little longer. My husband likes to brag. He said, "I sent for a hundred dollars and my brother sent two hundred."

There was another Italian guy from Cadore, and they had a speakeasy four or five blocks from where we lived, and they used to go there during the dry time [Prohibition]. John used to go down there, especially on Saturday and Sunday, play boccie and drink beer and that terrible whiskey. Anyway, he mixed all of these drinks, and he was loaded. Then, this Caladorino . . . he took off early . . . he was there too . . . and under the elevator on Second or Third Avenue where it was noisy and all the stores were closed, he hid there. When John came, he struck him in the head and knocked him down flat. It was 2:00 A.M., and I was worried and thought, "It's time for the place to close. John's supposed to come." And John came home with blood all over. I said, "Dear God. What happened? Who did that to you?" He said, "I don't know nothing. I don't know nothing." Because he drank mixed drinks, he was vomiting really bad. I said, "Look, you went down there and bragged because my brother sent you two hundred dollars. That guy thought you had it with you. That's why this happened to you." He just went into John's inside pocket and didn't find anything. John just had fifty cents left. When the other man didn't get anything, he just ran home. Then I said, "I hope that is a lesson." And Irena said to me, "Tell John not to go down there. It's a speakeasy. They really sell poison. It's bad for his health."

But he's a man who really feels pity for himself. "No work," he said. "I have to go to the breadline." I said, "That's not a breadline. They're not giving anything to you and me. It's just bread and butter for the children, and everybody goes." Anyway, we had it rough and tough in that way. I said, "I won't ask any more money from nobody. We'll have to pay it back." John said, "How? When? Can we do that?" I said, "We will get out of here like everybody else." So I said to the landlord, "Look, Mr. Doracher. I try to talk the best I know how. We're going to pay you later on, the best we can. Soon John will get a job, and even if it's fifty cents, I'll put it away until I get enough to pay you." He said, "You're a good woman. Okay. I trust you."

We moved from there, down from 101st Street to 106th Street, to be a janitor for a five-story-high building. There were twenty-five families, and they were all Sicilian. They had a vegetable stand outside the building. They started the eastside market, and they had everything you could ever think of and imagine. Everyone was Italian—butcher and everybody. I just used to go where I could express myself . . . all Italian in all the buildings. So I said, "John, I would like to move from here, because we'll never get a chance to learn English." But then, like I said, we were there, and I was scrubbing the stairs there, up and down, just for the rent. Then in this space of time I was taking in sewing. But the company didn't have much work because too many people were asking for jobs . . . too many Italian ladies.

Before we moved, there was a German family next to us. They spoke with a very thick accent. They had two beautiful children but they were arguing all the time. Anyway, one of the ladies who was working with her—I don't know whether she quit or was fired—anyway, the German lady told Hermann, the husband, to come and get me for the job. So—good. Hermann came over and said, "My wife has an opening where she works. She says you're a hard worker. Would you like to take it?" I said, "Yes." Well that job was from 11:00 P.M. to 7:00 A.M., before the company opened in the morning. The job was to clean Wall Street offices, empty the wastebaskets in a big bag, mop floors, and wipe the desks real nice. I didn't mind working. I was happy. I made seventeen, eighteen, and twenty dollars a week.

From New York to Detroit

When we moved from New York to Detroit, we wrote to one of our old friends in Detroit that we were tired of living in an apartment in New York. I said, "I would like a little yard to plant radishes and dandelion." But that year, it was a cold winter, and I remember the coal. We used to use the coal for the furnace, and it cost fourteen dollars a ton. It seemed like we were in the basement shoveling coal all the time. So the rent wasn't very high. Then, in those frame houses, especially upstairs when you have that much snow on top of the roofs, you know, it's like living in a refrigerator.

When we were living in New York, we were living among Italians from the south of Italy. All five floors of the apartment were from the South. They liked me. They respected me. We spoke in Italian, and I understood them. But when they spoke among themselves, I didn't understand anything.

When John went to Detroit and I stayed in New York, John stayed with my brother. I wrote to John and said, "Look for a little house in Detroit." In Detroit through a friend, Inez, who was born in America but whose parents were from Italy, John found out that there was a little house on the same street where Inez lived— on Lawrence Street. The house had three bedrooms. John talked with the owners, and they were willing to rent. So we came and brought all our furniture. It was a nice house. I liked it a lot, and we planted a garden there. We even have photographs of the place with Bruna, Benny, and John outside in the cabbage and bean patches. But like I said, in the winter it was so cold and long, and we kept putting more and more coal in the furnace. I said, "My God, it's so expensive and so cold, and John can't work with his rheumatic pains." It was impossible because of the rent and heating bills. You need a ton of coal a week to heat that house. It was fourteen or fifteen dollars a ton, so I said, "There's got to be a better way to heat a house. That's enough."

It was the time when we found a great selection of vegetables in the markets. We would get a bushel of tender, fresh string beans for sixty-five cents; a bushel of peaches or tomatoes was fifty cents. There was plenty of everything, because in Detroit every-thing grows . . . delicious apples . . . Hmmm . . . I remember when Bruna was teaching in a high school in Bangor, Michigan. She taught there for one year after she graduated from Wayne University. Anyway, a bunch of farmers had gone out to pick apples near Bangor, near the high school. . . .

On to Phoenix
You know, when I came to Phoenix twenty years ago, it was another thing. After our children got married, Benny left home and was busy with his business for seven or eight years. He and his father were tight, you know. Then Bruna got sick and died. And John's the kind of person who likes to be around lots of people. He was alone.

From New York, he went to Detroit to work. He had said, "If you want to come, come." He left me in New York with children and the furniture and everything to take care of. But thanks God, I don't know how to speak English well, but I went to Detroit.

We went to Detroit when we didn't have enough money to pay John's doctor bills for rheumatism and when the doctor injected water instead of medicine in his veins. On the second and third visits to the doctor, I said to John, "Ask the doctor what could be done if the treatment here is not doing anything. You have to have treatment because it's necessary for you to work. You have a family to support.'' The doctor said. ''John, the best thing you can do is to go out west.'' And so he did it. John came home and told me that the doctor said he could get better if he went out west, where there is dry air. John said, ''Pack my suitcase. I'm going to leave tomorrow.'' Just like that, ''I'll leave tomorrow.'' On the spot. After he came to Phoenix, he went to design school. Yes, John was a terrific artist. He exhibited his designs even before we were married.

Well, I said, ''Look for a house in Phoenix, John, with room.'' In June when Bruna and Benny finished school, we could all come out west. Bruna was in Bangor, Michigan. John went looking for rooms in Phoenix, and he didn't find anything, because it was a small town and there were lots of people there. Wives of soldiers, I mean. There were no houses to rent. John finally found this English family who had a big house and there wasn't even a fan there. You know, John doesn't suffer from the heat. He loves it. John said, ''I found three rooms. It's impossible to find a flat. Go to the doctor who treated me and ask him for a letter of recommendation, and I'll ask the city officials for some priority, so I can buy the materials and build a house.'' I said, ''Good.''

I went to the doctor and got the letter for John, and then John got permission to buy the materials. The real estate men brought John here, saw the lot for sale, and we bought the lot from neighbors. John ordered the materials and said, ''Now, I'll begin right away, and when you come with the children in June, the house will be complete.'' And the poor man worked so hard, because there was a lot of adversity. When we arrived, John was putting in the window sills. He worked so hard. Then Benny arrived, he was fifteen. He began to help his father, mixing cement, carrying bricks, and in that way we constructed the house, very slowly. Wood was very scarce and expensive, and so we constructed the entire house out of brick and masonry. It's a very strong house . . . eight inches of wall.

Socializing in New York and in Phoenix
Of course, the difference was that in Faller visiting in the stable

was the style of the town. But in New York, we were in an apartment with our own little family there. It was altogether different. We used to buy chestnuts and roast them and have a little wine. When it was a holiday, we would visit this good friend of ours and that was the desert after a good meal—roasted chestnuts and wine . . . Italian style . . . instead of cake and ice cream. In New York there weren't many people from northern Italy. Like I said, with the others it was hello and good-bye. In Detroit we used to go to the Venetian Club and the Friulani Club, and they used to go on picnics during the summer and stay inside during the winter. When a girl reached sixteen or seventeen, she was taken to the club to introduce her to society, to take her dancing. That's the way we used to do it.

In Phoenix we didn't know many people at all. We had to start from the beginning. Like at the Italian grocery store. We wanted Italian food, so we went there, and there were other Italians buying stuff too, you know. So little by little we met a lot of people, and then John joined the Italian Club. They were all professional people in the beginning . . . like DeConcinni . . . doctors and lawyers. They formed this club because there were not many Italian families there . . . no other kinds of people either. Around 1950, there were five hundred thousand people, and now the state is growing more than any other place.

Tale-Telling in America

Tale-Telling in New York
We used to go to the park, Central Park, in New York when Bruna was little. In fact, in the beginning we had a nice carriage for our baby, and we used to put her in, and she held her baby brother . . . when she was six or seven years old. Anyway, in other words everything she marked down under my name and that was the honest truth. All the stories I remember.

We started in New York. When Bruna was little, I used to tell her the story of Teofolo, a little boy who went to an island with his father to get nuts. I don't remember exactly, but they tied the boat to a little pole there. The father was collecting the fruit there, and the boy was picking it up from the earth. Soon a bad windstorm came. The boy ran from there and tried to make more

knots to secure the boat, but the wind was too strong. A story—
yet Bruna had tears down her cheeks. I said, "I feel sorry for
you. I don't want to tell anymore." She said, "I want to know.
Come on, keep going." When I tell a story, I almost forget who
is in front of me. I am there [in the story]. I want to be
Margherita or Barbarina and express with all my heart all the
trouble and suffering and injustice or whatever it was. And that's
why I really enjoyed telling the story the way I did.

In New York we didn't go visiting other people's houses. The
three friends I had in New York, we all would get together during
the holidays; we are like sisters. They're still alive, almost eighty
years old. One lives in the Bronx, New York. The other one lives
with her daughter whose husband just died—both she and her
husband. They just wrote me a card on Thanksgiving Day, saying, "Oh Clementina, I wish we would be near each other to
empty my heart to you. I've got a lot to tell you. John has gotten
old and forgets a lot." She told me all her sorrows. She lost two
brothers, son-in-law; it was very sad. She said to me, "You let
me breathe. I think how beautiful if would be if I could be near
you, like before." Every Sunday we would visit each other. We
would go to them, or they would come to us. So, in the summer
especially, we would go on picnics. There was also the Club Ita-
liani in New York, which would go on Long Island for the picnics
on Coney Island—all those children with popcorn and merry-go-
rounds.

All around us there was misery, because the men hadn't been
working for years. Another friend, who started to work with me
in a factory, said, "Tina, you know today it's penny ante," make
a dollar a day or a month. We worked here and there—sewing—
but you know, it was enough to buy the food to gèt along for the
week. Anyway, we still write to each other. The couple on Long
Island—Giuseppina and Attilio . . . there, they have an older
son like Benny. Attilio was born in Mestre, and Giuseppina was
born in Argentina. Irena and Giovanni are the others. When the
men were looking for work and didn't find any, sometimes Attilio
would come from Long Island and Irena would come, and we
women would put the three children in the carriage.

The men went pushing the carriages to Central Park, and they
would sit on the benches and play cards and tell stories and watch

the children. All the while, we three women were home, cooking. We really liked each other, like brothers and sisters. That's all. We suffered the consequences of the depression together. So, like I said, we are all old, but we always write to each other, we three women. We write about our children and grandchildren.

Religion, Love, and Children

Religion

I believe strongly in God, and I believe anything can happen. Maybe slowly, maybe in another direction, but you reach your goal if you really believe and pray to God to grant the grace. I have my own proof. When I was a young girl, I had a very unhappy childhood. I used to go to my girlfriend's house— Maria. They were poor, nine children, seven girls and two boys; her mother had a child every year. She was tired, but she always said honey and dear and gave her kisses and hugs. A child lives from the love of a mother. It is that love which nourishes and sustains the child, helps the child. [Clementina was crying here.] And I felt it in my heart. I said, "Why not me?" And Bruna said that too. "My friends have daddies. When is my daddy coming home?" She always asked me that question. And the years passed. It was a torment.

When I was a child, on Holy Friday I told myself to go to church and kneel before the altar and give thanks to God. I said to God, "As far as I know, I never did anything wrong, so you have to grant me this wish. If someday I would like to meet a man and get married, please make him good, not cruel or not one who doesn't believe in God." I said this prayer ninety-nine times that day in church on my bare knees with a lighted candle. I really did that. I had some young men courting me. Some were poor, some were ugly, and some were better looking than this one [John].

For sure, there is justice in heaven . . . honest to God. Otherwise, it doesn't pay to suffer. True love, the love of God, is the summit. Perfect love brings perfect joy in every way. Instead, if you don't believe in anything, you become selfish and think of yourself first. If you say, like the priest said this morning, you do

what you would like other people to do to you . . . if you share
equally whatever it is . . . When I can do something good, my
reward is that delicious feeling of being able to do something for
others. I'm sorry when I can't help or give. That's how I feel.

Sometimes on a Sunday morning, I listen to preachers on the
radio—the Lutherans and all the other denominations. They're
not priests, you know. Some are really intelligent. They don't
only talk about God; they talk about the poor conditions in
America and why the things are as terrible as they are—dope,
prisons. You know, there's a prison near here where they stick
four hundred prisoners when there is room only for one hundred
prisoners. They kill each other there. So, if one could see all the
suffering in the world . . . why? . . . for nothing!

Now, the first thing President Carter did was to pardon all the
draft dodgers. It's true that we shouldn't have sent Americans to
fight that way. To help those people in Vietnam, yes, but to send
Americans there to be killed . . . fifty-six thousand boys . . . the
best crop . . . the best young people, not the demented or dis-
abled or crippled. That was a human sacrifice. So, what can we
believe in now? It's the fault of the bad, but the good always suffer. Most of all, the poor suffer. When Benny went to Korea, I
said, "Son, you have to go to do your duty. I'm not going to cry.
I'll pray for your safety, but don't forget to tell your officer there,
you're the only son we've got, and if you die, our name will be
finished." I wanted them to know this, because in America this
doesn't matter. They don't keep score. In Italy they do. They put
only sons in the second line, out of danger.

The Devil

The devil has his own reign and his own power. And that's why I
think God put us in the world. God made people of all colors and
character. People like different things. People have different ways
of thinking. God put us all together. I think life is like purgatory
because we have to put up with each other.

In one story the girl was smart all right. She really played the
part of a very wise young girl, making the devil believe she was in
love with him, that she didn't mind being there and obeying as he
wanted her to. God has more power than Satan, and God over-
powered Satan with a rosary and crucifix in her hands. So the

284

devil had no power. The devil then had to back up and stay on the side. At least, that's what I think.

Was it in God's mind to make the devil as intelligent as God? Is the devil as intelligent as God?

Who can judge God? God is infinite; God is from the beginning to the end and forever. Who knows how many devils there are. Everybody who's condemned is still in hell.

Love and the Training of Children

You have to train a little child like a plant—straight up—with the name of Jesus, who wants the child to be good. And, after that, there is hell and then there's heaven. The child has to pick up the right or the wrong way. With encouragement and good example, the child grows up in the family, then goes to school to learn to read and write, and finds out that somehow it doesn't pay to be bad because, first of all, the child gets a licking from parents and finishes up in jail from the law or authority. It doesn't pay to do anything wrong. And plus, if you have a conscience, you sleep and relax and say that you're not afraid to do anything.

Love and good nourishment are needed and good teaching and good example. A little child's mind is tender. He looks up for guidance, for help, and for everything. What's important is to give your best. It's simple. Instead, those people who don't believe in God teach children to steal and lie. Those children don't know better. They love their parents or uncle or brother or whoever is the one who teaches wrong. And they do it without the fear of God or nothing, because they don't know better and don't believe in God. So, I think it's common sense. In fact, I keep thinking . . . even in America . . . to help priests and nuns, good people who believe in God and the Ten Commandments and so on. They really help one another and do good; these people are doing the most important things for the nation. To do right and not wrong . . . I think the authority of nuns and priests really helps a lot to conserve the goodness of people.

Now, when they bring in dope from all over the place, this ruins the crop of young people. Drugs are the ugliest thing to do to a person. Cocaine and the powerful drugs really ruin a good healthy young man and woman. With these drugs, poor, young, innocent girls are tricked into doing wrong and get a bad name.

Besides that, when they do wrong, it's not right, and sooner or later they're going to do worse. When they develop a bad habit, they can carry on when they have money, but when they don't have money, they rob and they kill. It's a mess. It's really a destruction of humanity. Finally, they finish by going inside of saloons, and now we have the courts and judges and lawyers who are all for money, money, money, money. They lie and cheat, corruption in every way, and that's the ruin of America. We are in bad shape. They believe in having a good time—eat, drink, sex. *Amore publico* [free love]. *La moglie può essere per tutti* [a wife is available for any man]. No, it's not right.

Romantic Love

That strong love, the love of the heart, is not easy to control. When people, like they say, experience love at first sight, they don't have control. Like the couples who go to death because they can't . . . the boy or the girl . . . they want so much. Romeo and Juliet, that was true love. They died from the anguish of not being able to get together.

Then there was the story of Paolo and Virginia of Rimini. Paolo was the son of a duke, and he had an older brother who was ugly, bad-looking, bad character, and very bad in every way. But Paolo was young, tall, handsome, *simpatico,* and a beautiful young man. The style in Italy says that the firstborn will inherit the title when the father passes away. This story I read in a book. As soon as I finished the book, I knew it by heart . . . when I was young. Now, I'm no good at that any more. Anyway, they were so much in love. I mean that they met and saw each other. They were so in love, they could hardly sleep or eat. What they wanted was to be together. Paolo used to go to the garden to meet her. The more he saw her, the more he was in love with her. So he went and proposed to her and said, "I can hardly wait to marry you."

He went home and told his older brother that he found the girl he wanted to marry. The foxy, good-for-nothing brother said, "I want to meet her. She must be a beautiful girl, because you deserve the best." Paolo said, "She is. She's better than anyone I have ever seen." So this guy went to meet the girl in the garden with his brother. She was such a beauty, and the older brother said, "Hey, I've got the title. This girl will be my bride, not yours." Anyway, the younger brother said, "We'll see." She was still young and didn't have a trousseau yet, so they had to wait.

Well anyway, the older brother made the younger brother an ambassador, and the younger brother protested, "I don't want to go. I don't want to go." "Oh yes, you're going," said the older brother and sent him away and went to court the girl. She was polite and everything, but she never dreamed he wanted to marry her. Finally he made her realize he was in love with her and wanted to marry her. She said, "Oh no, I want my Paolo or nobody. I love him very much. Where is he?" "Oh, he went on a mission, and he won't be back for years. So you had better make up your mind." "I did. I'll never marry anybody else but my Paolo, or I'll go to a monastery. But I don't want you or anybody else." He said, "I'm rich. I'm powerful. I've got a title." "That is nothing at all. I'd rather have Paolo without a penny than all the world that you can offer." Then he started to get fresh.

Of course, he had power, and he used his power at that time. You know how they were—so cruel. Remember the parents used to pick the boy for the girl and the girl for the boy and this and that. But she was determined not to marry him. Finally, she sent her maid to mail a letter. She found out where Paolo had gone. She wrote, "Please come. I can't stand the sight of your brother any longer. I want you to help me. You come home and we'll run away together."

Well, when Paolo received the letter, he came home. The brother ordered a couple of his guards to trick him. They grabbed him, taped his mouth, tied his hands, and put him down in the bottom of the jail and locked him up. "I want him dead," the older brother said. He was young and strong, and the two guards were young and strong. They put him down in the jail after he had talked with his sweetheart and said, "Yes, honey, tonight we'll get a couple of horses and carriage, and we'll run away." She was waiting and waiting for him. Oh, when they pushed him inside of the jail, he had cut his hands on the metal floor. He really hurt himself very bad. He was desperate; he was really going crazy. He said, "You've got the wrong man. I'm Paolo." Anyway, he cried himself to sleep for days. When he woke up, he realized he was bleeding badly. The first time the guards took food to him, they took care of his wounds. But they also tied him with a chain like he was a criminal.

The girl waited for years. But Paolo did not come back. She never heard anything. The older brother just had excuses for everything. He told her that Paolo forgot her, found another girl, or this or that. In the end, she made the sacrifice of marrying him on the condition that he find Paolo. Finally, he promised he would find Paolo. So they were married, and she, of course, despised him, and she was very unhappy. She went to the garden every day with her maid and cried.

The Miracle of the Apostles

The way the Church says, God is in three persons. And there is only one God. It's a mystery, and after that, we don't go too far to find out what and how and why. It's this way. So God the Father, and God the Son, who comes from the Father, because when Christ talked to the apostles, they asked him, "Show me your father." Christ said, "I am with the Father and he is with me." Then in the end, after he died and was resurrected, he sent the sign of the Holy Ghost, the third person of the Trinity. When they were in the room of the Last Supper, the apostles heard a wind. It was like a tongue of fire, just a little bit over their heads. And that fire was the Holy Spirit, and it penetrated into the body and soul of the apostles. After that, the apostles were able to speak Italian, German, and every tongue in the book. They said, "How in the world can we know all this?" They started to talk to each other, and they used to understand everybody in every language, because that fire was the Holy Spirit, the third person of the Holy Trinity. What else?

The Franciscans of Faller

In Faller it's pretty high, and in the winter it gets very cold. It would be pretty tough to be a hermit there. Besides that, in Faller we don't have many holy people who want to suffer that much. [Laughter.] But I remember now that there were many orders of monks, but there were more Franciscans than any other order. John, my husband, would help them. They had a monastery in Feltre and would go from village to village begging, and they in turn would give whatever they collected to the poor. The Franciscans would go from door to door in Faller. John would have a sack and wheelbarrow, and when they were filled with donations, he would take them to Feltre.

The Franciscans would offer food to the poor all during the winter. They cooked potatoes, beans, a minestrone in a great caldron of two hundred liters. And they gave a scoop to everyone. They were the real sons of Saint Francis because they believed in helping the poor. Now they stay inside the rectory, eating and drinking and taking it easy, and they are nice and fat. Everything has changed. I don't know. Maybe I'm wrong for criticizing, but the Franciscans today are not like they used to be in our time. They are still very, very good people, I know.

There were, in those days, some monks who used to beat themselves. They really starved. They did so more for the expiation of sins and sinners. But today they don't do that. They cancel this and they cancel that. Our priests in our parish until fifteen years ago had a big rosary. After Pope John, flagellations were no longer permitted. Pope John said we needed healthy, strong people to go to work and to help the poor and the sick and to teach young people, not to stay in their cells and beat themselves and starve, and do this or that. And so they changed. Especially since the Ecumenical Council II stressed that. Then everybody tried to examine whether that was right or not. When they made the change of having the priest face the people instead of the altar, that was one such change. Many things changed for the best.

Life and Death
Life is the most important thing. Nobody's ready to die. Isn't that something—to be so selfish? But really and truly, I'm not afraid of dying. I believe in God [bangs on the table], and I believe in heaven and hell. I'm not afraid. I keep saying, "Dear God, when my time comes, just let me go fast." If I have to be a cripple or a person who can't take care of herself, then I'd be a burden to somebody else. Oh, I don't want that. I pray to God to give me enough health to take care of my man. And I wish to live two days after John dies. The most important thing is life and to take care of your loved ones—the ones close by and the ones far away—and to know every day that they are healthy and happy,

and that makes me happy. Also, to be able to pray and just plain living. We were created free. We have to thank our parents, of course. We didn't ask to be brought into this world, but we are here and we are grateful to them. To take life away is the worst punishment—especially for criminals—and to live healthy and happy is the most wonderful thing, I think.

I ask the question of why do bad things happen to innocent people many times. To the eyes of a human being . . . even when Bruna was sick, I said, "God, why do you have to take away this young mother of these six small children? Why?" We don't know why. But God has a purpose. I think Bruna suffered enough, and then God said, "Now, Bruna, you come home." Her own children suffered too, and I suffered, but I deserved it because I'm a sinner, and I just don't complain about it. That was very, very hard to accept. What I suffered the most was to see my grandchildren suffer and not be able to help. And you just say that is unjust? Why? Someday, we'll know why. It's for our own good. If we believe in him, who is only good, you have to believe that. That's why. It's not an answer, but it is an answer, somehow.

Love, Fatalism, and the Social Order
In the beginning, like with the Jewish people, people related to God through the prophets, the holy men who believed in God. They had the gift of God, of being able to see right from wrong. Well, the one who knows how to run the boat becomes the captain. Ability is important. Or like Italy with all the big cities, it was run by a duke or count who came from the original king. If this king had three or four children, that makes a lot of princes and princesses. So it's just like an army without a leader; nobody wants to do anything. Nobody likes discipline, but they have to have it, and people have to obey it and punish those who violate the discipline. I think it's simple. He who has the ability and power to run other people, if they are good, they have a good nation. If they are bad, well, then it's very simple.

Love doesn't have any restraints. The power of real, strong love overcomes everything. They, under martyrdom, like the first Christians in Rome who believed in God so much, they just didn't give up. They were placed in the Pantheon [*sic*], and tigers

290

came out, hungry without food for three days, so they devoured them. These early Christians just embraced themselves and said, "Now is the time to be strong." That's what fate means, and that's what love is. Lucky is he who believes in God, and lucky is he who really falls in love strongly and says, "This is the lucky girl I choose and she will be the one till the end. Amen." Most of the time God permits people to suffer a lot, until somehow there's an end to everything. Who is true to God and asks for his help has a happy ending, if not in this life then for sure in the next life. I know I'm going to heaven, and I'm going to throw a little lasso to John to pull him up.

Bruna's Difficulties in America

Prejudice

When I was in Italy, I had nostalgia for my husband; I thought of him. Then when I came to America, I thought of my people in Italy. I always hoped that I could return one more time to see them again. So after World War II, there were planes from Arizona to Italy. The first flight was filled with schoolteachers. Almost all of them had relatives in Italy, and they wanted to see them because they had heard how hard they had suffered during the war. So Bruna went on this flight to spend her vacation in Italy in 1949.

She was planning to marry a nice young man of English descent. After the war, he became an architect and had finished the final year of college at Tucson, the University of Arizona. They were practically engaged. His name was Robert. His mother had been a widow from the time she was a young woman, right after she had Robert and his sister. The daughter fell in love with an Italian, and she became pregnant. She was only fifteen years old. The mother had a passionate hatred of Italians; they repelled her after that. When Robert told his mother he had met Bruna, a good girl whom he liked very much, a schoolteacher, the mother asked him to bring Bruna for a visit. So Bruna went to meet the mother. Everything went fine. Then the mother asked, "What is your nationality, Bruna?" Bruna said, "Italian. In fact, I was born in Italy." Bruna didn't tell her the name of the town because it was too small and the mother wouldn't have known it. So Bruna just said, "Venice, Italy. Northern Italy." "Ohhh," the mother said, her face becoming pallid, as if Bruna had said she was a whore or something to offend her. Anyway, there was a sudden change.

As Easter was drawing near, Bruna said to me, "Mama, is it all right if we invite Bob and his mother and sister for Easter dinner?" I said, "Sure." You know, they were really serious about getting married. The first year that Bruna came to California, the school board sent her to Buckeye, where Robert worked in a grocery store. You know, he didn't have a profession at that time. Anyway, Bruna used to go shopping in that store, and they met each other, and in a short time, they were serious about getting married. When Bob's mother saw how serious he was about Bruna, she said, "Nothing doing. An Italian ruined my family, ruined my daughter. No. No. You'll never have my consent, and I'll never accept her as part of the family." So then Bob didn't know what to say. He came here and said his mother was very opposed to the marriage, but he didn't care.

He had finished school and knew Spanish well. He wanted Bruna to go to Argentina with him. Bruna said, "No. No. Not in Argentina. Tell me why your mother hates Italians. I noticed her look of disgust when I told her I was Italian." So Bob told her the story. Bruna said, "I forgive her, and I feel pity for her because that was real bad. If that Italian really loved Bob's sister, he wouldn't have taken advantage of her innocence. That man was not a lover but a traitor! And that's not just." The Italian had run off with the girl but later divorced her because the mother was putting so much pressure on him. The mother couldn't stand him. The daughter had a little baby. The girl really loved that Italian. It was first love, but the mother made her divorce him. The mother said, "Enough. I am your mother, and I was both a mother and father to you. I helped you learn a profession. You're a young man without experience, and you don't know what's best for you." He, Bob, had lots of friends who were of English origin who had lots of pretty sisters. You know how things used to be done before; the mother wanted Bob to marry one of those girls. Love should be free. Isn't that right?

Bruna's First Day at School

As I said, Bruna was six and a half when John returned to Italy. We stayed in Faller for eight months, and then we came to New York in 1930. Before we arrived in New York, John had taught Bruna the English alphabet. That's all Bruna knew when she arrived in New York. I was pregnant when we landed in New York, and John had found some work.

I remember the day Bruna went to school for the first time in New York. She was accompanied by an interpreter, a little boy whose parents owned a bakery. They were from Rome. He was one year older than Bruna, so he accompanied her to school. He knew how to speak Italian because his mother and father spoke correct Italian at home. But the next day, this little dog of a kid took Bruna all over the school building, the second and third floor. You know, at a certain age little boys hate little girls. It's pitiful. For no reason did he do this, and it was really terrible. Then he left her in one of the halls and went to his own class. Bruna began to cry and she kept walking around and around looking for her classroom. Finally, she found the class, wiped her eyes, and entered the class. The teacher was a Jewish lady with red hair. She yelled at Bruna, "You are late! Why?"

I told the little boy to go into the class and tell the teacher that Bruna had just come from Italy and that she didn't speak or understand English, to please not send her to the blackboard, and please have patience. Instead, that little boy told the teacher on the first day that Bruna wanted to go to the board and write her answers to the assignment. That little beast! So this teacher said to Bruna, "All right, you are late." And she gave Bruna an assignment to do at the board. Such confusion. Bruna stood there looking at the teacher who thought that Bruna was too lazy. So the teacher got mad and said, "Here, kneel down in the corner!" This was the first day of class in America, and Bruna had to kneel down and look at the wall. Bruna was so upset and disgusted, along with being afraid and humiliated. She only told me this story when she graduated from high school.

Notes to the Text

Preface
1. The Clementina Todesco materials collected by Bruna Todesco may be found in the Wayne State University Folklore Archive, 1941 (16): Italian; U.S.; Michigan; Detroit; Todesco; 1940-41; folktales.

Introduction
1. In addition to the narratives, Clementina's daughter collected folk songs (Wayne State University Folklore Archive, 1941 [17], 1942 [17]: English and Italian; U.S.; Michigan; Detroit; 1940-41; Todesco; tales and songs of Clementina Todesco and other Italian immigrants), which are evenly divided into love and war motifs. We have excluded the folk songs as well as other short forms, such as folk cures and sayings, and limited our study to Clementina's narrative repertoire.
2. Fernand Braudel, "History and the Social Sciences," in *Economy and Society in Early Modern Europe: Essays from Annales,* ed. Peter Burke (London, 1972), pp. 11-41.
3. Eric Wolf, *Anthropology* (New York, 1974), p. 77.
4. Braudel, "History and the Social Sciences."
5. Eric Wolf, *Europe and the People without History* (Berkeley, 1982).
6. Antonio Gramsci, *Letters from Prison,* selected, translated from Italian, and introduced by Lynn Lawner (New York, 1973), p. 106.
7. Vladimir Propp, *Le radici storiche dei racconti di fate,* trans. Clara Coisson (Turin, 1949), pp. 572, 578. Cocchiara's comments are found in the preface to this volume. This important work by Propp has been translated into many languages, though not into English. The translation in the text is the authors'.

   We direct readers to the second edition of this work with its valuable introduction by A. M. Cirese (Turin, 1973.) Cirese sets the volume into the context of Propp's other published works, especially his major work *The Morphology of the Folktale,* published in Italian with an introduction by Claude Levi-Strauss (Turin, 1966). He discusses the development of Propp's thought and his analytical approach to the folktale between the publication dates of these major works. In addition, Cirese comments on the importance of rereading Propp's work in the light of current scientific theoretical orientations.

We are indebted to Carla Bianco, professor of anthropology and folklore at the University of Florence, for bringing this work to our attention.

Propp's text reads as follows:

> i racconti si capiscono soltanto con l'ananalisi della vita sociale, entrano in essa non soltanto come parti costitutive, ma agli occhi della tribú sono una delle condizioni della vita al pari degli attrezzi e degli amuleti, si conservano e si custodiscono come le cose piú sacre. (p. 572)

> Né la teoria delle migrazioni, né quella dell' unità della psiche umana, propugnata dalla schola antropologica, possono risolvere questo problema. Esso si risolve con l'indagine storica del folclore nella sua connessione con l'economia della vita materiale. (p. 578)

8. See Kenneth Goldstein, "On the Application of the Concepts of Active and Inactive Traditions to the Study of Repertory," in *Toward New Perspectives in Folklore,* ed. Americo Parades and Richard Bauman (Austin, Tex., 1972), p. 16.

9. Ruth Finnegan, *Oral Poetry* (New York, 1977), p. 210.

10. Linda Dégh, *Folktales and Society: Story-telling in a Hungarian Peasant Community,* trans. Emily Schossberger (Bloomington, Ind., 1969), p. 81.

11. See Joseph Lopreato, *Peasants No More: Social Class and Social Change in an Underdeveloped Society* (Scranton, Pa., 1967), p. 107.

12. Roger Abrahams, *African Folktales: Traditional Stories of the Black World* (New York, 1983), p. xvi.

13. Linda Dégh, "Folk Narrative," in *Folklore and Folklife,* ed. Richard Dorson (Chicago, 1972), p. 65.

14. Statement of Clementina Todesco, recorded February 20, 1977, Phoenix, Arizona (Wayne State University Folklore Archive, 1977 [24]: English and Italian; U.S.; Arizona; Maricopa; Phoenix; 1977; Italy; Veneto; Faller; 1974-76; Raspa; interviews with storyteller Clementina Todesco; interviews and tales of Faller residents). This quote and all subsequent quotes from Clementina are from this collection.

15. Abrahams, *African Folktales,* p. 2.

16. Dégh, "Folk Narrative," p. 64.

17. Dégh, "Folk Narrative," pp. 77-79.

Context and History

1. In *A Geography of Italy* (New York, 1958), D. S. Walker gives a complete physical and cultural geography of Italy.

2. The National Geographic Society's special publication *The Alps* (Washington, D.C., 1973) has a brief explanation of plate tectonics, pp. 120-55.

3. Walker, *A Geography of Italy,* p. 114.
4. The earliest extant documents on Faller are records of marriage licenses from 1523, found in the Archivio Vescovile di Feltre. The archivist at that church archive speculated that Faller was settled in the eleventh century by people originally from Feltre who traveled to the new area along the Roman road from Feltre to Trento.
5. See "Feltre," *Enciclopedia Italiana,* 1929 ed., for a brief history.
6. In *The Hidden Frontier: Ecology and Ethnicity in an Alpine Valley* (New York, 1974), Cole and Wolf study Tret in Trentino and St. Felix in Alto-Adige, two villages adjacent to Faller, and provide a political-economic history of the area in the eastern Alps. Their discussion is helpful in putting the intense religiosity of the zone into historical perspective.
7. A number of informants were interviewed in Faller in 1975 and 1976 (Wayne State University Folklore Archive, 1977 [24]).
8. Walker, *Geography,* pp. 118-19.
9. Personal interview with Stella Slongo, 26 August 1975.
10. Personal interview with Cecelia DalZot, 29 August 1975.
11. Walker, *Geography,* pp. 92-96.
12. See Sydel Silverman, "Agricultural Organization, Social Structure, and Values in Italy: Amoral Familism Reconsidered," *American Anthropologist* 70 (1968): 1-20, for an analysis of regional differences in the farming of southern and northern Italy.
13. See Leonard Moss, "The Passing of Traditional Peasant Society in the South," in *Modern Italy: A Topical History since 1861,* ed. Edward Tannenbaum and Emiliana Noether (New York, 1974), pp. 147-70.
14. Eric Wolf, *Peasants* (Englewood Cliffs, N.J., 1966), p. 20.
15. For an evocative ethnography of Italian migrant workers in northern Europe, see Ann Cornelisen, *Strangers and Pilgrims* (New York, 1980).
16. Regional crops are identified in Kish, *Italy,* pp. 55-58.
17. Douglas Holmes, "A Peasant-Worker Model in a Northern Italian Context," *American Ethnologist* 2 (1983): 743.
18. Narrative of Fiorentina Slongo, 30 August 1976 (Wayne State University Folklore Archive, 1977 [24]).

The Storyteller in Italy
1. For additional discussion on the daily life of villagers in a neighboring region, see Cole and Wolf, *Hidden Frontier,* pp. 128-32.
2. Personal interview with Fiorentina Slongo, 30 August 1976 (Wayne State University Folklore Archive, 1977 [24]).
3. Kish, *Italy,* p. 56.
4. Personal interview with Carolina Todesco, 29 August 1976 (Wayne State University Folklore Archive, 1977 [24]).
5. Personal interview with Maria Trento, July 1975 (Wayne State University Folklore Archive, 1977 [24]).
6. We are here in the trenches, while lying in ambush, eating, feasting, singing, and going crazy. Who is the victor? War is a game for rich men.

7. Finnegan, *Oral Poetry,* p. 210.
8. Cole and Wolf, *Hidden Frontier,* p. 11.
9. Dégh, *Folktales and Society,* p. 79.
10. Personal interview with Ruffino Todesco, 31 August 1976 (Wayne State University Folklore Archive, 1977 [24]).

The Storyteller in America

1. For a discussion of the commercialization of food, see Harry Braverman, *Labor and Monopoly Capital: The Degradation of Work in the Twentieth Century* (New York, 1974), pp. 274-75.
2. Sidney Pollard, "The Adaptation of the Labour Force," in *Genesis of Modern Management* (Cambridge, 1965), p. 160, as quoted in Herbert Gutman, *Work, Culture, and Society in Industrializing America* (New York, 1976), p. 14.
3. An analysis of the shift from agrarian to industrial societies is found in Gutman, pp. 3-78.
4. Joseph Lopreato, *Italian Americans* (Austin, Tex., 1970), p. 46.
5. Lopreato, *Italian Americans,* p. 36.
6. Oscar Handlin, *The Uprooted,* 2d. ed. (Boston, 1973), as quoted in Lopreato, *Italian Americans,* p. 41. Leonard Moss and S. C. Cappannari, "Patterns of Kinship, *Comparaggio,* and Community in a South Italian Village," *Anthropological Quarterly* 33 (January 1960): 24-32.
7. Carl Wittke, *We Who Built America: The Saga of the Immigrant* (Englewood Cliffs, N.J., 1939), as quoted in Lopreato, *Italian Americans,* p. 43.
8. See Carla Bianco, *The Two Rosetos* (Bloomington, Ind., 1974), for an analysis of persistence and change in an Italian-American settlement in Roseto, Pennsylvania, with comparative data from Roseto, Italy.

Annotations to the Tales

1. Barbarina and the Black Snake

Type 425, The search for the lost husband; Type 510, Cinderella and Cap O' Rushes; and Type 510B, Dress of gold, silver, and stars.

This tale combines Types 425, 510, and 510B as though they were integral episodes in a single narrative. All five episodes of Type 425 are observable, and of Type 510, episodes III, IV, and V are present. Two variants of the composite tale were collected in Faller (Wayne State University Folklore Archive, 1977 [24]). Unlike Clementina's version, the Faller tales lack a competing second woman who marries the prince and are without the persona of the witch who casts the spell on the young prince. In one variant, the penitential motif is absent.

Type 425 is diffused throughout the Veneto. There are three collected versions in the Discoteca (30 Ven. 1-3). In the Discoteca tales, it is the father who plucks a flower or vegetable from the monster's garden, which precipitates the monster's demand for the youngest daughter in marriage.

Type 425 is also represented in published collections: Penzer, *Pentamerone,* II. 2, V. 3, V. 4; Waters, *Straparola,* I, 129-33; Bernoni, *Fiabe,* 96-101; Crane, *Tales,* 322-24. These literary variants are closer to Grimm's Tale 127, "The Iron Stove," in that the young girl's laments on two successive nights with the drugged prince asleep next to her in bed are overheard by a faithful retainer; on the third night, the prince does not imbibe the drug and is reunited with the heroine. In Clementina's version the young prince sleeps through the third night. His ugly wife overhears his lament of their unhappy marriage and commits suicide, freeing the prince to marry the young heroine. In some literary variants, especially in Penzer, *Pentamerone,* the marriage ceremony precedes the disenchantment by the kiss. During that whole time, the young heroine, trapped in the skin of a pig or snake, is living with the prince in the palace with the rest of the royal family.

Type 510 is found in some literary variants: Penzer, *Pentamerone,* I. 6, II. 6; Crane, *Tales* 42-52. *Pentamerone,* "The Cat Cinderella," incorporates the motif of treachery on the part of a father toward his natural daughter. In both *Pentamerone,* II. 6, and Crane's "Fair Maria Wood," the full use of Motif T411.1, Lecherous father, may be found.

Variants from other regions of Italy include: Comparetti, *Novelline,* 38-39; Imbriani *XII Conti,* 176-81; Coronedi, *Novelle,* 37-41; Pitrè, *Novelle,* II, 44-45; Finamore, *Tradizione,* I, 5-8.

2. *The Cats under the Sea*

Type 480, The kind and the unkind girls.

Clementina's version contains some interesting motifs which are not properly a part of the international Tale Type 480. Clementina's lowly heroine, Maria, is glimpsed fleetingly by the prince as she speeds by in her splendid carriage pulled by a white pony. The pony drops one of his golden horseshoes, Motif F862.1, and almost immediately afterwards, the prince arrives at Maria's house, horseshoe in hand, and claims her as his bride before a baffled stepmother and stepsister. In episode VIII in this version, after the unkind girl returns with the horse's tail on her forehead, the stepmother dies from envy, Motif F1041.1.10.

The two variants collected in Faller (Wayne State University Folklore Archive, 1977 [24]) both lack the element of the heroine's marrying the prince. In one of the variants, the kind girl does not climb down a well nor does she encounter animals in a subterranean castle who ask for her help. In the second Faller version, the stepmother, in an interesting reflection of the village *ethos,* puts only clean clothes into the basket of the unkind daughter so as not to tire her.

The Discoteca version (45 Ven. 2), unlike Clementina's tale, lacks episode VII and in the end reconciles the kind and unkind girls, with money from the fairies being shared generously between the parents of both girls.

Type 480 is found in these literary variants. Penzer, *Pentamerone,* IV. 7, "The Two Cakes," is similar to Clementina's version, incorporating Motif L162 into the body of the story. *Pentamerone,* V. 2, differs from Clementina in directly centering the tale around episode VI (d), maintaining polite conduct under different conditions, as the kind and unkind young men address the personifications of the months of the year.

Other regional Italian variants are: Imbriani, *XII Conti,* 190-93; Bernoni, *Fiabe,* 101-8.

3. The Cherry Tree and the Pumpkin Vine

Type 480, The kind and the unkind girls.

Clementina has embellished the first and last episodes in this tale while eliminating completely episode III, The pursuit. After being cast out of the house by her stepmother and father, the young heroine is assisted by her poor but kindly grandmother and given a broom, a rope, and a crust of bread, Motif S351.1. The pumpkin vine suggests to the girl that she rob the witches of their treasures. Motif G610.3, Stealing from ogre as task, is found in Penzer, *Pentamerone,*, IV. 7, though used there for other reasons than alleviating the poverty of the kind girl's grandmother. When the unkind girl goes forth, Clementina ends the final episode in a particularly hideous way by using Motif S135, Murder by springing bent tree, as the witches congratulate themselves on having seized the culprit who stole their treasures both times.

Regional Italian variants include: Pitrè, *Novelle,* II. 189-95.

4. The Devil Gets Tricked

Type 311, Rescue by their sisters.

Clementina's version includes the details of domestic life—sewing, cooking, cleaning, and so on—which characterize her heroine's relationship both to her parents and to the devil. In Grimm's Tale 46, and in the literary variants, Bernoni, *Fiabe,* 16-21, and Crane, *Tales* 78-81, the devil/ogre loses power over the third girl after she cleverly passes the test and is not trapped by curiosity into opening the forbidden door. In contrast, Clementina develops the devil's growing infatuation with the girl, who is able to manipulate him by appealing to his vanity, coquettishly flattering him for his agility and strength. Before the third girl leaves, she and the devil act like a newlywed couple.

In the Faller version (Wayne State University Folklore Archive, 1977 [24]), the devil comes in the form of a rich gentleman, courting the young girl in the stable where they are spinning yarn. He appears immediately after prayers are said and offers to help her with the task.

The Discoteca variant (19 Ven. 5) treats the devil as a disguised, prosperous gentleman, entering the house of the three sisters and publicly proposing to them one by one, leaving the parents happy on each of the successive occasions. Like the Faller variants, the civilities of ordinary social exchange are heightened, and each time the devil visits with a chest, the parents invite him to stay and join them for the evening. In the Discoteca variant, there is an additional gulling of the devil. As he tries to kiss the look-alike doll, he tastes sugar on her lips, and, unable to restrain himself, he consumes the whole doll.

Regional Italian variants include: Coronedi, *Novelle,* 111-14; Gradi, *Racconti,* 56-63; Imbriani, *XII Conti,* 7-10; Penzer, *Pentamerone,* I. 5.

5. The Ducks That Talked

Type 403, The black and the white bride.

Clementina employs all six episodes in her tale, except II, Kind and unkind, which appeared in other variants. In one Faller version (Wayne State University Folklore Archive, 1977 [24]), for example, the girl is kind to a magician with a thorn in his throat, and in another version, to a toad who asks for a kiss. In still another, she is kind to an old lady who asks that lice be removed from her head.

Unlike other variants, Clementina treats the substituted bride using Motif M225.1. The stepmother drugs the food and water and exchanges them for the heroine's beautiful wedding gown, then hurls her into the river. In one version from Faller, the supplanted bride is hidden in a pigsty.

Clementina's version differs from Penzer, *Pentamerone,* IV. 7, in using the talking ducks instead of geese and in deleting the use of the heroine's picture as a dramatic device for introducing her into the story.

The punishment scene incorporates a dimension of communal belief absent in other Italian versions. The revelation of the deception occurs during the wedding banquet, when the king narrates the history of the treachery. It is the community which insists on burning the women at the stake. The stepmother's fears of community opinion are justified here, recalling the incident in the first scene when the stepmother insisted that the stepdaughter wear her shoes in public but tie them around her neck when she was out of sight.

Regional Italian variants include: Gradi, *Racconti,* 20-25; Comparetti, *Novelline,* 124-26.

6. The Forty-One Robbers

Type 676, Open sesame.

There are two Faller versions (Wayne State University Folklore Archive, 1977 [24]) and one in the Discoteca collection (31 Ven 2). Unlike Clementina's story, the Faller versions pair up the husband and wife as a team who, sitting high in a tree, observe the forty-one robbers gathering below for their dinner. In both versions the robbers are scared off by what they regard as the work of the devil when, in fact, it is the door upon which the couple has been sitting in the tree which falls among them.

The Discoteca version (31 Ven. 2) parallels Clementina's tale but incorporates Type 954, The forty thieves, after the episode of sewing up the dead body for burial.

Regional Italian variants include: Visentini, *Fiabe,* 27-33; DiFrancia, *Fiabe,* III, 59-65.

7. The Gourd of Blood

Type 1535, The rich and the poor peasant, and Type 1115, Attempted murder with hatchet.

Type 1115 becomes a part of episode IV (b) of Type 1535 in Clementina's version. The trickster resuscitates his wife by prayer after the potential murderer stabs the gourd of blood placed on his wife's chest. Clementina's version differs from the three Discoteca versions (27-29 Ven. 2) in some respects. Clementina focuses on the evil of the rich peasant, especially using Motif S21, Cruel son, and makes the suffering of the older brother the result of his greed. In the Discoteca versions the stress is upon the cleverness of the poor peasant's devices, which fool the rich peasant. Another difference in Clementina's version is that the rich peasant initiates the treacheries against the poor one, who devises the obstacles for self-defense. In two of the three Discoteca versions, the poor peasant is the aggressor and torments the rich one with his stratagems.

Other Italian regional versions include: Cozzani, *Leggende,* 155-64.

8. Margherita

Type 403, The black and the white bride.

The treatment of the heroine's kindness to a fish allows Clementina a basis from which to develop an intricate pattern, particularly in the substitution and disenchantment episodes. Before replacing the heroine with her own daughter in the wedding scene, the stepmother mutilates Margherita, Motif S165, by putting out her eyes, a brutal event that is paralleled in Waters, *Straparola,* I, 302-39. Then the fish that Margherita saved reappears, transforms itself into an old lady—similar to the forest maiden in another *Straparola* variant, I, 242-62—and step by step, justice is meted out. The fish buys back Margherita's eyes with figs and strawberries, Motif M225, and then creates a beautiful castle next to the palace of the heroine's deceived king, Motif D1132.1. In the end Clementina uses the old lady to tell the story of the black and the white bride, and the heroine is restored to her rightful position at the side of the king.

In the one Faller variant (Wayne State University Folklore Archive, 1977 [24]), the difficult task the young girl is assigned is to find strawberries in the winter on top of a mountain. As in Clementina's story, the heroine marries a prince who sees her calmly gathering flowers in the garden after the stepsister has returned. Unlike Clementina's story, the unkind girl goes unpunished.

Other regional Italian variants include: Finamore, *Tradizioni,* I, 234-35; Pitrè, *Novelle,* I, 19-31; Penzer, *Pentamerone,* III. 10.

9. The Old Magician Sabino

Type 1640, The brave tailor; Type 1060, Squeezing the (supposed) stone; Type 1062, Throwing the stone; and Type 1085, Pushing a hole into a tree.

Three versions were collected in Faller (Wayne State University Folklore Archive, 1977 [24]), and one was found in the Discoteca collection (22 Ven. 1). All versions except one incorporate the episodes of squeezing the supposed stone, which is actually ricotta, and pushing a hole in a tree.

There are some differences in the versions in the treatment of the relationship between the magician/ogre and the hero. In one Faller version the young boy is kept in a pigsty. In another the ogre and the young boy become friends, and it is only due to the excessive harassment of his mother that the ogre attempts murder.

There are also some differences between Clementina's version and the others in the ending. One Faller version concludes with Motif D672, Obstacle flight: fugitives throw obstacles behind them which magically become obstacles in pursuer's path. In the Discoteca version, the hero in his escape kills a sheep for its intestines, meets a woodsman, borrows a pruning knife, and pretends to cut out his intestines in order to run faster. The ogre is tricked into following suit and dies.

Another Italian regional version is Imbriani, *XII Conti,* 574-75.

10. The Stone of Gold

Type 875, The clever peasant girl.

Clementina works with only the first two episodes of the international type. Unlike other versions, the theme of equality is developed throughout this tale. A prince is introduced who loves mingling with peasants and threatens to become one himself if he cannot secure the king's consent to marry the heroine, a peasant's daughter. It is the king who then imposes a riddle on the young girl. Later, when the king makes a claim on the gold stone because it was discovered in his kingdom, instead of having the peasant sent to jail, Clementina has all the peasants sign a petition which urges the king to relent.

In the end it is not the peasant's daughter but his wife who discovers a solution to the riddle.

Other Italian variants include: Crane, *Tales,* 311-14; Nerucci, *Sessanta,* 120-27; Pitrè, *Novelle,* I, 111-17.

11. The Story of Little Peter

Type 327, The children and the ogre.

There was one version in Faller (Wayne State University Folklore Archive, 1977 [24]) and one version housed in Rome in the Discoteca collection (38 Ven. 5). However, there were seven variants of Type 327A, Hansel and Gretel, in Faller and the Discoteca.

All three variants of Type 327 contain only episodes I, Arrival at ogre's house, and II, The ogre deceived. In the Faller version, Motif S326, Disobedient child cast forth, is not present, and in the end the old witches are merely burned slightly. In the Discoteca version, the hero is caught and escapes on two different occasions and is helped by a farmer and a bricklayer.

In Clementina's tale, there is a strong moral tone which is absent in other versions. The boy reflects upon the suffering he has caused his mother and sees his encounters with the witch as just punishment for his sins.

Regional Italian variants include: Imbriani, *XII Conti,* 277-78; Coronedi, *Novelle,* 10-14; Busk, *Rome,* 40-45; Visentini, *Fiabe,* 138-41.

12. The Three Brothers and the Fig Tree

Type 300, The dragon-slayer.

There are two Faller versions (Wayne State University Folklore Archive, 1977 [24]), and, like Clementina's tale, they begin and end with life on the farm cultivating the fig tree. However, Clementina's version contains more supernatural helpers, including Motif D1254, Magic staff, Motif D1081, Magic sword, and Motif D1415.2.6, Magic lute causes dancing.

In one Faller version, after slaying the ogre with seven heads, the hero does not marry the princess but goes home to his parents with lots of money and with his two brothers freed from prison.

Some Italian regional variants are: Comparetti, *Novelline,* 80-82; Visentini, *Fiabe,* 85-89; Bernoni, *Fiabe,* 50-58; Finamore, *Tradizioni,* I, 105-9; Penzer, *Pentamerone,* I. 7.

13. *The Twelve Doves on the Mountain of the Sun*

Type 400, The man on a quest for his lost wife.

The story is consistent with episodes II through V of Type 400. However, Clementina departs from the usual episodic opening by having her hero entangled in the service of a rich and greedy man who assigns him the task of securing precious stone at the top of the slippery glass mountain. The two motifs, H1114, Task: climbing glass mountain, and K1861.1, Hero sewed up in animal hide so as to be carried to height by bird, are characteristic of Type 314, The youth transformed into horse.

There are some other interesting features of this tale. In searching for his lost wife, the young man enters the house of the seven winds and is helped by their mother. Then, to thicken the plot, Clementina enters the young hero in a good-natured contest with the wind to race past the fallen oak tree to the Mountain of the Sun. The young boy's joking continues into the recovery episode. While the twelve princesses leave the dinner table momentarily to wait for the food to cool, the young boy eats his wife's soup and drinks her wine. Then later, in a sweep of confidence, he hides the magic cloak which makes him invisible and approaches the mansion, hands in pocket, whistling loudly and merrily, to ask the magician for a job as his servant, Motif G462.

In the final treatment of Motif D1745, Magic power rendered ineffective, the hero enters the magician's room as he is asleep—bloodred eyes open—finds a variety of magical ointments, searches closets, sifts through clothing, and by the light of the moon reads the directions for the flight and the killing of the magician. All disenchantments were accomplished while the severed head was still bouncing.

In the Faller version (Wayne State University Folklore Archive, 1977 [24]), the young dove is given back her shirt immediately and not taken away from her sister prisoners. Unlike Clementina's story, the Faller version relies more heavily upon formulaic action—the young boy wandering for seven years and being given three nuts by an old hermit. The ending also differs from Clementina's. The young man does not marry a transformed princess but returns home rich to support his poor mother.

The Discoteca version (14 Ven. 4) is called "Monte Cristallo" and was collected from an informant from Falcade, a small village near the mountain resort town of Cortina d'Ampezzo, where the ten-thousand-foot Monte Cristallo is located. This tale is a composite of Type 400 and Type 530, The princess on the glass mountain. The tale is distinguished from Clementina's in its substitution of an uncle from America who urges the young boy to ascend the mountain of glass, for it is his destiny to marry the daughter of the king of the wizards there. Unlike Clementina's story, it is the hero Giovanni who is transformed into a talking horse rather than other boys.

Regional Italian versions include: Imbriani, *XII Conti,* 440-54.

14. *The Bloodred Evil Elf*
Motifs:
C25.1	Child threatened with ogre
F236.1.1	Fairies in red clothes
F365.3	Fairies occupy peasant's house

15. *The Dark Men*
Motifs:
E542.1	Ghostly fingers leave mark on person's body
F80	Journey to lower world
F471	Dream demons
Q501.1	Punishment of Sisyphus

16. *The Good Priest and the Rich Stranger*
Motifs
D2140	Magic control of the elements
G283	Witches have control over weather
G303.3.1.2	Devil as well-dressed gentleman
G303.16.14.	The devil exorcised

17. *The Monk and His Cloak*
Motifs:
D830	Magic object acquired by trickery
E121.5.2	Resuscitation through prayers of holy man
V331.4	Conversion to Christianity through repentance

18. *The Monk and the Mason*
Motifs:
D2149.4	Magic control of gravitation
W181	Jealousy

19. *The Old Man Who Couldn't Die*
Motifs:
D771.7	Disenchantment by rosary or scapular
Q223.1	Neglect to pray punished
Q558.4	Blasphemer stricken dead
Q558.13	Mysterious death as punishment for opposition to holy person

20. *Saint Peter Gets His Way*
Type 774P, Saint Peter and the nuts.
Motifs:
J755   All aspects of a plan must be foreseen

21. *The Story of the Black Sheep*
Motifs:
C949.2   Baldness from breaking tabu
Q221.3   Blasphemy punished
Q558.4   Blasphemer stricken dead
V331.4   Conversion to Christianity through repentance

22. *The Old Man and the Rosary*
Motifs:
D771.7   Disenchantment by rosary or scapular
G303.3.1.12 Devil in form of woman
G303.4.5.4.1 Devil is betrayed by his goat hoofs
G303.4.8.1   Devil has sulphurous odor
Q424   Punishment: strangling

Bibliography

Aarne, Antti, and Stith Thompson. *The Types of the Folktale*. Folklore Fellows Communication, no. 184. Helsinki, 1961.

Abrahams, Roger. *African Folktales: Traditional Stories of the Black World*. New York, 1983.

Agonito, Rosemary. "Il Paisano: Immigrant Italian Folktales in Central New York." *New York Folklore Quarterly* 26 (1967): 52-64.

Austin, J. L. *How To Do Things with Words*. 2d ed. Cambridge, Mass., 1975.

Azadovskii, Mark. *A Siberian Tale Teller*. Translated by James R. Dow. Center for Intercultural Studies in Folklore and Ethnomusicology, Monograph Series No. 2. Austin, Tex., 1974.

Bateson, Gregory. *Steps to an Ecology of Mind*. New York, 1972.

Bauman, Richard, and Joel Sherzer, eds. *Explorations in the Ethnography of Speaking*. Cambridge, 1974.

Ben-Amos, Dan, ed. *Folklore Genres*. Austin, Tex., 1976.

————, and Kenneth Goldstein, eds. *Folklore: Performance and Communication*. The Hague, 1975.

Bernoni, Giuseppe. *Fiabe popolari veneziane*. Venice, 1875.

Bianco, Carla. "Italian and Italian American Folklore: A Working Bibliography." *Folklore Forum*. Bibliographies and Special Series, no. 5. Bloomington, Ind., 1970.

————. *The Two Rosetos*. Bloomington, Ind., 1974.

Braudel, Fernand. "History and the Social Sciences." In *Economy and Society in Early Modern Europe: Essays from Annales*. Edited by Peter Burke. London, 1972.

Braverman, Harry. *Labor and Monopoly Capital: The Degradation of Work in the Twentieth Century*. New York, 1974.

Brendle, Thomas, and William Troxell. *Pennsylvania German Folk-Tales, Legends, Once-upon-a-time Stories, Maxims, and Sayings*. Pennsylvania German Society Publications, no. 50. Norristown, Pa., 1944.

Briggs, Katharine, and Ruth Tongue, eds. *Folktales of England.* Chicago, 1965.

Busk, Rachel. *The Folklore of Rome.* London, 1874.

Carrière, Joseph, ed. *Tales from the French Folk-Lore of Missouri.* Evanston, Ill., 1937.

Cirese, Alberto, and Liliana Serafina, eds. *Tradizioni orali non cantate.* Rome, 1975.

Cole, John W., and Eric Wolf. *The Hidden Frontier: Ecology and Ethnicity in an Alpine Valley.* New York, 1974.

Comparetti, Domenico. *Novelline popolari italiane.* Turin, 1875.

Cornelisen, Ann. *Strangers and Pilgrims.* New York, 1980.

Coronedi, Carolina. *Novelle Popolari Bolognesi.* Bologna, 1874.

Cozzani, Ettore. *Leggende della Lunigiana.* Milan, 1942.

Crane, Thomas F. *Italian Popular Tales.* New York, 1885.

Creighton, Helen, and Edward D. Ive. "Eight Folktales from Miramichi as Told by Wilmot MacDonald." *Northeast Folklore* 4 (1962): 3-70.

Cronin, Constance. *The Sting of Change: Sicilians in Sicily and Australia.* Chicago, 1970.

D'Aronco, Gianfranco. *Le fiabe di magia in Italia.* Udine, 1957.

――――. *Indice delle fiabe toscane.* Florence, 1953.

Dégh, Linda. "Folk Narrative." In *Folklore and Folklife.* Edited by Richard Dorson. Chicago, 1972.

――――. *Folktales of Hungary.* Chicago, 1965.

――――. *Folktales and Society: Story-telling in a Hungarian Peasant Community.* Translated by Emily Schossberger. Bloomington, Ind., 1969.

DiFrancia, Letterio. *Fiabe e novelle calabresi.* 3 Vols. Turin, 1929.

Discoteca di Stato. *Tradizioni Orali non Cantate.* Rome, 1975.

Dorson, Richard. *American Folklore.* Chicago, 1959.

――――. "Oral Style of American Folk Narrators." In *Style in Language.* Edited by Thomas Sebeok. Cambridge, Mass., 1960.

――――. "Polish Wonder Tales of Joe Woods." *Western Folklore* 8 (1949): 25-52, 131-45.

Douglas, Mary. *Purity and Danger.* New York, 1966.

Dundes, Alan. *The Morphology of North American Indian Folktales.* Folklore Fellows Communications, no. 195. Helsinki, 1964.

Enciclopedia Italiana. 1929 ed. Rome, 1929.

Ets, Marie. *Rosa: The Life of an Italian Immigrant.* Minneapolis, Minn. 1970.

Falassi, Alesandro. *Folklore by the Fireside: Text and Context of the Tuscan Veglia.* Austin, Tex., 1980.

Finamore, Gennaro. *Tradizioni popolari abruzzesi.* Lanciano, 1882.

Finnegan, Ruth. *Oral Poetry.* Cambridge, 1977.

Foerster, R. F. *The Italian Emigration of Our Times.* Cambridge, Mass., 1919.

Georges, Robert. "Toward an Understanding of Storytelling Events." *Journal of American Folklore* 82 (1969): 313-28.

Gertz, Clifford. *The Interpretation of Cultures.* New York, 1973.

Goldstein, Kenneth. *A Guide for Field Workers in Folklore.* Hatboro, Pa.: Folklore Associates, 1964.

Gradi, Temistocle. *Racconti.* Florence, 1864.

Gramsci, Antonio. *Letters from Prison.* Selected, translated from Italian, and introduced by Lynn Lawner. New York, 1973.

_____. *Osservazione sul folklore nella ed. crit. dei Quaderni del carcere.* Turin, 1975.

Gumperz, John, and Dell Hymes, eds. *Directions in Sociolinguistics: The Ethnography of Communication.* New York, 1972.

Gutman, Herbert. *Work, Culture, and Society in Industrializing America.* New York, 1976.

Handlin, Oscar. *The Uprooted.* 1951. Reprint. Boston, 1973.

Holmes, Douglas R. "A Peasant-Worker Model in a Northern Italian Context." *American Ethnologist* 2 (1983): 734-48.

Hoogasian Villa, Susie. *100 Armenian Tales and Their Folkloristic Relevance.* Detroit, 1966.

Imbriani, Vittorio. *XII Conti pomiglianesi, con varianti avellinesi, montellesi, bagnolesi, milanesi, toscane, leccesi.* Naples, 1877.

Jones, Maldwyn. *American Immigration.* Chicago, 1960.

Kirshenblatt-Gimblett, Barbara, ed. *Speech Play: Research and Resources for the Study of Linguistic Creativity.* Philadelphia, 1976.

Kish, George. *Italy.* New York, 1969.

Klymasz, Robert. *Folk Narratives among Ukrainian-Canadians in Western Canada.* Center for Folk Culture Studies, no. 4. Ottawa, 1973.

Lomax, Alan. *Folk Song Style and Culture.* Washington, D.C., 1968.

Lopreato, Joseph. *Italian Americans.* New York, 1970.

_____. *Peasants No More: Social Class and Social Change in an Underdeveloped Society.* San Francisco, 1967.

Luthi, Max. *Once upon a Time: On the Nature of Fairy Tales.* Translated by Lee Chadeayne and Paul Gottwald. New York, 1970.

Macksey, Richard, and Eugenio Donato, eds. *The Structuralist Controversy.* Baltimore, 1970.

Milanovich, Anthony. "Serbian Tales from Blanford." *Indiana Folklore* 4 (1971): 1-60.

Moss, Leonard. "The Passing of Traditional Peasant Society in the South." In *Modern Italy: A Topical History since 1861.* Edited by

Edward Tannenbaum and Emiliana Noether. New York, 1974.

Moss, Leonard, and S. C. Cappannari. "Patterns of Kinship, *Comparaggio,* and Community in a South Italian Village." *Anthropological Quarterly* 33 (January 1960): 24-32.

National Geographic Society. *The Alps.* Washington, D.C., 1973.

Nerucci, Gherardo. *Sessanta novelle popolari montalesi.* Florence, 1891.

Noy, Dov. "The Universe Concept of Yefet Shvili, a Jewish-Yemenite Story-Teller." *Acta Ethnographica* 14 (1965): 259-75.

Papanti, Giovanni. *Novelline popolari livornesi.* Leghorn, Italy, 1877.

Paredes, Americo, and Richard Bauman, eds. *Toward New Perspectives in Folklore.* Austin, Tex., 1972.

Pelley, Francine. "Gypsy Folktales from Philadelphia." *Keystone Folklore Quarterly* 13 (1968): 83-102.

Penzer, N. M., ed. *The Pentamerone of Giambattista Basile.* London, 1932.

Pira, Michelangelo. *La rivolta dell'oggetto.* Milan, 1978.

Pitrè, Giuseppe. *Novelle popolari toscane.* 2 vols. Florence, 1941.

Propp, Vladimir. *Morphology of the Folktale.* 2d ed. Austin, Tex., 1968.

———. *Le Radici storiche dei racconti di fate.* Translated by Clara Coisson. Turin, 1949. 2d ed. Introduced by A. M. Cirese, 1973.

Re, Vittorio. *Michigan's Italian Community: A Historical Perspective.* Monographs in International and Ethnic Studies. Detroit, 1981.

Ricoeur, Paul. "Narrative Time." *Critical Inquiry* 7, no. 1 (Autumn, 1980): 169-90.

Rooth, Anna. *The Cinderella Cycle.* Lund, Sweden, 1951.

Rotunda, D. P. *Motif-Index of the Italian Novella in Prose.* Bloomington, Ind., 1942.

Silverman, Sydel. "Agricultural Organization, Social Structure, and Values in Italy: Amoral Familism Reconsidered." *American Anthropologist* 70 (1968): 1-20.

Smith, Dennis Mack. *Italy: A Modern History.* Ann Arbor, Mich., 1969.

Stahl, Sandra. "The Personal Narrative as Folklore." *Journal of the Folklore Institute* 14 (1977): 9-30.

Stewart, Susan. *Nonsense: Aspects of Intertextuality in Folklore and Literature.* Baltimore, 1979.

Swahn, Jan-Ojvind. *The Tale of Cupid and Psyche (AaTh425 and 428).* Lund, Sweden, 1955.

Taylor, Archer. *The Black Ox: A Study in the History of a Folktale.* Helsinki, 1927.

Thompson, Stith. *Motif-Index of Folk Literature.* Bloomington, Ind., 1966.

Visentini, Isaia. *Fiabe mantovane.* Turin, 1879.

Walker, D. S. *A Geography of Italy.* New York, 1958.

Waters, W. G., ed. *The Facetious Nights of Giovanni Francesco Straparola.* London: Society of Bibliophiles, 1894.

Wayne State University Folklore Archive, 1941 (16): Italian; U.S.; Michigan; Detroit; Todesco; 1940-41; folktales.

Wayne State University Folklore Archive, 1977 (24): English and Italian; Italian; U.S.; Arizona; Maricopa; Phoenix; Italy; Veneto; Faller 1974-76; Raspa; interview with storyteller Clementina Todesco; interviews and tales of Faller residents.

Wolf, Eric. *Anthropology.* New York, 1964.

_____. "Cultural Dissonance in the Italian Alps." *Comparative Studies in Society and History* 6 (1968): 1-14.

_____. *Europe and the People without History.* Berkeley, 1982.

_____. *Peasants.* Englewood Cliffs, N.J., 1966.

Index of Motifs

Motif numbers are from Stith Thompson, *Motif-Index of Folk Literature* (6 vols., Bloomington, Indiana, 1955-58).

Motif		Tale
	B. ANIMALS	
B11.2.3.1	Seven-headed dragon	12
B11.11	Flight with dragon	12
B325.1	Animal bribed with food	3
B375.1	Fish returned to water: grateful	8
	C. TABU	
C25.1	Child threatened with ogre	14
C611	Forbidden chamber: person allowed to enter all chambers of house except one	4
C920	Death for breaking tabu	21
C949.2	Baldness from breaking tabu	21
	D. MAGIC	
D191	Transformation: man to serpent	1
D361.1	Swan maiden: swan transforms herself at will into a maiden	13
D721.2	Disenchantment by hiding skin	13
D771.2	Disenchantment by rubbing with magic grease	13
D771.7	Disenchantment by rosary or scapular	19
D791.3	Disenchantment fails because conditions are not fulfilled	1
D822	Magic object received from old man	1
D830	Magic object acquired by trickery	17
D832	Magic object acquired by acting as umpire for fighting heirs	13

Index of Tale Types

Type numbers are from Antti Aarne and Stith Thompson, *The Types of the Folktale* (Helsinki, 1961).

Type		Tale
	II. ORDINARY FOLKTALES	
	A. Tales of Magic (300-749)	
300	The dragon-slayer	12
311	Rescue by their sisters	4
327	The children and the ogre	11
400	The man on a quest for his lost wife	13
403	The black and the white bride	5, 8
425	The search for the lost husband	1
480	The king and the unkind girls	2, 3
510	Cinderella and Cap o' Rushes	1
510B	Dress of gold, silver, and stars	1
676	Open sesame	6
	B. Religious Tales (750-849)	
774P	Saint Peter and the nuts	20
	C. Novelle (Romantic tales, 850-999)	
875	The clever peasant girl	10
	D. Tales of the Stupid Ogre (1000-1199)	
1060	Squeezing the (supposed) stone	9
1062	Throwing the stone	9
1085	Pushing a hole into a tree	9
1115	Attempted murder with hatchet	7

Type   Tale

III. JOKES AND ANECDOTES

Stories about a Man (Boy) (1525-1874)

Elizabeth Mathias and Richard Raspa have a long
association with Italian culture and ethnography. They
were both Fulbright scholars in Italy. They have done
field work in Italy, taught at Italian universities, and
lived in the Dolomite region, birthplace of Clementina
Todesco.

Elizabeth Mathias is associate professor in the
department of sociology and anthropology at St. John's
University, Jamaica, N.Y. She has studied at the
University of Akron (B.A., 1962), Kent State
University (M.A., 1964), and the University of
Pennsylvania (M.A., 1972; Ph.D., 1974). She has
published several articles on various aspects of Italian
culture.

Richard Raspa has published three books and
numerous articles in language, literature, and folklore.
He received his Ph.D. from the University of Notre
Dame in 1971. He is currently professor of
communication at Wayne State University.

The manuscript was edited by Doreen Broder. The
typeface for the text and display is Baskerville, based on
the original design by John Baskerville in the eighteenth
century.

Manufactured in the United States of America.